C0-BWY-154

DISPENSATIONAL TRUTH:

OR

THE PLACE OF ISRAEL AND THE CHURCH

IN

THE PURPOSE OF THE AGES.

By

CHARLES H. WELCH

Author of
Dispensational Truth
The Apostle of the Reconciliation
The Testimony of the Lord's Prisoner
Life Through His Name
(an exposition of the Gospel of John)
Just and the Justifier
(an exposition of the Epistle to the Romans)
The Prize of the High Calling
(an exposition of the Epistle to the Philippians)
An Alphabetical Analysis
(10 volumes)
etc., etc.

First Published 1912
Second Edition 1927
Third Edition 1959
Fourth (Revised) Edition 1981

THE BEREAN PUBLISHING TRUST
THE CHAPEL OF THE OPENED BOOK
52a Wilson Street, London EC2A 2ER

The Berean Publishing Trust 1981
ISBN 0 85156 082 2

Phototypeset by H.M. Repros
163 St. Vincent Street, Glasgow G2 5PG
Printed and bound by
Bell & Bain Limited, 303 Burnfield Road, Thornliebank, Glasgow G46 7UQ

CONTENTS

DEDICATION

IN LOVING AND GRATEFUL MEMORY OF

ADAM MOSS M.D. 1868-1959

dear to his son and to many who were associated with this witness during his lifetime.

Dr Adam Moss, formerly of West Kirby, was closely associated with Mr Charles H. Welch, who, in his autobiography, referred to the doctor as "The Beloved Physician".

(Col. 4: 14; 2 Tim. 4: 11)

PREFACE TO FIRST EDITION

Few words of introduction to the following pages will be necessary.

The difficulty, uncertainty and confusion resulting from failure to apportion the Scriptures according to the various phases of the divine purpose are so manifest, that an attempt to clear away some of the traditions of men, and at the same time to exhibit the purpose of the ages as revealed in the Scriptures, cannot be considered uncalled for nor untimely.

Although the Author's name stands alone upon the Title Page, the present Volume is by no means a single-handed work. Its production, whether viewed from the financial standpoint, or the standpoint of actual labour, is the result of much self-sacrificing and loving fellowship. The whole of the manuscript has been reviewed by one or two interested brethren, who by their criticisms, annotations, and typographical corrections, have largely contributed to any lucidity of expression which the book may contain. The valuable indexes, which we trust will make the book of greater service to the student, are the fruit of the labour of a sister in Christ.

We feel that we cannot do better than quote from the works of Miles Coverdale, as explanatory of the method followed in the preparation of this Volume:

> "It shall greatly helpe ye to understande Scripture, if thou mark
> not only what is spoken, or wrytten,
> but of whom,
> and to whom,
> with what words,
> at what time,
> where,
> to what intent,
> with what circumstance,
> considering what goeth before, and what followeth",

in other words, we have sought "rightly to divide the Word of truth" (2 Tim. 2: 15), and to be guided by the fact that *God always means what He says*.

We would here acknowledge our indebtedness to the following Works for helpful suggestions during the writing of this Volume:

The Companion Bible (Structures from this source appear on pages 10, 12, 51, 53, 54, 57, 61, 77, 91, 106, 107, 128),
The Analysed Bible (Dr Campbell Morgan),
The Emphasized New Testament (Rotherham),
The Two Babylons (Hislop),
Addresses on the Atonement (Pastor Geo. Aldridge), and
The One Baptism of the Church Age (Amplius).

The book is now sent forth with prayer that it may bring glory to God, and prove a blessing to the reader. We are grateful for the privilege of being permitted to expound in some small way the purpose of Him Who worketh all things after the counsel of His own will.

CHARLES H. WELCH.

Denmark Park,
London, S.E.
1912.

PREFACE TO SECOND EDITION

For some time a reprint of *Dispensational Truth* has been called for, and we are thankful at length to be able to respond. With the exception of one or two minor alterations the book remains as it was first published in 1912. We believed its message to be true then, and fifteen years' further study and conflict have but given added confirmation.

We humbly yet confidently commend the Volume to any who seek rightly to divide the Word of truth, and pray that through this second edition many hearts may be touched, eyes enlightened, and lives dedicated to Him Who hath blessed us with all spiritual blessings in the heavenly places in Christ.

CHARLES H. WELCH.

"Shalom",
Hutton, Essex.
1927.

PREFACE TO THIRD EDITION

We are profoundly glad that a third edition of "Dispensational Truth" is called for. To some, the word 'dispensation' is heresy. We would remind such that it is one of the words the "Holy Ghost teacheth" (1 Cor. 2: 13), occurring some nine times in the New Testament.

In Ephesians we have the dispensation of the grace of God, given by the Ascended Christ to the Apostle Paul to make known to sinners of the Gentiles (Eph. 3: 1). This must be in contrast to law, human merit and works, for such cannot mix (Rom. 11: 6). We have the dispensation of the Mystery or Secret (Eph. 3: 9 R.V.), previously hidden by God in Himself and now revealed to and through the Apostle of the Gentiles. In chapter 1: 10 the dispensation of the fulness of the seasons is a Divine goal, when all things in heaven and earth will be gathered under the Headship of the Lord Jesus Christ and He shall reign supreme everywhere.

Here are at least three different dispensations or administrations of God, concerning which no true believer can afford to be ignorant. If we obey the Divine command of Philippians 1:10 margin and "try the things that differ", we shall surely "approve things that are excellent" and get to know the exceeding riches of grace and glory which are treasured up in our Saviour (Eph. 1: 7, 8; 2: 7; Col. 2: 3).

This Scriptural principle Mr Welch has faithfully followed out in this volume, and all who wish to get to know the best and highest that God has revealed in His Word will reap great benefit if they carefully and prayerfully read this book without bias and prejudice, being willing to learn and unlearn if need be.

May many be led, as a result of this, to handle correctly the Word of Truth and so be approved unto the Lord (2 Tim. 2: 15). All else is secondary.

Stuart Allen
October 1959.

PREFACE TO FOURTH (REVISED) EDITION

Many years ago, when in my late teens, certain Bible problems were causing concern and no one seemed able to give satisfactory help. One part of the New Testament discouraged marriage — another part encouraged it; one part said keep the sabbath — another part said there was no need; there were two, if not three baptisms in the Acts yet Ephesians spoke of only one; at one point Paul healed everyone yet in others he could not heal his closest friends.

It was at this time that a friend gave me Mr C. H. Welch's *Dispensational Truth* and, just like that, these difficulties disappeared. One saw God as the all wise Father Who did not treat all His children exactly alike. Different instructions were given to His different children at different times. There was not confusion in the Bible but a clearly defined plan and purpose, centred in the Lord Jesus Christ, which God was slowly revealing to mankind and in which man had a place!

It is perhaps significant that this fourth edition has had to be Revised — or better, slightly expanded for nothing has been abridged. When this book was first written in 1912 most Christians had a good knowledge of the Bible but since then there has been a tremendous decline in Bible study and so some of the terminology, which nowadays would be confusing and not understood, has been expanded. As such we pray that every reader will benefit from this new edition and will start to appreciate some of the deeper truths of Scripture which exalt our Lord Jesus Christ to that high and lofty position of "Head over all things to the church which is His Body, the fulness of Him that filleth all in all".

Mike Penny 1980

CHAPTER ONE

The inspiration and right division of Scripture

The opening chapter of a book purporting to unfold some of the wonders of the purposes of the God of all grace seems a fitting place wherein to describe the attitude of mind and heart of the writer towards the Holy Scriptures, inasmuch as a constant appeal is made throughout the book to those writings which we call *The Bible.*

We are surrounded by those who deny or doubt the truth of the Word of God. Some totally deny the existence of inspiration, and consider the Bible as having no more miraculous origin than the writings of Shakespeare; others deny the universality of its inspiration, and pick out the portions which they are pleased to label "inspired", and leave the rest as being merely "sacred literature"; others again have denied its plenitude; these last, whilst admitting a notion of inspiration to the whole Bible, deny its fulness. They speak of the "inspiration of superintendence", the "inspiration of elevation", the "inspiration of suggestion". All these, and many other man-made definitions, are in opposition to the continual and unqualified claim of the books of Scripture themselves to the full, verbal inspiration of God, which we proceed to show is clearly set forth in its pages.

In the first place we would not be misunderstood. Believing that all Scripture is inspired, we do not deny the fact that every word in it was written by man. The epistle to the Galatians, *e.g.*, is in one sense altogether a letter of defence and entreaty coming from the Apostle Paul, while in another sense it is absolutely and altogether the inspired and authoritative "Thus saith the Lord". There is a passage in Psalm 12 which may help us to consider this relation of the human and divine in the Bible in the right way. It is found in verse 6, but we will first exhibit the structure of the whole Psalm, which in itself will help the reader to see that the order, the design, and the inter-relation of parts are factors of great importance in this question of the divine inspiration of Holy Writ.

Psalm 12

A 1. Decrease of good
  B a 2. Man's words (Falsehood)
    b 3, 4. Their end — "Cut off"
      C 5—. Oppression
        D 5—. Sighing
        D 5—. I will arise (for the sighing)
      C 5. I will deliver (from oppression)
  B a 6. Jehovah's words (Truth)
    b 7. Their end — "Preserved"
A 8. Increase of bad.

We now expand *B a* (verse 6) as follows:

a c The words of Jehovah are pure words
  d As silver tried in a furnace
  c (Words) pertaining to the earth
  d Purified seven times.

This verse teaches us that, while the language of the Bible is in "words pertaining to earth", yet divine inspiration has taken hold of them, and used them in such a way that by the time they are placed on the page of Scripture they become "as silver purified seven times", every word being indispensable, every word being "given by inspiration of God". This full and exact inspiration is denied by many simply because, of necessity, it involves a stupendous miracle in its production. We must remember the words of the Lord Jesus to those who denied the resurrection on similar grounds, "Do ye not therefore err, because ye know not *the Scriptures*, nor the *power of God*?" (Mark 12: 24-27).

Some find a difficulty in accepting the full inspiration of Scripture in the fact that the individuality of the writer is found in the various passages. None can fail to observe the intense impress of personality, with its resulting modification of style, on the books of Scripture written by David, by Isaiah, by John, by Paul; yet this in no wise militates against the most absolute inspiration of their respective writings. There is intense individuality in the bitter spite of a degenerate Caiaphas when he cried, "Ye know nothing at all, nor consider that it is expedient for us that one man should die for the people"; yet of these words it is written, "He spake this not of himself; but being High Priest that year, *he prophesied*" (John 11: 49-52). If then the Spirit of God can use and overrule the enmity of man, shall we deny His power and willingness to use the sanctified affections of those among men who are His own?

In providence the Lord makes "all things to work together" to the accomplishment of His wondrous purposes. "Herod and Pilate, with the Gentiles, and the people of Israel (each influenced and actuated by so many differing motives), were gathered together, for to do whatsoever Thy hand and Thy counsel had predetermined to be done" (Acts 4: 27, 28). Shall we then deny that the same sovereign will should govern the writing of the self-same prophecies which He so marvellously brought to pass?

Enoch, the seventh from Adam, prophesied, "Behold, the Lord came with ten thousands of His holy ones, to execute judgment" (Jude 14 R.V.); but already, before the mind of God, there was a John in the Isle of Patmos writing in perfect harmony therewith, "Behold, He cometh with clouds, and every eye shall see Him" (Rev. 1: 7). Between the first recorded utterance and the last, all other inspired writers were ranged, and when the time came, another human instrument was taken up by the Lord, through whom He caused to be written another portion of His infallible truth. Thus Moses said, "Oh, my Lord, I am not eloquent". The Lord's answer was, "Who hath made man's mouth? . . . Now therefore go, and I will be with thy mouth, and teach thee what thou shalt say" (Exod. 4: 10-12).

Then again, to Jeremiah the Lord says, "*Before* I formed thee in the belly, I *knew* thee; and *before* thou camest forth out of the womb I *sanctified* thee, and I ordained thee a prophet unto the nations" (Jer. 1: 5). Overwhelmed with the awful magnitude of such a thought, and considering his own frailty rather than the omnipotence of the Lord, Jeremiah exclaims, "Ah, Lord God, behold, I cannot speak, for I am a child". The Lord answers his fears by the promise of absolute inspiration. "Say not, I am a child . . . for whatsoever I command thee, thou shalt speak . . . I have put My words into thy mouth" (Jer. 1). Or listen to the apostle of the Gentiles, "When it pleased God, Who separated me from my mother's womb, and called me by His grace, to reveal His Son in me, that I might preach Him among the Gentiles; immediately I conferred not with flesh and blood" (Gal. 1: 15, 16).

There is a remarkable and important passage to be found in 2 Peter 1: 20, 21, "Knowing this first, that no Scripture is of any private interpretation. For the prophecy came not of old time by the will of man, but holy men of God spake as they were moved by the Holy Ghost". Note the four important items in this verse.

(1) It relates to that which is written (*propheteia graphes*).

(2) That *never* by any means (*ou pote*) did these written prophecies come by the will of man.

(3) That the great cause was the "bearing along" by the Holy Spirit (*phero*, cp. Acts 27: 15, "we let her drive").

(4) That the written prophecy is "not of its own unfolding" (*i.e.*, it was a matter of revelation, not the clever reasoning or foresight of the person who wrote the messages).

This passage refers to the origin of Scripture, rather than its unfolding. We cannot afford the space to set out the structure of this epistle as a whole, but we point out one or two sections as bearing upon our subject.

The prophetic Word (2 Peter 1: 19, 20)

A a 19—. The prophetic Word as a whole
  b —19—. Exhortation (general) to take heed to it
    c —19—. Its character — A light in a dark place
    c —19—. Its duration — Until the day dawn
  b — 19. Exhortation (particular) to take heed in heart
a 20—. Prophecy in particular.

The reason (2 Peter 1: 21)*

B d Man's part in it e How it did *not* come	Negative.—Not by will of man, or own unfolding.
e How it *did* come *d* Man's part in it.	Positive.— Holy men spake as moved by the Holy Ghost.

Much as we would wish to give a full witness to this Book of Books, we must refrain from multiplying quotations and proofs, owing to the ultimate purpose of this volume, which is to seek to open up the treasures of these *wonderful* Scriptures. The unceasing and united testimony throughout Scripture is to its inspiration. "The Lord hath spoken"; "Thus saith the Lord"; "Hear the Word of the Lord"; "The Spirit of the Lord spake by me, and His Word was in my tongue" (2 Sam. 23: 2). Peter, addressing the disciples, said, "Men and brethren, this Scipture must needs have been fulfilled, which the *Holy Ghost, by the mouth of David*, spake before concerning Judas" (Acts 1: 16). Again, in Solomon's Porch he cried, "But those things which *God before had showed by the mouth of all His prophets*, that Christ should suffer, He hath so fulfilled" (Acts 3: 18). Gaussen, in his *Theopneustia,* by which we have been greatly helped, says:

> "A man prophesied sometimes without foreseeing it, sometimes without knowing it, and sometimes without desiring it. I have said, without foreseeing it, and often at the very moment when he could least expect it. Such was the old prophet of Bethel (1 Kings 13: 20). I have said, without knowing it. Such was Caiaphas (John 11: 51). Finally, I have said, without desiring it. Such was Balaam, when, wishing three times to curse Israel, he could not, three successive times, make his mouth utter any words but those of benediction" (Numb. 23, 24).

* This order follows the inspired original, *not* the English translation.

Thus we would seek, most unreservedly and wholeheartedly, to subscribe to the doctrine of the full verbal inspiration of Scripture. "All scripture is given by inspiration of God" (2 Tim. 3: 16). The word "Scripture" means "that which is *written*" (*graphe*). The words "given by inspiration of God", may be literally rendered "God-breathed" (*Theopneustos*). This is very important. If the *written* Word is God-*breathed*, there can be no possibility of human error creeping into "that which is written for our learning". We have not to consider the *men* as being inspired, so much as the *words* that they wrote down. It is not that they beheld a vision of truth and recorded it in their own way, but that they wrote down that which God told them, and searched their own writings afterwards to endeavour to fathom their depths (*cp.* 1 Peter 1: 10-12). Speaking in the terms of our schools days, it is "dictation", not "composition".

The Revised Version has rendered 2 Timothy 3: 16 as follows: "Every Scripture inspired of God is also profitable", but has not consistently rendered a similar construction in other places. Lest any readers may have been unsettled by the Revisers' translation, we give one or two passages which exhibit the same order and usage, and which vindicate the translation of the Authorised Version:

Romans 7: 12

He entole		*hagia*	*kai*	*dikaia*
The commandment	*is*	holy	and	just

1 Corinthians 11: 30

Polloi		*astheneis*	*kai*	*arrhostoi*
Many	*are*	weak	and	sickly

2 Timothy 3: 16

Pasa graphe		*Theopneustos*	*kai*	*ophelimos*
All Scripture	*is*	given by inspiration of God	and	*is* profitable.

Hebrews 4: 13

Panta de		*gumna*	*kai*	*tetrachelismena*
But all things	*are*	naked	and	opened.

With the exception of 2 Timothy 3: 16, the Revisers have translated the above, with 2 Corinthians 10: 10; 1 Timothy 1: 15; 2: 3; 4: 4, and 4: 9 consistently, supplying the verb "to be", and translating "*kai*" as joining the two predicates together. If the Revisers had been consistent with their exceptional treatment of 2 Timothy 3: 16, we should have had such trite statements as the following:

> Romans 7: 12 would have read, "The commandment (being) holy *is* also just".
>
> 1 Corinthians 11: 30 would have read, "Many *ones* (being) weak *are* also sickly".
>
> Hebrews 4: 13 would have read, "All things (being) naked *are* also opened".

We do not ask why the Revisers made such a prominent exception, but we value the truth of an infallible Bible above the reputation of ourselves, or even of Revisers, and seek to show that in deed and in truth *all Scripture is God-breathed.*

Having, we trust, given sufficient evidence to show that our belief in the inspiration of the Bible is fully warranted, we would now address ourselves to one special command given by the Lord, obedience to which is largely responsible for the subject matter of this volume. The passage is found in the same epistle in which we read, "All scripture is given by inspiration of God", and occurs in chapter 2, verse 15: "Study to show thyself approved unto God, a workman that needeth not to be ashamed, *rightly dividing the Word of truth*". What does the Apostle mean by this command? What is our attitude with regard to it? Are we obedient or disobedient?

There are some who seem to think that this "dividing" of the Scriptures is like to that of Jeremiah 36: 23, where we read of Jehoiakim and his penknife, "And it came to pass that when Jehudi had read three or four leaves, he (Jehoiakim) cut it with the penknife, and cast it into the fire"; but the "dividing" of 2 Timothy 2: 15 is not of this character. Neither is it of the kind that to-day parades itself under the name of "Higher Criticism", which so mutilates and dismembers the Word of God, for 2 Timothy 2: 15 says, *rightly* divide, and adds that this division is concerning the Word of *truth.* Consequently, accepting the Scriptures as the "Word of truth", our next concern must be, how are we to divide it aright? To enable the reader to understand this important passage, we will consider (1) the words used; (2) the place in which they occur; (3) two important reasons for dividing the Word aright set forth in the Scriptures; (4) some illustrations of a right and wrong division of Scripture.

Firstly, the words used

"*Study*". — To the minds of many this word seems to preclude any but those who are of a studious turn of mind from obeying this command. This is not the case, however, for the word rendered "study" signifies rather "be diligent", "labour", "endeavour", and is addressed to a "workman" rather than to a "student". The Greek word is *spoudazo*, and occurs eleven times in the New Testament. It is translated "be diligent", twice; "labour", once; and "endeavour", three times. In passing, we would refer to Ephesians 4: 3, where the word is translated "endeavouring", "endeavouring to keep the unity of the Spirit". *Only* as we rightly divide the Word can we hope to keep this unity. The confusion all around us, that anomaly — "Christendom" — with all its "bodies" and "parties", is but the offspring of the failure rightly to apportion the Scriptures, and the vain endeavour to fit "kingdom" teaching into the dispensation of the Mystery.

Again, in 2 Timothy 4: 9, 21 the word is rendered, "Be diligent". This endeavour, this study, is not child's play, far less is it a mere hobby, it pertains to the attainment of full knowledge and perfect manhood in Christ, and our earnest prayer is that every reader may be convinced of the importance of this endeavour and study.

The next word (we follow the order of the Original) is "approved". The Greek word is "*dokimos*", and has the force of "assaying, examining, and testing metals". We are before the eye of the Lord; He it is that examines us; He it is Who infallibly distinguishes between "the vessels of gold and silver, and vessels of wood and earthenware" (2 Tim. 2: 20). Our fellow-men sometimes attempt to assay us, but this should be considered by the Lord's workman as a "very small thing" (1 Cor. 4: 3). Paul was not ashamed even though all in Asia deserted him (2 Tim. 1: 15). Onesiphorus was not ashamed of Paul's chain (verses 16-18); and Timothy is exhorted not to be ashamed (2 Tim. 1: 8; 2: 15).

The next word which we have to consider is translated "show", and literally means, "to make to stand beside". If we turn to 2 Timothy 4: 17 we shall see a notable lesson, for the word again occurs there, "the Lord *stood with* me". Paul as good as says to Timothy, "Take your *stand with* God and His truth; you need not fear man, for the Lord will surely *stand with* you as He has with me". This was the secret of Elijah's strength; it is in this character that he appears upon the page of Scripture. "And Elijah the Tishbite, who was of the inhabitants of Gilead, said unto Ahab, As the Lord God of Israel liveth, *before Whom I stand*, there shall not be dew nor rain these years, but according to my word" (1 Kings 17: 1; 18: 15; *cp*. 2 Kings 3: 14; 5: 16). This, too, shall be our strength. Fearing God, let us fear naught else, but fearlessly and faithfully let us endeavour to divide aright the Word of truth.

We now approach the words which contain the great exhortation. What are we to understand by the term, "rightly dividing"? The word in question is "*orthotomonta*", from *orthos*, right, and *temno*, to cut. The word *apotemno* occurs in the Septuagint version of Jeremiah 36: 23, the passage already referred to, where Jehoiakim *wrongly* cut up or divided the Word of truth. We mention this because it shows that the idea of "cutting" and "dividing" is an essential meaning of the word. The Septuagint supplies us with another helpful passage for in Proverbs 3: 5, 6 we read:

> "Trust in the Lord with all thine heart,
> And lean not unto thine own understanding:
> In all thy ways acknowledge Him,
> And He shall *rightly divide* thy paths".

Here we have a close parallel with 2 Timothy 2: 15. In both cases the fear of man and the assistance of man are put aside, and the Lord divides or opens up aright the tangled pathway. There are some who seek to turn the edge of 2 Timothy 2: 15 by rendering it, "cutting a straight pathway along the Word of truth". Now although this is good advice, it is a false interpretation. It is the Word itself that has to be divided, not the pathway of the believer, in this passage.

It will be seen that the Word of God must not only be considered as a whole, but also that the separate parts must be clearly distinguished the one from the other. So far we have briefly considered the meaning of some of the words used in this command. We consider:

Secondly, the place wherein the passage occurs

It is of great importance in the study of any passage to carefully note in what portion of the Bible it is found. As we have seen, the command under consideration occurs in 2 Timothy. This second epistle to Timothy is in many ways unique. It is the last inspired message from Paul before his death, and the last epistle of the dispensation of the Mystery. Like Ephesians, Philippians, and Colossians, it is a *prison* epistle, and was written by the Apostle during his last Roman imprisonment.

Ephesians gives us the first full revelation of the glorious truth of the Mystery (which will be explained in a subsequent chapter), and 2 Timothy shows us the well-nigh universal desertion of Paul and his message. It speaks of the corporate failure of the church on earth. Ruin is its setting; individual faithfulness its exhortation. Perilous times, formalism, and fables are among its prophetic warnings. Amid all the perfidy and faithlessness of the creature, the faithfulness of the Lord shines in all its unsullied splendour (2 Tim. 1: 12; 2: 13, 19; 3: 11; 4: 8, 17, 18), and the truth of the Scriptures is interwoven in the epistle in a way that emphasizes its position and purpose.

Like all God's ways and works, His Word is perfect, and the passages which contain the word *truth* in this epistle are arranged in such perfect symmetry, that, although we desire to consider more particularly the passage which contains the first occurrence of the word, we believe it will be of service to exhibit the structure of the six passages containing the term.

"Truth" (2 Timothy).

A 2: 15. Rightly dividing the Word of truth. — *Result.* — The unashamed workman
  B 2: 18. Concerning the truth have erred. — *Two examples* (modern). — Hymenæus and Philetus
    C 2: 25, 26. Repentance unto knowledge of truth. — *Condition of such.* — Taken captive
    C 3: 7. Never able to come to knowledge of truth. — *Condition of such.* — Led captive
  B 3: 8. Withstand the truth. — *Two examples* (ancient). — Jannes and Jambres
A 4: 4. Turn away ears from truth. — *Result.* — False teachers.

We believe that this arrangement will be clear to all, but we would seek to emphasize the teaching of the first and last members (A and *A*). Here we have a definite contrast, and an awful alternative. On the one hand the true servant of the Lord, seeking above all things to be faithful to the truth; on the other the false teacher, pandering to popularity, and turning from the truth unto fables.

The more we consider these things, and note the trend of events, the more we are convinced that the professing church will finally be found under one or other of these two descriptions. They will either obey 2 Timothy 2: 15, and apportion aright the Word of truth, or failing to do this they will continue their work of confounding Zion, Israel, and the earthly kingdom with the Body of Christ, until, becoming heartily sick of the jangle and jumble that they will have made, they will throw over the truth and believe *the lie*. O, that the many believers who mourn the infidel tendency of the times, who realize that the apostasy is at our very doors, O, that they may see that the divine safeguard set up by the Lord is the Word of truth *rightly divided*! We now turn to the consideration of our next heading.

Thirdly, two important reasons for dividing the Word aright set forth in the Scriptures

We are about to draw attention to the strongest indictment that can be made against a believer, viz., *the denial of his Lord*! Surely nothing can be worse than this! We crave the reader's most earnest attention to the following Scriptures, as we believe they will demonstrate that failure to discern that which is termed "dispensational truth", failure to "rightly divide" the Word of truth, failure to realize the special message and Apostle of this dispensation, brings a believer perilously near to denying his Lord.

We are often met by the statement made by those who do not perceive the importance of dispensational truth (a term which will be explained presently), that they are satisfied with the words of Christ Himself. In the first place we desire to record that we do not doubt the heart's desire underlying these words. We feel that such believers desire, above all things, to be loyal to the Lord. We ask them to put aside for a moment any prejudice that they may have, for surely, if their loyalty can be called in question, they should be the very first to search the matter to the bottom.

There is a fallacy in this satisfaction with the "words of Christ", for it really amounts to the assumption that the words recorded in the Gospels are of greater value, are of a higher order of inspiration than those written in the epistles. Christ Who spoke in the four Gospels, as surely spoke in the Acts of the Apostles, and in the epistles of Paul, of John, of Peter, and in the Revelation. Further, we find by comparing the Scriptures, that some of the words spoken in the Gospels are countermanded in the Epistles. Is it obedience, therefore, if we persist in seeking to obey a command of the Lord which He Himself has abrogated or modified? Let us illustrate our meaning. The law given through Moses, with all accompaniments of divine majesty at Sinai, is inspired truth. Why do we not still render obedience to its every command? Because the Lord Who spake at Sinai has spoken again. We are not disobedient to Him or His Word if we hear and follow His later commands. The reader will see it is not a matter of doubting the inspiration of Mosaic ritual that absolves us from Tabernacle service and Levitical rites, it is the coming and the offering of Christ, in other words, the later revelation sets aside the earlier. The four Gospels give us a marvellous record of the personal ministry of Christ, but it is unscriptural to believe that therein is recorded the last and final utterance of God to us.

Following the Gospels we have the Acts, wherein the Lord is seen at work by the power of the Holy Spirit, but this is not all. There came a time when the people of Israel were set aside as a *nation*, and again a new set of instructions, a new revelation was given, this time to the Apostle Paul, as set forth in the Prison Epistles: Ephesians, Philippians, Colossians, and 2 Timothy. These contain the words of Christ *to us*. We were never connected with the Jewish nation, we were never members of that church which was endued with miraculous gifts. We belong to the church of the dispensation of the Mystery, and while we fully believe that all Scripture is *for* us, we do not believe that all is *about* us, and we have to be faithful to those portions which are expressly sent *to* us, if we would follow the Lord our God.

In Romans 15: 8, 9 we have the inspired statement as to the ministry of the Lord Jesus Christ while on earth:

> "Now I say that Jesus Christ was a minister of the circumcision, for the truth of God, to confirm the promises made unto the fathers, and that the Gentiles might glorify God for His mercy".

It was never a mystery that in Abraham's seed all families of the earth should be blessed. It formed a part of the unconditional covenant made with Abraham as recorded in Genesis 12. Israel was to be the "great nation", a "kingdom of priests", and the other nations were to be blessed through them. This is part of what is called kingdom truth, but has no relation to the church of the Mystery. When the Lord Jesus was on earth, in the capacity of a minister of the circumcision, He said:

> "Whosoever shall be *ashamed* of Me and of My words, in this adulterous and sinful generation, of him also shall the *Son of man* be ashamed, when He cometh in the glory of His Father, with the holy angels" (Mark 8: 38).
>
> "Whosoever shall *deny* Me before men, him will I also *deny* before My Father which is in heaven" (Matt. 10: 33).

Here we have two solemn passages, ashamed of the Lord and His Word, and denying Him. Now turn to 2 Timothy 1: 8, "Be not thou therefore ashamed of the *testimony of our Lord*, nor of me His prisoner". It is still the same Lord as in Mark 8: 38, but not the same message or mouthpiece. Note the change of the title of Christ.* In Mark 8: 38 it is the Son of man; in 2 Timothy 1: 8 it is the Lord. Which title is it that God has linked to the church, and which to the earthly kingdom? We leave our readers to the inevitable result of their answers to these questions.

(**See* Chapter 2 for different Titles of Christ.)

As we read on in 2 Timothy we find, in chapter 2: 11-13, words which still further link up the question of denying the Lord and of rightly dividing the Word.

> "Faithful is the Word; for if we died together, we shall also live together.
> If we endure, we shall also reign together;
> If we shall deny, He also will deny us;
> If we are faithless, faithful He remaineth, for deny Himself He cannot".

The passage goes on from these tremendous statements and says, "Of *these things* be putting them in remembrance, adjuring them before God, not to be waging word battles, useful for nothing, but to the subversion of the hearers", but rather, remember that which will make you unashamed, which will prevent you from denying the Lord and His testimony, viz., "divide the Word aright".

If there has taken place a complete change in the administration of God's dealings with man subsequent to that period covered by the Gospels and the Acts; if a different piece of God's "good news" has been sent by an especially chosen Apostle; if higher hopes and richer grace have been revealed; if we are definitely told that to the Apostle Paul has been committed this present dispensation; if he had the apostleship to the Gentiles, and the proclamation of the Mystery or secret, which had been hidden from before the foundation of the world, committed to him, then it is perfectly clear that if we seek to put into practice the commands, to entertain the hopes, or proclaim the good news pertaining to another dispensation, we shall be as guilty of denying the Lord, and of being ashamed of His testimony, as the Judaisers were who sought to enforce the Mosaic law upon Gentile believers, as recorded in Acts 15.

These Judaisers could quote chapter and verse for their teaching, but the evil lay in the fact that the dispensation had changed, and consequently the Apostle Paul, referring to *the very law of God* from this aspect, calls its precepts and ordinances "weak and beggarly elements" (Gal. 4: 9). If the Holy Spirit can speak of the very ordinances given by God under such a title when they are applied in an undispensational manner, the reader should not rest satisfied with the current opinions concerning the church and its ordinances, until he is assured that such are not only to be found *in Scripture*, but also found in the Scriptures positively applying to this present time; in other words, he must "rightly divide the Word of truth".

Passing to the other important reason for "rightly dividing the Word of truth", we would point out that we shall not be clear as to the *gospel*, if we are uncertain as to *dispensational* truth. Many seem to think that a knowledge of the different dispensations and ways of God is unessential; all that they feel called upon to do is to "preach the gospel". Without questioning the worthiness of their motives we might ask, which gospel? The word translated "gospel" in the New Testament means "good news". The word itself does not say to whom the good news is addressed, nor what the good news is about, hence we have:

> The gospel or good news of the *kingdom.*
> The gospel or good news of God concerning *His Son.*
> The gospel or good news of the *circumcision.*
> The gospel or good news of the *uncircumcision.*
> The gospel or good news of the *grace of God.*
> The gospel or good news of the *glory of Christ.*
> The gospel or good news of the *glory of the blessed God.*
> The *everlasting (eonian)* gospel or good news.

We may illustrate our meaning by taking the extreme case of the "everlasting (*eonian*) gospel". This is found in Revelation 14: 6, 7. It is set in a scene of judgment. It says nothing about the very essentials of the gospel which we have received. There is not a word as to faith, justification, redemption, pardon, or peace. Its terms are, "Fear God, and give glory to Him, for the hour of His judgment is come, and worship Him that made the heavens and earth, the sea and the fountains of waters". It is a message of "good news" to the nations on the earth under the awful reign of antichrist. As many as will not worship the image of the beast shall be killed (Rev. 13: 15), hence the angel preaches this peculiar gospel to them, viz., to fear, give glory to, and worship God as *Creator.*

Again, take the expressions of Galatians 2: 7, "the gospel of the *uncircumcision*" and "the gospel of the *circumcision*". It is *not* the same gospel sent in the same way *to* different hearers; it is not the gospel *to* the circumcision, but the gospel *of* the circumcision. Paul tells us that when he went up to Jerusalem, and "communicated unto them *that* gospel which *I* preach among the Gentiles", the Apostles at Jerusalem were perfectly satisfied that the gospel which Paul preached had the authority of God equally with Peter's. Peter tells us in Acts 15: 7 that the message he delivered to Cornelius was "the gospel". If we turn to Acts 10 we shall discover what was the gospel as preached by Peter. The opening words of Peter are enough to tell us that we are to hear a message expressed differently from the gospel as preached by Paul.

"Of a truth I perceive that God is no respecter of persons, but in every nation he that feareth God, and *worketh righteousness* is accepted with Him" (Acts 10: 34, 35). Place these words beside Titus 3: 5, "*not* by *works* of *righteousness* which we have done, but according to His mercy He saved us". Peter commences with the preaching of John the Baptist, and the earthly life of the Lord Jesus, and concludes with the "remission of sins". The character of Cornelius ("a devout man", one who "prayed to God always"), is quite different from the "ungodly", the "sinners", the "enemies" (Rom. 5), who are the only ones to whom the Apostle Paul directs his message of salvation.

We will not tarry longer to speak of the still further differences that are clearly discernible both between the doctrine and dispensation of the ministry of Peter and Paul; all should feel that if there is a peculiar message sent through the Apostle of the Gentiles, *that* should be the gospel for the time in which we live, and not the gospel of the earthly kingdom. Needless to say there are no discrepancies here. Peter is perfectly right in Acts 10; Paul is perfectly right in Titus 3. Both are inspired and both are true, but Peter's message would be *untrue* in Titus 3 or Ephesians 2, even though true in the Pentecostal period, simply because the dispensation had been changed, and a new order inaugurated. As the reader considers the teaching of the Scriptures set forth in the following chapters, we believe the tremendous importance of this subject will grow upon him; hence we reserve any further comment upon this point, and proceed to consider some illustrations of a right and wrong division of Scripture.

Fourthly, some illustrations of a right and wrong division of Scripture

The chapter headings of our English Bible supply a good example of wrongly dividing the Word of truth. Over Isaiah 29 we read: "1. God's heavy judgment upon Jerusalem. 9. The senselessness. 13. And deep hypocrisy of the Jews"; whereas over Isaiah 30 we read: "18. God's mercies towards His church". In Isaiah 29: 1 we read of "The city where David dwelt". In Isaiah 30: 19 we read, "For the people shall dwell *in Zion at Jerusalem*", yet while the *judgments* are reserved for the Jew, the *blessings* in the self-same passages are appropriated by the church. If we will but look for ourselves, and believe that which we see, we may discover in Isaiah the people *to* whom and *concerning* whom this prophecy was written. Isaiah 1: 1 says, "The vision of Isaiah, the son of Amoz, which he saw concerning *Judah and Jerusalem*".

This appropriation, or rather mis-appropriation, of Scriptures written concerning Israel and the earthly kingdom is a fruitful source of confusion among believers. Think of the many who have stumbled over the epistle of James. Those who have seen "justification by faith, without legal works of any kind" (Gal. 2: 16), to be vital to the integrity of the gospel of grace, have had considerable difficulty in deciding what to do with the teaching of James. Some have laboured to harmonize the teaching of James, and the teaching of Paul. Others, seeing the futility of this, discredit the epistle of James. Luther called it an "epistle of straw"; while others, of equal orthodoxy, questioned its canonicity. On the other hand, there are those to whom the emphasis upon works is more palatable than Paul's emphasis upon "grace", who have used James to water down the teaching of Romans or Ephesians.

If we will but rightly divide the Word of truth, all this "vain jangling" will cease. *We* are saved Gentiles. *We* never have had any connection with the people, land, or promises of Israel. God has sent to *us* an apostle — Paul, the apostle for *you Gentiles*. We are responsible for the way in which *we* receive his message. James did not write his epistle to saved Gentiles, nor to the "church, which is the body of Christ". James, as the first verse tells us, wrote thus: "James, to the twelve tribes which are scattered abroad". If any reader should be a member of one of these twelve tribes, he may feel that the epistle has a word for him, although even in that case we hope to show that the dispensation in which we (whether Jewish or Gentile believers) find ourselves is not connected with the epistle of James; but if he be a believer of the Gentiles, then although he may learn much and profit much by reading this epistle, he will only make confusion unless he rightly divides the Word of truth.

If we consider the "address on the envelope" a little more closely than we have done, we shall not be found appropriating the promises and blessings of others, and confusing our own hopes. Suppose a father, having several sons, sends to them letters of advice, words of encouragement, promises of help, and reward. We can quite understand that one son, John, would be glad to read the letter written to his brother William, and *vice versa*. Both would doubtless find much in the letter written from their father to the other that would be profitable, but neither would think of claiming the promises made to the other, nor of obeying the other's instructions.

If John were a bank clerk, and William were an artist, the instructions given to the brother in the bank would be of little service to the brother at his easel. So it is with the children of God. The same Father in heaven has many sons. Some have been placed under "law", and have as their hope a share of the promises "made unto the fathers", whilst others have been placed under "grace", and have an inheritance concerning which Abraham, Isaac, and Jacob knew nothing. All the messages of love, cheer, hope, instruction and warning may be profitably read by all, but each one must see, at the same time, that the words sent *to* him, and written *about* him, are duly considered and placed foremost. The failure to realize that God has dealt with man under different economies or administrations (*see* meaning of *Dispensation*, chapter 2), is at the root of much of this confusion.

Another fruitful cause of misunderstanding is the forgetfulness or ignorance of the fact that this present dispensation is "the dispensation of the Mystery (or secret) which had been hidden away from all ages and generations by God" (Eph. 3). Of this we shall speak more fully in subsequent chapters, but we refer to it here because the knowledge of this will help us with regard to many of the passages of Scripture that are wrongly applied to-day, and perhaps prevent us from too hastily condemning the division of Scripture called by some "The Gap Theory".

The Lord Jesus, at the commencement of His ministry as recorded in Luke 4: 16-20, shows very clearly the principle which we seek to emphasize. Entering the synagogue at Nazareth, He stood up and read Isaiah 61: 1, 2, but the noteworthy fact is that the Lord did not complete the latter verse. Immediately upon reading the words, "the acceptable year of the Lord", "*He closed the book*". Why did the Lord stop just here? Why did He not read on to the end of the verse? The reason is that the next words belong to *a yet future dispensation.* The Lord was about to make a most important statement. His words were, "*This* day is *this* Scripture fulfilled in your ears". This could not have been said if He had read on and included the words, "the day of vengeance of our God". The day of vengeance will not be ushered in until the Lord Jesus steps forward and "opens the book", as recorded in Revelation 5 and 6.

So far as dispensational truth is concerned, we have to remember the "closed book", and to see that this present dispensation comes in between the acceptable year of the Lord, and the day of vengeance of our God. The Lord seems to have given a hint of an impending change by the words which He spoke to the people after the action cited above. He emphasized the fact that although there were many widows and many lepers in Israel, yet it was a *Gentile* leper, and a *Gentile* widow that were blessed, as recorded in the Scriptures. The "gap" and the emphasis upon *Gentile* blessing come together in this chapter in a way that demands careful consideration. So also with other prophets who wrote beforehand "of the *sufferings* for Christ, and the glories which should follow" (1 Peter 1: 10, 11). So far as we can tell from their writings, there was nothing to guide them as to whether days or centuries would come between the "sufferings" and the "glories".

Much more could be written on this important subject, but we hope that sufficient has been put forward in this chapter to show that not only is it incumbent upon the reader of the Bible to accept its every statement as absolute truth, but also to see to it that the varied manners and times, the differing dispensations and economies that qualify the different commands and promises made, be given due consideration. By thus apportioning the Word of truth according as it is written respecting the Jew, the Gentile, or the dispensation of the Mystery (secret), they will obtain a grasp of its wonderful harmony, perceive something of the manifold grace that pervades the whole of God's purposes, and find themselves approved unto God, workmen having no need to be ashamed, *rightly dividing the Word of truth.*

CHAPTER TWO

A definition of terms

In the former chapter we have sought to establish, and to illustrate, that (*a*) the Scriptures are fully and verbally inspired, and (*b*) that to understand their teaching, appreciate their fulness, and proclaim a consistent gospel, they must not only be believed *en masse*, but must also be "rightly divided" or apportioned as to their various dispensations.

We have mentioned, in passing, two important sections, named respectively, "the truth of the earthly kingdom", and "the truth concerning the Mystery". The consideration of these will occupy the greater part of this volume, but we feel that before we go any further with these subjects it will be helpful if we try to explain briefly some of the terms that are continually used in this particular line of study, not attempting to give a full exposition of the various subjects (for that will occupy the remainder of the book), but to define the terms as concisely as possible.

The word "dispensation"

The Greek word translated "dispensation" is *oikonomia*, and signifies the *act of administering*. *Oikonomia* is a compound made up of *oikos* (a house), and *nemo* (to dispense, to deal out as a steward or housekeeper). The Greek word is preserved in our English tongue in the words "economy", "economics". Let us consider the occurrences of this word. In Luke 16: 2, 3, 4 it is rendered "stewardship". In 1 Corinthians 9: 17; Ephesians 1: 10; 3: 2, 9 (R.V.); Colossians 1: 25, and 1 Timothy 1: 4 (R.V.), it is rendered "dispensation". These are all the passages where the word *oikonomia* occurs, nine in all, and those who are acquainted with the significance of numbers will recognise that nine, "the number of finality of judgment" both in relation to God and man, is in part explanatory of the goal of the various dispensations of God.

By *dispensational truth* we mean that particular revelation of God's will to man during some particular administration or economy, and specially appertaining thereto. When we speak of some teaching or practice as being *undispensational*, we mean that owing to the introduction of a new administration, certain things that obtained under a previous régime have become obsolete. By the term undispensational teaching, therefore, we mean that the teaching peculiar to one dispensation has been imported into another and differing dispensation, where the conditions of divine dealing render the practical application of such teaching quite inadmissible.

The dispensation of law is in many respects in entire opposition to the principles that underlie the dispensation of grace. "*Do* and thou shalt live" is the condition of blessing under law. "And it shall be our righteousness if we observe to *do* all these commandments before the Lord our God, as He hath commanded us" (Deut. 6: 25). "*Live* and then do" is the blessed fact of the present dispensation of grace. "*Not* by works of righteousness which we have done, but according to His mercy He saved us, by the washing of regeneration, and renewing of the Holy Ghost" (Titus 3: 5). "Therefore by the deeds of the law there shall *no flesh* be justified in His sight, for by the law is the knowledge of sin" (Rom. 3: 20). Certain rites (*e.g.*, circumcision), observances (*e.g.*, sabbaths), and sacrifices were enjoined upon Israel under law, but these are entirely set aside, nay, are made false and untrue if carried over into the present dispensation. "Let no man therefore judge you in respect of . . . the sabbath" (*see* Col. 2, and Heb. 10).

If we do not rightly divide the Word of truth, we are in danger of falsifying the gospel, and of misrepresenting the Lord. The false teachers who disturbed the Gentile believers with their words, "Except ye be circumcised after the manner of Moses, ye cannot be saved", could point to chapter and verse for their doctrine. Circumcision was not only a divinely-appointed ordinance, but the Lord had said of the man child who was not circumcised, "That soul shall be cut off from his people, he hath broken My covenant" (Gen. 17: 14). Nevertheless, the Apostle Paul, when speaking of this very thing to the Galatians, says of the divinely-appointed ordinances when brought over out of their true place — under law — into the dispensation of grace, that they are "weak and beggarly elements", and that the believers' subjection to such is to be placed upon a parallel with the idolatrous service of their unconverted heathen days (*see* Gal. 4: 8-11; 5: 1-3; and 6: 12-16). If the words of the Bible are not to be divided according to their dispensational setting, then we must all be circumcised, all keep the sabbath, the passover, the day of atonement, the feast of tabernacles, and the other observances of the Mosaic ritual, thus setting one passage of Scripture in conflict with another, and ultimately find ourselves in utter confusion.

The word "church"

The word translated "church" is *ekklesia*, and means "an assembly or congregation of called-out ones", and is derived from *kaleo* (to call or summon), and *ek* (out of). The Greek word occurs some 111 times in the New Testament. It has several phases:

(1) A future assembly prophesied of in Matthew 16: 18 (*see* chapters on the kingdom for explanation).

(2) The assembly of the people of Israel called out from all other nations (Acts 7: 38).

(3) The "church of God" which was persecuted by Paul when a Pharisee (Acts 8: 3; 1 Cor. 15: 9).

(4) An assembly of people called out by some common cause (Acts 19: 32-40).

(5) An assembly of the people called out by the civil magistrate (Acts 19: 39).

(6) The synagogue of believing Jews during the transitional period of the Acts, and also of Revelation 2, 3, (James 2: 2; 5: 14).

(7) The assembly of the dispensation of the Mystery (the church, which is His Body) as used by Paul in Ephesians, Philippians, and Colossians.

It will be at once seen that it is not sufficient merely to use the word "church"; we must know when such church was formed, the nature of its fellowship, and the dispensation under which it originated. The "church in the wilderness" was under *law*. The "church which is His Body" is absolutely under *grace*. The one abounded in rites and ordinances, the other has none. The hopes of the first were connected with earthly blessings (even though they were to be enjoyed in resurrection); the hope of the second is found in heavenly places.

When, however, we use the term "church truth" in the following pages, we shall limit our meaning to cover the following idea. Church truth is that system of doctrine revealed in a special manner to the Apostle Paul as the divinely-appointed channel. It is contained particularly in the epistles written during his imprisonment at Rome, which for the sake of brevity we may speak of as "Prison Epistles". These epistles were written by him after the date of Acts 28: 28 and reveal a new calling resting upon the finished work of Christ. This "Church truth" will be used in antithesis to "earthly kingdom truth", which will be taken to mean that system of doctrine revealed in the Old Testament, the Gospels, the Acts, the Epistles of Paul prior to Acts 28, the Epistles of Peter and James, John and Jude and the Revelation. This kingdom on earth covers the whole field of Abrahamic promises, Davidic promises, the hopes of Israel and the nations, and the future millennial kingdom. We hope to show that just as there was a church connected with *this* kingdom, so now the church of the Mystery is connected with a kingdom in heaven and not in the earth.

Acts 28: 25, 26

We shall make continual reference to this important passage as being the divinely-appointed dispensational landmark. We cannot attempt to set out the Scriptural argument for this statement here, but we will show the arrangement of the epistles of Paul on either side of this dividing line, and this will obviate lengthy explanations in subsequent chapters. The dates are those which are received by all competent judges; they have not been altered to suit our own personal ideas. The reader will understand that when we mention the bearing of the chronological order of the epistles upon their doctrine, it is to this arrangement that we refer.

1 Thessalonians.	A.D. 52	*Pentecostal and transitional period.*
2 ,,	,, 53	
1 Corinthians.	,, 57	*"Earthly Kingdom truth" and preparatory teaching by Paul for impending change.*
2 ,,	,, 57	
Galatians.*	,, 57	
Romans.	,, 58	

Acts 28: 25, 26 (A.D. 62).

The Dispensational Boundary.

Ephesians.	A.D. 62		*The dispensation of the mystery. "Church truth", and the standard doctrine for the present period.*
Colossians.	,, 62	*Prison*	
Philippians.	,, 62		
1 Timothy.	,, 67		
Titus.	,, 67		
2. Timothy.	,, 68	*Prison*	

The epistle to the Hebrews has a mission and message peculiarly its own. It was written about A.D. 64. We do not speak of it as "church" truth, but will seek to explain its relation to the Mystery in the course of this book.

---

*For a fuller discussion of Galatia and the date of Galatians, *see The Apostle of the Reconciliation* by the same Author and Publisher where reasons are given for putting Galatians first.

The foundation of the world

In the text of this book the reader may be surprised to find that, instead of quoting the Authorised Version or Revised Version, "Before the *foundation* of the world", we give it as "Before the *overthrow* of the world". The explanation of this somewhat drastic change is here given. There are two Greek words rendered "foundation": *themelios*, which occurs some 16 times, and *katabole*, which occurs some 11 times. "Foundation" is a correct translation of *themelios* (*see* 1 Cor. 3: 10, 11, 12; Eph. 2: 20; 2 Tim. 2: 19). "Foundation" is not a true translation of *katabole*, as we will seek to show. The verb from which *katabole* is derived is *kataballo*, and occurs in 2 Corinthians 4: 9, "cast down"; Revelation 12: 9, "cast down"; Hebrews 6: 1, "laying"; here also it should be rendered "cast down", as we shall explain when dealing with Hebrews 6. The Septuagint (Greek translation of Hebrew Old Testament) uses this verb as a rendering of words, all of which mean to overthrow, destroy, pull down, etc.; ***none* means to lay a foundation or build up.**

> "They battered the wall *to throw it down*"! (2 Sam. 20: 15).
>
> "I will *overthrow* the throne of kingdoms" (and so in all its occurrences) (Hag. 2: 22).

The expressions "from" and "before" the overthrow of the world relate to that period indicated in Genesis 1: 1, 2, and 2 Peter 3: 6. "In the beginning God created the heavens and the earth". This is "the world that then was" of 2 Peter 3: 5, 6. This "perished", and is described in Genesis 1: 2, "And the earth *became* without form and void; and darkness was upon the face of the deep". The word "was" is really "became" (*see* Gen 2: 7, "Man *became* a living soul"; Gen. 4: 3, "It *came* to pass"; Gen. 9: 15, "*Become* a flood").

The words "without form and void" are in the Hebrew *tohu va bohu*. Isaiah 45: 18 definitely tells us that the earth was *not* thus created *tohu*; 2 Peter 3: 5, 6 explains that it *became* so. Thus Genesis 1: 2 is the dividing line between the periods designated "*before* the overthrow of the world", and "*since* the overthrow of the world". It must also be remembered that the word translated world (*kosmos*) refers not merely to the material earth, but to the whole order and constitution of the universe. It was this order and constitution, primarily, which became involved in the "overthrow".

The Mystery

We reserve any comments upon the various mysteries of Scripture until we deal with that subject, but we would here take the opportunity of giving a word or two as to the meaning of the word. It may be set out thus:

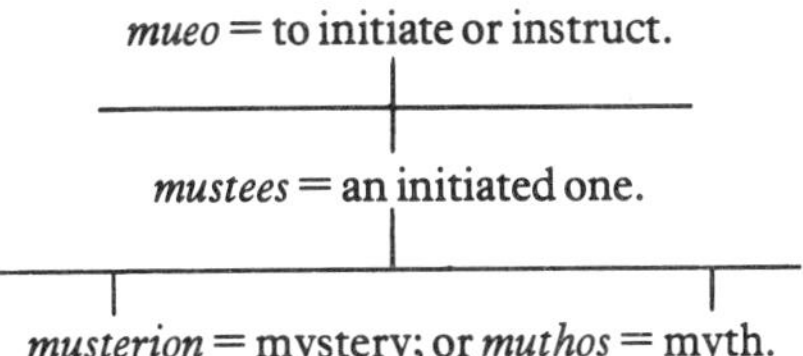

It is intensely significant that the "myths" (translated "fables" in 2 Timothy 4: 4, "they shall *turn away* their ears from the truth and shall be turned unto fables"), are placed in contrast with the truth, viz., the Mystery which was entrusted to Paul. "All they which are in Asia be *turned away* from me" (2 Tim. 1: 15).

The word simply means "a secret"; in Scripture a *divine* secret. Hence, in the New Testament a mystery was not something that in itself was necessarily mysterious or hard to understand; but, to put it simply, something one could not know until one was told. A reference to 1 Corinthians 2: 6-10; Matthew 13: 11; Colossians 2: 2 and Revelation 10: 7, will confirm this. There have been many secrets or mysteries revealed in Scripture at different times. They relate to widely differing portions of truth, and we do well to remember the futility of endeavouring to find in Scriptures written beforehand anything which God kept secret until a later period. The following is a list of the most prominent "mysteries" in the Scriptures:

(1) The mysteries of the *kingdom of heaven* (Matt. 13: 11).
(2) The mystery of Israel's *blindness* (Rom. 11: 25).
(3) The mystery of *resurrection*, and change (1 Cor. 15: 51).
(4) The mystery of *iniquity* (2 Thess. 2: 7).
(5) The mystery of *godliness* (1 Tim. 3: 16).
(6) The mystery of *Christ* (Eph. 3: 4).
(7) The mystery of *this dispensation* (Eph. 3: 3-9).
(8) The *great* mystery (Eph. 5: 32).
(9) The mystery of *God* (Rev. 10: 7).

Bible Numerics

Occasional reference will be found to what is called Numerics. In the works of God in nature number is a prominent factor, so also is it in the Word of truth. Every word, syllable, and letter is found to be subject to a most involved and marvellous law of numerics. Take, for example, the number of occurrences of certain words:

Mercy seat occurs in the Old Testament 27 times (3 × 3 × 3).

Frankincense occurs {in Leviticus 7, elsewhere 14} 21 times (3 × 7).

Manna occurs 14 times (2 × 7).

The "sevens" here are emphasized. Before leaving the subject we give a brief note on the spiritual significance of numbers.*:

> *One* denotes *unity* and *commencement*. First occurrences of words give their essential significance in interpretation.
>
> *Two* denotes *division, opposition*. See the work of the second day. Note use of "double" applied to "heart", "tongue", "mind", &c.
>
> *Three* denotes *completeness* and *resurrection*, and when applied to the Godhead speaks of *redemption* rather than creation.
>
> *Four* denotes *creation*, the *world*, things under the sun.
>
> *Five* denotes *grace*. It is 4 + 1. It is God adding His gifts and blessing His works. The Gematria of *charis* (grace) is a multiple of five. The Gematria of the Hebrew "the heavens" is also a multiple of five, while the Gematria of the Hebrew "the earth" is a multiple of four.
>
> *Six* is the number of *man*. Man was created on the sixth day. Antichrist is 666. Nebuchadnezzar's image, and Goliath and his armour, are marked by the same number. 6 is one short of 7.
>
> *Seven* denotes *spiritual perfection*. Seven is the hall-mark upon the Scriptures and the work of the Spirit. He is the Giver of life.
>
> *Eight* denotes *resurrection, regeneration*. It is the octave, a new beginning.
>
> *Nine* denotes *finality of judgment* (3 × 3).
>
> *Ten* denotes *ordinal perfection*.
>
> *Eleven* denotes *disorder, disorganization*, being one short of twelve.
>
> *Twelve* denotes *governmental perfection*. Twelve tribes, twelve apostles, twelve gates, &c.
>
> *Thirteen* denotes *rebellion* and *apostasy*. The titles of Satan are multiples of thirteen.

Other numbers follow the laws which govern smaller factors. The four *perfect numbers* (3, 7, 10 and 12) have for their product the remarkable number 2,520, which is the number of days in the seven prophetic years which are yet to run their course in relation to Israel, and concerning which the Book of the Revelation is written. (The 3½ years, or 42 months, or 1,260 days, is one half of this period).

There is also beyond the evident design exhibited in the number of occurrences, the *significance* of the numbers themselves, as exhibited by what the ancients call *Gematria*. This is the use of the letters of the alphabet instead of figures. Both in the Hebrew and the Greek languages the letters of the alphabet were used to represent numbers. Thus, using the English alphabet, A = 1, B = 2, C = 3. The numerical value of the word "cab" would be C = 3, A = 1, B = 2, = 6.

**See* Appendix 10 to *The Companion Bible*.

Revelation 13: 18 tells us that the number of the *beast* is the number of *man*, and is 666; Nebuchadnezzar's image, which foreshadowed this exaltation of man, was 60 cubits high and 6 cubits wide. Six is the number of man. Cain's descendants are given to the *sixth* generation. Athaliah's reign of usurpation was for *six* years. *Six* words are used for "man" in the Hebrew Bible. *Six* names are found in the Hebrew Bible for the *serpent*. Six denotes imperfection, whereas seven denotes spiritual perfection. Abraham had 8 sons, and eight is a factor in the Gematria of their names:

Abraham = 248 (8 × 31)
Isaac = 208 (8 × 2 × 13) } 456 (8 × 57).

Jacob = 182
Leah = 36
Rachel = 238 } 456 (8 × 57).

Notice the difference emphasised between Rachel's two sons and those of her handmaid and Leah's.

Joseph = 156
Benjamin = 152 } 308 (77 × 4).

Rachel's maid (Rachel = 238 (7 × 34).)

Bilhah = 42
Dan = 54
Napthali = 570 } 666.

Leah's maid (Leah = 36 (6 × 6).)

Zilpah = 122
Gad = 7
Asher = 501
Add *Leah* = 36 } 666.

The fact that the addition of Leah to the names of the children of her handmaid makes 666 is a commentary in itself. Rachel though received after Leah, was the wife for whom Jacob toiled.

We could pursue this subject with interest, but we must desist. Sufficient has been given to show that *Bible Numerics* contain a tremendous amount of teaching, and consequently we shall from time to time give any instances that may be relevant to our subject, although we are quite conscious that through our many limitations we shall pass over passages that teem with instruction and interest. The numerics *always* refer to the original Hebrew or Greek, *never* to the English version. We would further remark that numerics alone are not to be taken as sufficient of themselves to establish a doctrine, but when a doctrine is established by Scripture, the numerics are valuable as confirmatory evidence.

The kingdom of heaven
and
The kingdom of God

A word or two here may be well, in briefly explaining the meaning of the two expressions, the "kingdom of the heavens", and the "kingdom of God". The word *basileia* (kingdom) refers not so much to the country, or the subjects, as to the sovereignty and rule of the king. The termination "*dom*" is an abbreviation of "doom", meaning judgment, then office, power. Hence the kingdom refers to the rule of the king. In this sense we speak of wis-dom, Christen-dom.

"The kingdom of the heavens" signifies that blessed period on earth when the prophetic type of Daniel 4: 25, 26 shall be fulfilled: "the heavens do rule"; "the Most High ruleth in the kingdom of men", and there shall be realised what is spoken in Daniel 2: 44, "In the days of these kings shall the God of heaven set up a kingdom which shall never be destroyed"; and in Daniel 7: 13, 14, "I saw in the night visions, and behold, one like the *Son of man* came with the clouds of heaven ... and there was given Him dominion, and glory, and a kingdom, that all peoples, nations, and languages should serve Him"; and in Daniel 7: 27, "and the kingdom, and dominion, and the greatness of the kingdom *under the whole heavens* shall be given to the people of the saints of the Most High"; and in Revelation 11: 15, "And the seventh angel sounded and there were great voices in heaven, saying, The kingdoms of *this world* are become our Lord's and His Anointed's"; and in Psalm 2: 2-6, "The kings of the earth set themselves, and the rulers take counsel together, against the Lord, and against His Anointed ... Yet have I set My King upon My holy hill of Zion".

The kingdom of the heavens refers to that kingdom which shall be set up on earth when the Lord Jesus returns to the Mount of Olives, destroys antichrist, and brings blessing to His people Israel. The term "kingdom of the heavens" is confined to the Gospel according to Matthew, and hence the Gospel opens with the words, "The book of the generations of Jesus Christ, *the Son of David*, the Son of Abraham". The kingdom of the heavens will be the rule of heaven's king upon earth, the millennial earth will be its sphere, but the rule of heaven its law, "Thy will be done on earth as it is in heaven". It will belong to "a people" and "a nation", indeed to "a kingdom of priests", viz., redeemed Israël.

The "kingdom of God" is a wider term. Nothing is outside this sovereignty. This kingdom is limited by no bounds of time or space. The sovereignty or kingdom of God includes all ages and dispensations, past, present, and future; all realms, earth, heaven, and the universe; all creation, dominions, principalities, powers, angels, and men, things temporal, and things spiritual. It includes the kingdom of the heavens, and the church. "The church" is not "the earthly kingdom," but both are within the kingdom of God, and rest upon the same rock foundation. Thus it is that while we read in the Gospels of the wider term, the kingdom of God, and in the epistles of the Mystery, of the kingdom of God, and the heavenly kingdom, we never read in the epistles of the Mystery of the narrower and Jewish name, "the kingdom of the heavens". Those who speak of "extending the kingdom" by missionary effort doubtless mean well, but use terms that are unscriptural and misleading.

The gospel

Not only are there observable in Scripture various dispensations and purposes, but there are also, in relation to these varying administrations, varying gospels. Let us examine the word and its occurrences. The Greek word translated "gospel" means "good news". Good news is comforting, but good news may be concerning a multitude of things. It is "good news" to the anxious mother to hear from her son at the end of a long sea voyage that he is doing successfully in his foreign home. Yet again it is "good news" of a different type which tells her that within 24 hours, she may welcome her son back. So with the "good news" of the Bible. There is a message regarding the earth, and the future blessings of the earth; this is the gospel of the kingdom.

There is a message of free salvation, forgiveness, justification, and future glory, resting solely upon the redeeming work of Christ; this is the good news or gospel of grace. There is a message relating to, and linking us with, the exalted Son of God in His heavenly glory and ultimate purposes; this is the good news or gospel of the glory of Christ, and of the blessed God.

Our readers must not infer that we preach a "yea and a nay gospel". What they must understand is that they are not to assume that the word "gospel" (no matter what may be its setting, its terms, or its name) has reference to one and the same thing. Let us not join together that which God has kept distinct.

The titles of Christ

The titles of Christ are never used promiscuously, but are in perfect conformity with their setting.

Son of man. — This title is of frequent occurrence, and is found for the first time in Psalm 8. This Psalm opens and closes with a reference to the *earth*, and concerning the Son of man it says, "Thou madest Him to have dominion over the works of Thine hands". The reference backwards is to Adam, the first man, who failed, and forfeited his dominion; the forward reference is to Christ, the second Man, the last Adam, the Lord from heaven, Who brings this kingdom to a perfect consummation. The last occurrence of the title shows the fulfilment of Psalm 8, and is found in Revelation 14: 14, "And I looked, and behold a white cloud, and upon the cloud one sitting like unto the Son of man, having upon His head a golden crown, and in His hand a sharp sickle". The harvest is the harvest of the earth. As the lowly Sower, the Son of man had not where to lay His head (Matt. 8: 20 is the first occurrence of the title in N.T.). As the Man of sorrows He was cruelly crowned with thorns. All that, thank God, is past. Revelation 1: 13 and 14: 14 show us the Son of man about to "take the kingdom", and to "execute *judgment*, because He is the Son of man" (John 5: 27).

This title occurs 84 times. Eighty-four = 4 × 7 × 3. Four is the number of the world; seven represents spiritual perfection; three signifies redemption and resurrection. The title Son of man means just this very thing, viz., that the *world* is to be brought under the beneficent sway of Christ in resurrection power. Another important set of factors is 12 × 7. Twelve speaks of Israel, while seven tells of perfection. As Son of man, before His death and resurrection, He declined all idea of kingship or judgment, but this He claims as His prerogative "hereafter" (Matt. 26: 64). It is remarkable to note that although this title occurs 84 times in the New Testament, it is *never once found* in the epistles of Paul written to the churches. It occurs eighty times in the Gospels, once in the Acts, once in Hebrews, and twice in Revelation. If the title "Son of man" relates to earth and things of the earth, the next title refers to heaven and things of heaven.

The Son of God. — We do not intend to deal here with the question of the deity of the Lord Jesus Christ. We believe with all our heart that "this is our God", and confess Him, with Thomas of old, as "Lord and GOD", but our subject will not allow us to deal with this wonderful theme. The first and second occurrences are in Matthew 4: 3, 6, in the words of the tempter, "If Thou be (or since Thou art) Son of God". The third occurrence is in Matthew 8: 29 where the demons cried, "What have we to do with Thee, Jesus, Thou Son of God?" It will be seen by these passages that the title shows us that the Lord Jesus is the Lord of the spirit realm, and of the unseen. It is His title as related to things *in* the heavens, even as the title "Son of man" relates to His connection with things *on* earth. The title occurs once only in the epistles of the Mystery. Ephesians 4: 13, "Till we all come unto the unity of the faith, and of the knowledge of the Son of God, unto a perfect man, unto the measure of the stature of the fulness of the Christ".

The Son of David. — This title is specifically linked with Israel. As Son of God the Lord Jesus is contemplated as "Heir of all things" in heaven and earth. As Son of man the Lord Jesus is seen in relation to the earth, the millennium, and judgment. As Son of David He is seen as the Heir of David's throne, the rightful King of Israel. The title occurs only in the synoptic Gospels, Matthew, Mark, and Luke; and has no connection with the promises and blessings of the Body of Christ. The angel Gabriel in announcing the birth of the Saviour to Mary says:

> "Thou shalt call His name *Jesus* . . . He shall be great, and shall be called the Son of the Highest, and the Lord shall give unto Him the throne of His father David, and He shall reign over the house of Jacob for ever, and of His kingdom there shall be no end" (Luke 1: 31-33).

The name "Jesus" is linked with all His titles. He carries it from the lowly manger to the cruel cross. He bears it now as Head of the church. He will in that name receive universal homage, and be crowned as Lord in the yet glorious future (Phil. 2: 10, 11).

Whereas Luke tells us, "Thou shalt call His name Jesus" in relation to the Davidic covenant Matthew 1: 21 says, "Thou shalt call His name Jesus, for He shall save *His people* from their sins". "His people" are primarily the same as the "house of Jacob" of Luke 1, the emphasis in Matthew 1 being not so much upon the King, as upon the Saviour. This exclusive character of the title "Son of David" is strikingly illustrated in Matthew 15: 21-28. A woman of Canaan cried:

> "Have mercy on me, O Lord, thou Son of David. But He answered her not a word! . . . He answered and said, I am not sent *but* unto the lost sheep of the *house of Israel*".

Davidic covenanted blessings are restricted to the house of Israel. Neither the covenant made with David or with Abraham have reference to "The church which is His Body", which is blessed neither in David, nor Abraham, but in *heavenly* places, with spiritual blessings, in Christ alone.

The Canaanite woman continues to ask for blessing, but the Lord emphasizes the exclusiveness of the blessings thus covenanted, referring to the house of Israel as the "children", and to the Gentiles as the "little dogs". The Lord does not say "dogs", but "*little* dogs", or puppies, which were kept in the house and petted by the children, whereas dogs were expelled and ran wild. The faith of the woman caught hold of the Lord's words. She confessed that Israel was superior; she said that she was not desiring the peculiar blessings of Israel, even though she had, perhaps unwittingly, used the title "Son of David"; she would be grateful for some of the crumbs that fall from their table. She drops the title of Son of David, and uses the wider term "*Lord*", and then the Saviour says, "O woman, great is thy faith, be it unto thee, even as thou wilt". This woman learned a lesson concerning dispensational truth that we need to learn also. An undispensational conception prevents blessing; remember this, O Christian reader!

The Head. — The title which seems to be connected as closely almost as any with the church of the Mystery is *The Head*:

> "And gave Him to be the Head over all things to the church, which is His Body" (Eph. 1: 22).
> "The Head, even Christ" (Eph. 4: 15).
> "Christ is the Head of the church" (Eph. 5: 23).
> "He is the Head of the Body, the church" (Col. 1: 18).
> "Not holding the Head" (Col. 2: 19).

Structures

A word or two may be of service regarding that which we call Bible *Structures*. The Word of God is so perfect that upon analysis it will be found to be built upon a most elaborate and wonderful plan, embracing not only verses and chapters, but whole books, and even sets of books. An illustration, evident at once, is found in Isaiah 6: 10, viz.:

a Make the *heart* of this people fat,
  b and make their *ears* heavy,
    c and shut their *eyes,*
    c lest they see with their *eyes,*
  b and hear with their *ears,*
a and understand with their *heart*.

Sometimes the actual words do not re-appear, but the underlying thought is there; thus in 1 Corinthians 1: 24, 25:

a *Power.* Christ the *power* of God
  b *Wisdom.* and the *wisdom* of God
  b Wisdom. Foolishness of God *wiser* than men
a Power. Weakness of God *stronger* than men.

Sometimes the structure affords valuable assistance in arriving at the meaning of a passage or a word. Especially is this the case when a word in the original can have more than one meaning. When seeking to discover the meaning of a word or clause, to find its place and answering member in the structure is often half the battle. Further, the structure of a passage will emphasize the important points. Thus, when we come to consider Genesis 3 (chapter 6), we shall find that the structural arrangement of that chapter places the *serpent* and the *Seed* as the central members; this is the central teaching of the chapter, around which the other members are grouped. The first member is the serpent; the last is the cherubim. These claim our attention, and largely assist us to a true interpretation.

The discovery of the structures is the result of much painstaking labour, and although some used in this book are of our own finding, and for which we must be held responsible, many, though slightly modified, are the fruit of the labours of the compilers of *The Companion Bible*, a book which we would urge all our readers to procure. The diligent reader might try to discover for himself the underlying structure of a short psalm, or epistle (*e.g.*, Jude).

CHAPTER THREE

The two-fold purpose

We now approach the main purpose of this book, viz., the exhibition of the distinctive characteristics of "The kingdom of the heavens", and "The church of the Mystery". The sphere of the one is the earth; the sphere of the other is the heavens. The kingdom of the heavens will be "the days of heaven upon earth" (Deut. 11: 21). It will not be *in* the heavens, whereas the church is heavenly in its calling, in its blessing, and in its destiny, and looks for nothing from the earthly promises and blessings.

There are many indications, if we will but heed them, of this two-fold division in the purpose of God. Let us take the two phrases, "Before the foundation (overthrow) of the world", and "From (or since) the foundation (overthrow) of the world". These mark two distinct phases of redemption. We have given our reasons in chapter 2 for translating "foundation" by *overthrow*; we will now give every occurrence of the two expressions, and seek to exhibit wherein they differ.

Before the overthrow

"Father, I will that they also whom Thou hast given Me, be with Me where I am, that they may behold My glory, which Thou hast given Me. For Thou lovedst Me *before* the overthrow of the world" (John 17: 24).

"But with the precious blood of Christ, as of a lamb, without blemish, and without spot. Who verily was foreordained *before* the overthrow of the world, but was manifested in these last times for you" (1 Peter 1: 19, 20).

From (or since) the overthrow

"All these things spake Jesus unto the multitudes by parables, and without a parable spake He not unto them; that it might be fulfilled which was spoken by the prophet, saying, I will utter things which have been kept secret *since* the overthrow of the world" (Matt. 13: 34, 35).

"Then shall the King say unto them on His right hand, Come, ye blessed of My Father, inherit the kingdom prepared for you *since* the overthrow of the world" (Matt. 25: 34).

Before the overthrow

"Blessed be the God and Father of our Lord Jesus Christ, Who hath blessed us with all spiritual blessings in the *heavenlies* in Christ, according as He hath chosen us in Him *before* the overthrow of the world, that we should be holy and without blame before Him" (Eph.1: 3, 4).

From (or since) the overthrow

"I will send them prophets and apostles, and some of them they shall slay and persecute, that the blood of all the prophets which was shed *since* the overthrow of the world may be required of this generation; from the blood of Abel . . . " (Luke 11: 49-51).

"As I have sworn in my wrath, if they shall enter into My rest; though the works have been taking place *since* the overthrow of the world" (Heb. 4: 3).

"For then must He often have suffered *since* the overthrow of the world" (Heb. 9: 26).

"And all who dwell on the earth will worship Him, each one whose name hath not been written *since* the overthrow of the world in the book of the Lamb slain" (Rev. 13: 8).

"The beast which thou sawest was, and is not, and is about to ascend out of the abyss, and go into perdition; and those who dwell on the earth shall wonder, whose name is not written in the book of life *since* the overthrow of the world" (Rev. 17: 8).

The reader cannot fail to see the different range covered by these two expressions. *Three* passages only are found wherein is used the word "before", while *seven* passages give the number of occurrences of the word "since". Both of these numbers have the significance of perfection,* three signifying divine perfection, and seven signifying spiritual perfection. Seven is 4 + 3; earth (4) with the addition of divine perfection (3). Hence, while the three occurrences of the word "before" have entirely to do with Christ Himself, or the members of His Body chosen before the overthrow of the world, and related only to the "heavenlies", the seven, on the other hand, refer to that kingdom and people whose destiny is linked with the blessing of the earth.

Take two passages by way of illustration. Matthew 25: 34 speaks of a kingdom prepared *since* the overthrow of the world. Hebrews 4: 3 takes up this with deeper suggestiveness, and shows that the six days'

**See* Chapter 2.

creation was but the beginning of the work of the redemption of the earth which will be consummated when "the rest that remaineth" takes the place of creation's groan (Rom. 8). This leads us to a further consideration, that just as two grand divisions of *time* are indicated by the expressions "before" and "since" the overthrow of the world, so Scripture testifies to two *places* of redemptive operations, viz., *the heavens*, and *the earth*. Theologians have largely limited sin and redemption to the earth, whereas sin appeared first in the heavens. Genesis 3 records the fall of man by the temptation of an *already* fallen spirit being. Prophetic students have stopped at the millennial kingdom, whereas Scripture leads on to a kingdom which eclipses the millennium as noonday does a candle flame.

Let us look at one or two Scriptures, and learn therefrom what the Lord has said concerning the heavens. According to Job 15: 15 the *heavens* are not clean in His (God's) sight. Now we are fully aware that although the Scripture record of these words is inspired, yet Eliphaz, the Temanite may have made an untrue statement; for in Job 42: 7 we read "The Lord said to Eliphaz, the Temanite . . . Ye have not spoken of Me the thing that is right, as My servant Job hath". However, we must not think that this means that every utterance of Eliphaz was wrong. Job's utterances are also condemned elsewhere. The statement in Job 42: 7 has peculiar reference to the great theme of the book. We do not pin our faith to a disputed passage, however, but we find elsewhere the same teaching, stamping this passage in Job 15: 15 as being truth (*cp*. Job 25: 5). If we had found no other mention of this, then we must have left the matter as being too uncertain.

There is a singular, and to us eloquent, omission in the first chapter of Genesis. After the 1st, 3rd, 4th and 5th day's work we read the divine comment "it was good". The statement does not follow the creation of man in quite the same way, but the omission there may be accounted for by the reference to the "image of God". After the creation of the firmament, which God called "the heavens" (always plural, except in one instance), He does not say "it was good". Our belief in the inspiration of Scripture precludes all idea of a lapse of memory; the omission is as much by inspiration as the inclusion in the other verses. One would have thought that "the heavens" would have been pronounced as "good" rather than the earth, but it is not so. In order to show the tremendous import of this passage, we shall have to make a digression to examine the Scriptural teaching concerning Satan and his angels, their present abode, and condition.

Satan is named in Scripture "That old serpent, the devil", "The wicked one", "Your adversary", and among the many marvels of the letter of Scripture is the fact that 13, a number of ill-omen, apostasy, and rebellion, is a factor in his names. Thirteen first occurs in Genesis 14: 4, "The thirteenth year they rebelled". The first occurrence of a word generally gives its significance, which in this case we find to be rebellion. The second mention is connected with Ishmael (Gen. 17: 25). Satan in Hebrew = 364 (13 × 28), showing that in the very numerics God has fixed this arch-rebel's character. Dragon in Greek = 975 (13 × 75). Serpent in Greek = 780 (13 × 60). Tempter in Greek = 1,053 (13 × 81). Fowler (Psalm 91: 3) = 416 (13 × 32), and the complete passage, "But against principalities, against powers, against the rulers of the darkness of this world, against spiritual wickednesses in heavenly places" (Eph. 6: 12) = 16,211 (13 × 1,247). Many more examples could be given, but we have given enough to show that there is something more here than mere coincidence, even if mere coincidence were possible in the sphere of divine inspiration. Satan is called, "The prince of the power of the air" (Eph. 2), and Ephesians 6: 12 tells us that there are spiritual wickednesses in the heavenlies.

Daniel, in the third year of Cyrus, received a visit from a mighty being — "A certain man clothed in linen, whose loins were girded with fine gold of Uphaz, his body also was like the beryl, and his face as the appearance of lightning, and his eyes as lamps of fire, and his arms and his feet like in colour to polished brass, and the voice of his words like the voice of a multitude". The effect upon Daniel was overwhelming — "there remained no strength in me, for my comeliness was turned in me to corruption, and I retained no strength" (Dan. 10: 5-8, *cp.* Rev. 1). This mighty visitant declares to Daniel that he was sent from the first day that he (Daniel) had set his heart to understand, but he adds, "The prince of the kingdom of Persia withstood me one and twenty days, but lo, Michael, first of the chief princes, came to help me" (Dan. 10: 13). He refers later to "The prince of Grecia" (verse 20).

If a man like Daniel could not endure the sight of this visitant, surely the prince of Persia who withstood him for twenty-one days must have been no earthly monarch. Michael is called here "first of the chief princes", and as such was placed by the Lord over Israel. Of him it is written, "Michael your prince" (Dan. 10: 21). Again, in Daniel 12: 1 we read, "And at that time shall Michael stand up, the great prince which standeth for the children of thy people". In Jude 9 we have further light given us, for there he is called "Michael the archangel", and is connected with the raising of the dead, just as in Daniel 12: 1, 2, and 1 Thessalonians 4: 16. All this points conclusively to the fact that the mighty opponents of God's messenger in Daniel 10 are also angelic beings — princes ruling over Persia and Grecia in the interest of Satan, who claimed, without receiving reproof, that the kingdoms of the world were his to give to whomsoever he willed (Luke 4: 6). Satan and his angels are here discovered in opposition to the purposes of God. This has ever been Satan's attitude.

Satan, the prince of the power of the air, the spirit that now worketh in the children of disobedience, is a fallen being, and his fall took place prior to the creation of man. Satan's place is in the heavens, and not until Revelation 12: 9 do we read that he and his angels are cast down to the earth. We can now appreciate the divine omission in Genesis 1. God, beholding this mighty rebel and his angels, could not look upon the place of their abode and say "it was good". The majestic purpose of God moves on; sin that entered the heavens and the earth is to be finally removed from both. At the coming of the day of God, "the *heavens* being on fire shall be dissolved", as well as the earth and its works. Then will follow a new heaven and a new earth, wherein (both in heaven and earth) dwelleth righteousness.

Still following up this line of thought we note the commentary upon the Tabernacle in Hebrews 9. Its typology regarding redemption has been noted by many, but few seem to have realized how vast is its scope.

> "It was indeed therefore necessary for the figurative representation of the *things in the heavens*, with these (sacrifices offered under law) to be purified; but the *heavenly things themselves* with an infinitely better sacrifice than these. For Christ has not entered into the holiest of all made with hands, the antitype of the real one, but into *heaven itself*, now to appear before the presence of God for us" (Heb. 9: 23, 24).

Thus it will be seen that the Tabernacle contained in type and symbol the purpose of redemption, both regarding earth and heaven.

When we consider the "mystery of Christ" we shall see how God has purposed that in the dispensation of the fulness of the seasons, He will head up all things in Christ, the things in the heavens, and the things upon the earth (Eph. 1: 10); these will have been fully reconciled by the blood of Christ, whether things upon the earth, or things in the heavens (Col. 1: 20).

Three passages should be noted, where the heavens and the earth are mentioned together, viz., Genesis 1: 1, Genesis 2: 4 and Revelation 21: 1. Genesis 1: 1 refers to the period covering the time from the original creation to the "overthrow of the world". Revelation 21: 1 refers to that future day when creation shall once again be seen in all its loveliness secured for ever by redemption. Genesis 2: 4 refers to the "world that now is", during which the mighty purpose of the ages is being accomplished.

We may now link together the two subjects considered in this chapter, viz., the things spoken of as being *before*, and the things spoken of as being *since*, the overthrow of the world. Below we bring together in two columns the two sets of passages.

Things in the heavens. (Before the overthrow of the world)	*Things on earth. (Since the overthrow of the world)*
John 17: 24; 1 Peter 1: 19, 20; Ephesians 1: 3, 4.	Matthew 13: 34, 35; 25: 34; Luke 11: 49-51; Hebrews 4: 3; 9: 26; Revelation 13: 8; 17: 8.

It will be seen that the church of the one Body is ranged under the heavenly heading, and consequently it is "blessed with all spiritual blessings in the heavenlies". The "kingdom of heaven" comes under the heading of the things on earth, and Israel's blessings are to take place there. Israel and the kingdom are connected with the blessing and regeneration of the earth. The church which is the Body of Christ is connected with the reconciliation of the heavens. Israel's witness is before the nations; the church's witness is "unto principalities and powers in heavenly places" (Eph. 3: 10). Thus it will be made clear, we trust, that the creation and making of the "heavens and the earth which are now" (2 Peter 3: 7) may be considered as being the first step in the purpose of redemption.

The place and position forfeited by Satan and his angels, God will fill by a redeemed people. Some — Israel and the nations — will occupy the new earth, while others — the Body of Christ — will occupy the new heavens. Although all are partners in this mighty plan, all have not the same destiny. Do we not slight our gracious God when we ignore His revelation of the high calling of the church of the Mystery, and occupy ourselves with the things which pertain to the earthly people? Let us seek "rightly to divide the Word of truth", and we shall get to know what is the hope of His calling, and what the riches of the glory of His inheritance in the heavenly holiest of all.

It is possible that some may anticipate our conclusions with an objection. The term "heavenly" is not confined to the church of the Mystery, it is found, *e.g.*, in connection with Abraham's faith and hope, so before we close this chapter we will give a list showing the use of the word "heavenly", and we believe that the truth of the distinctly heavenly connection of the church of the present dispensation will thereby be the more emphasized. The following list has been collected by a writer for his own purposes, but we feel quite sure that he will be only too glad for it to be of service here.

"Much confusion is the result of the lameness of the English language, when attempting to convey the accuracies of the original. We are at a loss, for instance, to determine whether the 'heavenly calling' of Hebrews 3: 1 refers to calling *from* heaven, or calling *to* heaven . . . *epouraniou*, heavenly, in the genitive (which marks *that from which everything proceeds*) simply calls our attention to the *origin* of that which we are considering; while *epouranio*, heavenly, in the dative (which indicates *that towards which anything tends*) marks the *location* of the matters in hand. Below we give a concordance of each".

Genitive

Epouraniou (Gen. sing.).

"The image of the *heavenly*" (1 Cor. 15: 49).
"Partakers of the *heavenly* calling" (Heb. 3: 1).
"Tasted of the *heavenly* gift" (Heb. 6: 4).
"A better (country), that is an *heavenly*" (Heb. 11: 16).

Epouranion (Gen. plural).

"(There are) also *celestial* bodies" (1 Cor. 15: 40).
"Of (things) *in heaven*, and (things) in earth" (Phil. 2: 10).
"The example and shadow of *heavenly* things" (Heb. 8: 5).

Dative.

Epouranio (Dat. sing.).

"The *heavenly* Jerusalem" (Heb. 12: 22).

Epouraniois (Dat. plural).

"In *heavenly* (places) in Christ" (Eph. 1: 3).
"At His own right hand in the *heavenly* (places)" (Eph. 1: 20).
"In *heavenly* (places) in Christ Jesus" (Eph. 2: 6).
"Powers in *heavenly* (places)" (Eph. 3: 10).
"In *high* (places)" (Eph. 6: 12).

"We are immediately struck with the fact that the dative, which speaks of location, is confined to the epistle to the Ephesians (just what we should expect if we 'rightly divide the word of truth'), and the present location of the new Jerusalem which will yet *come down out of heaven*" (Rev. 21: 10).

"On the other hand, the shadows of the tabernacle were 'heavenly', but not 'in heaven'. The gifts which even the apostate Israelite tasted, as recorded in the early chapters of Acts, were 'heavenly', but assuredly not *in* heaven. The emphasis is always upon the *source* or *character* in the Genitive, even when the object itself may be in heaven. Abraham did not look for an inheritance *in* heaven, but he did look for a 'heavenly country' (Heb. 11: 16). So also the 'heavenly calling' is heavenly in character, but it does not call *to* heaven; that would need to be expressed in the dative case". (A.E.K.).

The millennial kingdom, and the new heavens and new earth (Rev. 20-22), were before the eyes of the "father of many nations". He and his seed shall yet inherit the promises in all their blessed fulness. Israel will be honoured then. The twelve tribes will have their names emblazoned upon the twelve gates, and the twelve foundations will bear the names of the twelve apostles of the Lamb. No temple will be there, for the Lord God Almighty and the Lamb will be the temple of it. No need for sun or moon to shine there, for the glory of God will lighten it, and the Lamb will be the light thereof. The nations of them which are saved shall walk in the light of it, and the kings of the earth shall bring their *glory* and *honour* into it, and the gates of it shall not be shut at all by day, for there shall be no night there.

This it is for which creation groans and waits, for which Abraham looked and waited, an inheritance that seems enough to satisfy any heart, and yet we have to write — this inheritance is not ours. The hope, calling, blessing, and inheritance set before us are all of them not only heavenly in *character*, but they are *in* heaven as to *locality*. We hope to establish these statements in subsequent chapters.

CHAPTER FOUR

An exhibition of the plan and theme of the Bible

In our last chapter we saw that the Scriptures clearly speak of two *periods* of time in the dealings of God with man, viz., before and since the overthrow of the world, and two *spheres*, the heavens and the earth. Much confusion has resulted from the failure on our part to clearly distinguish between these definitely separated sections of God's redemptive purposes. The next thing for us to learn is that these different periods of time, and different spheres of activity, are connected with two distinctly different classes of men, who are alike as to nature, but diverse as to destiny. Alike by reason of a common salvation, but unlike as to their hopes, and the sphere of their operations. These two different companies of the redeemed, with their distinct sets of doctrine, we have named "the earthly kingdom" and "the church" (*see* chapter 2).

This *kingdom* is connected with the earth and its reconciliation. Its point of contact and channel of blessing is the peculiar *nation* — Israel; its purpose and ultimate goal is the restoration and reconciliation of "things on earth". The *church* on the other hand is connected with the heavenlies. Its present manifestation and foreshadowing, as also its future channel of blessing, is the *one body*, the church of the Mystery which was hidden by God from all ages and generations; its purpose and ultimate goal is the restoration and reconciliation of "things in heaven". Our first consideration will be the *earthly kingdom*, but it seems difficult to know quite where to begin our study. One of the passages already cited (Matt. 25: 34, "Come . . . inherit the *kingdom* prepared for you since the overthrow of the world") sends us back to the opening verses of the Bible, where we read of the creation of the heavens and the earth, the entrance of sin, the promise of the Redeemer, and many wonderful developments of God's mighty purpose. So let us, with our Bibles open before us, begin at the beginning and seek to learn what the Lord would teach us.

To understand any part of the Bible it is absolutely essential that we should first of all view it in its relation to the context, and to the rest of the Scriptures, and then discover, if possible, the internal arrangement and disposition of its subject matter. The first thing to which we would draw attention is the wonderful sympathy and correspondence that is everywhere seen between Genesis, the *first* book of holy writ, and Revelation, the *last*. If we note the things in Genesis that are repeated in the book of the Revelation, we shall have the divine emphasis upon the main features of the past and intervening books. We set out the corresponding items in two columns, and are indebted to *The Companion Bible* for this valuable collection.

Genesis	*Revelation*
(1) Genesis, the book of the beginning.	(1) The Revelation, the book of the end.
(2) The earth created (1: 2 — 2: 3).	(2) The earth passed away (21: 1).
(3) Satan's first rebellion.	(3) Satan's final rebellion (20: 3, 7-10).
(4) Sun, moon, and stars for earth's government (1: 14-16).	(4) Sun, moon, and stars connected with earth's judgment (6: 13; 8: 12; 16: 8).
(5) Sun to govern the day (1: 16).	(5) No need of the sun (21: 23).
(6) Darkness called night (1: 5).	(6) No night there (22: 5).
(7) Waters called seas (1: 10).	(7) No more sea (21: 1).
(8) A river for earth's blessing (2: 10-14).	(8) A river for the new earth (22: 1, 2).
(9) Man in God's image (1: 26).	(9) Man headed by one in Satan's image (13).
(10) Entrance of sin (3).	(10) Development and end of sin (21; 22).
(11) Curse pronounced (3: 14, 17).	(11) No more curse (22: 3).
(12) Death entered (3: 19).	(12) No more death (21: 4).
(13) Cherubim first mentioned in connection with man's fall and expulsion (3: 24).	(13) Cherubim finally mentioned in connection with man's redemption and restitution (4: 6).
(14) Man driven out from Eden (3: 24).	(14) Man restored (22).
(15) Tree of life forfeited (3: 22-24).	(15) Right to tree of life restored (22: 14).
(16) Sorrow and suffering enter (3: 17).	(16) No more sorrow (21: 4).
(17) Man's religion, art, and science resorted to for enjoyment, apart from God (4).	(17) Man's religion, luxury, art, and science, in their full glory, judged and destroyed by God (18).
(18) Nimrod, a great rebel and king, and *hidden* anti-God, the founder of Babylon (10: 8, 9).	(18) The beast, the great rebel, a king, and *manifested* anti-God, the reviver of Babylon (13 — 18).

	Genesis		*Revelation*
(19)	A flood from God to destroy an evil generation (6 — 9).	(19)	A flood from Satan to destroy an elect generation (12).
(20)	The rainbow, the token of God's covenant with the earth (9: 13).	(20)	The rainbow, betokening God's remembrance of His covenant with the earth (4: 3; 10: 1).
(21)	Sodom and Egypt, the place of corruption and temptation (13; 19).	(21)	Sodom and Egypt again, spiritually representing Jerusalem (11: 8).
(22)	A confederacy against Abraham's people overthrown (14).	(22)	A confederacy against Abraham's seed overthrown (12).
(23)	Marriage of first Adam (2: 18-23).	(23)	Marriage of last Adam (19).
(24)	A bride sought for Abraham's son (Isaac), and found (24).	(24)	A bride made ready and brought to Abraham's Son (19: 9). *See* Matthew 1: 1.
(25)	Two angels acting for God on behalf of His people (19).	(25)	Two witnesses acting for God on behalf of His people (11).
(26)	A promised seed to possess the gate of his enemies (22: 17).	(26)	The promised seed coming into possession (11: 18; 21: 12).
(27)	Man's dominion ceased, and Satan's begun (3: 24).	(27)	Satan's dominion ended, and man's restored (22).
(28)	The old serpent causing sin, suffering, and death (3: 1).	(28)	The old serpent bound for 1,000 years (20: 1-3).
(29)	The doom of the old serpent pronounced (3: 15).	(29)	The doom of the old serpent executed (20: 10).
(30)	Sun, moon, and stars associated with Israel (37: 9).	(30)	Sun, moon, and stars associated again with Israel (12).

A careful comparison of the above passages would seem fully to establish the fact that Genesis and Revelation are the first and last links in a mighty chain, that all apparent accident and frustration of purpose are omnipotently overruled and omnisciently anticipated. If we are really to understand the Bible we must read it as the *revelation* of a *purpose*, the *working-out* of a *plan*. Further, we must intelligently grasp the fact that the creation of Genesis 1: 2-2: 3 was not, as popularly supposed, the goal God had in view, but the first step towards it, which goal will not be reached until there shall be "the new heavens and the new earth, where in dwelleth righteousness". Where we have so signally failed is at the very threshold of the Bible. We have endeavoured to understand its detail, while we were all the time ignorant of its purpose.

So far we have glanced from one end of Scripture to the other; we must now limit our view to the Old Testament itself. The Hebrew canon is divided into three great sections, viz., (1) The Law (*Torah*);

(2) The Prophets (*Nebi'im*); and (3) The Psalms (*Kethubim* — Writings). Apart from the antiquity and universal recognition of this threefold division, the Lord Jesus Himself has endorsed and sanctioned it in the remarkable resurrection exposition recorded in Luke 24: 44-51:

> "These are the words which I spake unto you, being yet with you: that all the things that are written in the *Law of Moses*, and the *Prophets*, and the *Psalms* concerning Me, must needs be fulfilled. Then opened He their mind that they might understand the Scriptures".

O, that the same Lord would open our minds, too, so that casting away our prejudices and preconceived ideas we might believe *just what is written*, without the restraint imposed upon the Scriptures of truth by the folly of men. The Law of Moses, the first great section of the Old Testament, is composed as we know of five books. Let us look at them together, and see whether we cannot discover what is their theme. As some of the following statements may not at first be evident to the reader, we would here point out that we give Scriptural reasons for all that we advance.

The structure of the Pentateuch

(The numerics (5 books) signify grace and redemptive activities)

A *Genesis.* — *The beginning.* — The nations and the "great nation" — Israel

B *Exodus.* — *Redemption.* — The making of a nation and its redemption.

C *Leviticus.* — *Worship.* — The training of the "kingdom of priests."

B Numbers. — *Wandering.* — The failure of the nation — finally blessed.

A Deuteronomy. — *The end.* — "The second time." The nation ready to enter the land.

The whole of this history, while being a record of actual facts, is at the same time a prophetic picture also. In Genesis we see the preparation of the earth for the nations, but in complete subservience to the great nation chosen in Abraham. In Exodus this nation is fashioned in the furnace of Egypt, and redeemed by the blood of the passover lamb. In Leviticus the nation is alone with God, and its training commences in view of the special purpose for which as a nation it was chosen — "A kingdom of priests". It was not, however, the intention of the Lord to allow the creature more than an opportunity to witness its own inability and weakness, hence before we read Deuteronomy, we have Numbers, the book of failure and wandering, typical of the present character of Israel. Then

Deuteronomy emphasizes the truth of prophetic Scripture, that "the second time" Israel will believe and be saved. The five books do not go further than the nation. The last book gives instruction as to their behaviour in the land, but neither Moses himself enters it, nor is the nation's entry recorded in his writings. *The land* is the great feature of the next section, the Prophets.

We have mentioned in chapter 2 the significance of number in Scripture, and in the five books of Moses we have the number of grace and redemption. True, law is opposed to grace, but the whole purpose of law was nevertheless actuated by grace, and the people though under law had ample evidence that the Lord was "merciful and gracious". Scripture reveals three persons in the Godhead, (1) Father, (2) Son, (3) Spirit. The next number (4) signifies creation. Five is 4 + 1, the divine activity brought to bear upon creation. This second putting forth of power subsequent to creation is redemption and grace. When the Lord changed the name of Abram and Sarai to Abraham and Sarah, the letter "h" was added. Now "h" in the Hebrew represents 5, and it is in this same chapter that God reveals Himself as *El Shaddai*, God all sufficient, God all bountiful. In the fifth book (Deuteronomy), where the people are assembled again after their 40 years' wandering, the Lord emphasizes His grace toward them particularly in relation to the very subject of the five books — their calling as a *nation*.

> "For thou art an holy people unto the Lord thy God. The Lord thy God hath chosen thee to be a special people unto Himself, above all people that are upon the face of the earth. The Lord did not set His love upon you, or choose you because ye were more in number than any people, for ye were the fewest of all people, but because the Lord loved you, and because He would keep the oath which He had sworn unto your fathers" (Deut. 7: 6-8; *see also* 4: 7, 20, 32, 37; 8: 11, 17 etc.).

When we turn to the next section of the Old Testament, the Prophets, we find the number of books entirely harmonizes with the significance of this section. Eight books compose the Prophets, and eight is associated with resurrection and regeneration. Noah, "the eighth person", and the "eight souls" saved in the ark, were those who came through the waters of death to the new world, typical of resurrection and regeneration.

The first book in the Prophets is the book of Joshua. He it is who leads the *nation* into the *land*. But this first entry was a failure, and it is reserved for Another of the same name, but mightier than Joshua the son of Nun, ultimately to lead them in a *second time*. Then there will be no failure, but the purposes of God with regard to the nation will be fulfilled. Stephen in Acts 7: 45, and Paul in Hebrews 4: 8 speak of

Joshua, but rendered into English from the Greek it of course reads "Jesus", exactly the same as Matthew 1: 21, "Thou shalt call his name *Jesus*". Joshua the Son of Nun figures in the first book of the Prophets; Joshua the son of Josedech figures in the last book — the Minor Prophets, for these form one book. The first Joshua is a leader and warrior, and acts in some ways as a *king*; the second is *priest*. Here again a tremendous lesson is emphasized; God's King is also God's Priest, "He shall be a *priest* upon His *throne*". (Zech. 6: 13). "A *priest* after the order of the *king* of righteousness". This is the emphatic witness of the Gospel of Matthew, as will be seen by the structure in a later chapter.

The structure of the Prophets

(The numerics (8 books) speak of resurrection and regeneration)

The Former Prophets:

- A *Joshua* "The Lord of all the earth". Failure to possess the land (18: 3). The Canaanite still in the land (15: 63)
  - B *Judges* Failure. Thirteen judges. Israel forsaking and returning to God. "No king" (21: 25)
    - C *Samuel* Saul (type of antichrist). David (type of Christ). Israel want to be "like the nations"
      - D *Kings* Decline and failure under kings. Removal from the land

The Latter Prophets:

      - *D Isaiah* Israel's only hope, final blessing and restoration. Messiah — God's King
    - *C Jeremiah* Nebuchadnezzar (type of antichrist). David's "righteous Branch" "raised up" — the Deliverer. Israel sent into captivity among the nations
  - *B Ezekiel* The glory of God forsaking and returning to His land and people. *Jehovah Shammah,* the Lord is there
- *A Minor Prophets* "The Lord of all the earth" restoring Israel to the land. "No more the Canaanite in the house of the Lord of Hosts" (Zech. 14: 21).

God's purpose was that the nation's history in the land should be bounded at either end by these two men who, in office and in name, prefigured the One Who, in God's time, would indeed give them rest — Jesus, the Son of God. The fact that the Gematria of the Greek word "Jesus" is 888 (*see* chapter 2), brings the thought of resurrection all the more emphatically before us.

The first half of this section is a dismal drifting, a failure, and a fall. It soon becomes evident that the purposes of God with regard to the great nation and the promised land are not to be brought about by mere human effort. The arrangement of these four books tells its own story only too plainly.

Structure of the "Former Prophets"

A *Joshua.* — Israel entering the land. Joshua and *priests*
  B *Judges.* — Israel's failure under *priests*
A *Samuel.* — Israel in the land. Samuel and *kings*
  B *Kings.* — Israel's failure under *kings.*

Here priest and king alike are seen to be failures, and if the burdens of the Former Prophets were not answered by the Lord with the glories of the "Latter Prophets", Israel and the earth would be without hope, for our subsequent studies will show us that the blessing of the earth has been divinely connected with "a kingdom of priests" — Israel, who will be ruled over by the Royal Priest, the Lord Jesus Christ. This is the burden of both Old and New Testaments, with the exception of the one portion which is connected with the Mystery of the present dispensation.

The burden of the "Latter Prophets" is as follows:

A *Isaiah.* — Restoration of the throne of David through the priestly work of Messiah. The two tribes
  B *Jeremiah.* — Political disruption and Gentilization. Final restoration of Judah and Ephraim by the new covenant
  B *Ezekiel.* — Ecclesiastical disruption. The glory departing, yet final restoration of Israel
A *The Twelve Minor Prophets.* — Restoration of the throne of David through the priestly work of Messiah. The ten tribes.

Isaiah, Jeremiah, Ezekiel, Haggai, Zechariah, and Malachi, while speaking against Israel's sins, cry out "Turn ye unto Me, saith the Lord of Hosts, and I will turn unto you, saith the Lord of Hosts", and look forward to the days of millennial glory when "every pot in Jerusalem and in Judah shall be Holiness unto the Lord", and the cry of gratitude will go up:

> "Who is a God like unto Thee, that pardoneth iniquity, and passeth by the transgression of the remnant of His heritage? He retaineth not His anger for ever, because He delighteth in mercy . . . the mercy to Abraham, which Thou hast sworn unto our fathers from the days of old" (Micah 7: 18-20).

These two sections, The Law, and The Prophets, summarize the working-out of the main purpose of the Lord regarding Israel and the kingdom. The remaining section, The Psalms or The Writings, give the inner working and cause of the apostasy, and the divine order of overruling and ultimate blessing. This element can be well illustrated by the parallel passages of 1 and 2 Samuel and 1 and 2 Kings with 1 and 2 Chronicles. Samuel and Kings record the history viewed from the human standpoint, that which we might call the *exoteric* narration, while Chronicles gives the same history viewed from the divine standpoint, revealing the hidden workings and overrulings of the Lord, which we might call the *esoteric* standpoint.

The Writings give us the inner life of the people, the inner feelings of the heart, the inner cause of their corruption, and the inner secret of their marvellous preservation. The book of Kings, as we have seen, is the conclusion of The Former Prophets, it marks the lowest step. Starting with the glories of the throne of David, it ends in the gloom of Zedekiah's blindness. The book opens with the building of the Temple, and closes with its burning. So it is with the other books of this section. Chronicles is just the reverse. The very first name recorded is "Adam"; it starts with human failure. The last man mentioned is "Cyrus, king of Persia", who was raised up in order that "the word of the Lord spoken by the mouth of Jeremiah the prophet might be accomplished". There have been tabulated 111 parallel passages between the books of Samuel and Kings on the one hand, and the books of Chronicles on the other. We give a few in order to demonstrate the standpoint of each book.

Samuel and Kings *History from human standpoint.*	**Chronicles** *History as the outworking of God's purpose.*
"Then Saul said to his armour bearer, Draw thy sword, and thrust me through therewith . . . But his armour bearer would not. *Therefore Saul took his sword and fell upon it*" (1 Sam. 31: 4).	"So Saul died *for his transgression* which he committed against the Lord, even against the word of the Lord, which he kept not, and also for asking counsel of one that had a familiar spirit to enquire of it, and enquired not of the Lord, *therefore He slew Him*" (1 Chron. 10: 13, 14).
"Then came all the tribes of Israel to David unto Hebron . . . and they anointed David king over Israel" (2 Sam. 5: 1-3).	"Then all Israel gathered themselves to David unto Hebron . . . and they anointed David king over Israel, *according to the word of the Lord by Samuel*" (1 Chron. 11: 1-3).

Samuel and Kings *History from human standpoint.*	**Chronicles** *History of the outworking of God's purpose.*
"And again the anger of the Lord was kindled against Israel, and he moved David (or David was moved) against them to say, Go, number Israel and Judah" (2 Sam. 24: 1).	"And *Satan* stood up against Israel, and provoked David to number Israel" (1 Chron. 21: 1).
"So the king commanded Benaiah, the son of Jehoiada, which went out and fell upon him (Shimei), that he died. And the kingdom was established in the hand of Solomon" (1 Kings 2: 46).	"And Solomon, the son of David, was strengthened in his kingdom, *and the Lord his God was with him*" (2 Chron. 1: 1).
"And the days which Jeroboam reigned were two and twenty years; and he slept with his fathers" (1 Kings 14: 20).	"Neither did Jeroboam recover strength again in the days of Abijah; *and the Lord* struck him, and he died" (2 Chron. 13: 20).
"And it came to pass in the fifth year of king Rehoboam, that Shishak, king of Egypt, came up against Jerusalem" (1 Kings 14: 25).	"And it came to pass that in the fifth year of king Rehoboam, Shishak, king of Egypt, came up against Jerusalem, *because they had transgressed against the Lord*" (2 Chron. 12: 2).
"The king of Syria commanded ... saying, Fight ... only with the king of Israel. And it came to pass, when the captains of the chariots saw Jehoshaphat, that they said, Surely it is the king of Israel. And they turned aside to fight against him; and Jehoshaphat cried out. And it came to pass when the captains of the chariots perceived that it was not the king of Israel, that they turned back from following him" (1 Kings 22: 31-33).	"Now the king of Syria had commanded, saying, Fight ... only with the king of Israel. And it came to pass when the captains of the chariots saw Jehoshaphat, that they said, It is the king of Israel. Therefore they compassed about him to fight, but Jehoshaphat cried out, *and the Lord helped him, and God moved them to depart from him* ... they turned back from pursuing him" (2 Chron. 18: 30-32).

We will not multiply instances, those given above are sufficient to show the different standpoints of the two books. Now what is true of Chronicles is also true of the whole section of which Chronicles is the conclusion. The Writings, give the inner working of the history of the kingdom. Once again the number of the books is suggestive, there being eleven in the section. We are prepared for the spiritual significance of the number eleven by reading Deuteronomy 1: 2. "There are eleven days' journey from Horeb by the way of Mount Seir unto Kadesh Barnea". Eleven days! One more day's march, *i.e.*, twelve days, would have led Israel into the promised land, twelve being stamped upon Israel as is a hall-mark upon gold. There were twelve patriarchs from Shem to Jacob, and Jacob's twelve sons give their names to the twelve tribes, also the twelve foundations and twelve gates of the heavenly Jerusalem, as well as the twelve thrones of the twelve apostles, etc. Eleven is just one short, and thus the very number of the books of this third section gives its testimony to its message and purpose.

The way in which these eleven books are arranged, however, conveys a still more important lesson: the five central books are grouped together under the title of the five *Megilloth*, or smaller scrolls. Five, as we have seen, signifies grace, and six is the mark of

The structure of The Writings

(The numerics (II books) speak of Israel's failure, but show God's hand in the midst).

A *Psalms (Praises).* — The vanity of opposing the Lord's purposes. His final triumph

B *Proverbs (Rules).* — Advice to a ruler. At the end a righteous king and a virtuous woman

C *Job.* — "The end of the Lord". Satan defeated. The remnant of Israel typified

The Megilloth.

D *Canticles.* — Read at the passover (Pharaoh the oppressor). The bride

E *Ruth.* — Read at Pentecost. The stranger

F *Lamentations.* — Read at the feast of the 9th Abib. Israel's failure (Note the multiples of eleven in the acrostic chapters, which contain 22 verses, or 66 verses respectively)

E Ecclesiastes. — Read at the feast of Tabernacles. "Vanity." "The conclusion of the matter" (Eccles. 12: 13, 14)

D Esther. — Read at the feast of Purim (Haman the Jew's enemy). The queen

C Daniel. — "God is Judge." Defeat of antichrist. Deliverance of Israel

B Ezra-Nehemiah. — Civil and ecclesiastical government, looking forward to Messiah's rule.

A Chronicles. — The subservience of all things to the working out of the divine purposes.

human imperfection; again the truth is enforced upon us that the whole history of Israel is one of divine grace working amidst human failure, silently yet certainly working out the purposes of redemption, for which creation, Israel, and the kingdom were planned and brought into being. This will be more evident when we have the entire set of books before us.

This brings us to the end of the Old Testament canon. We believe that it is patent to all our readers that the whole book is the record of one mighty theme, the carrying out of the purpose of redemption so far as it relates to the earth. The Hebrew canon has not been framed by modern men, it has come down to us from antiquity. All that we have done is to point out the lessons which may be gathered by the mere recognition of the grouping of the books; that lesson will be amply confirmed when we consider the teaching of the books themselves.

The structure of the New Testament

A — *The Four Gospels.* "The acceptable year of the Lord."	*The first advent.* — The coming of the Son of man in humility. The presentation and rejection of the kingdom. "The king of the Jews" crowned with thorns.
B *The Acts. The earlier Pauline epistles, and the epistles of Peter, James, and John.*	*Transitional period.* — During which forgiveness is proclaimed to Israel, and a further proclamation of the kingdom is given, accompanied by signs and wonders (Acts 3: 19, 20; Heb. 2: 3, 4; 1 Cor. 12: 9); the hope being "the *parousia*" (1 Thess. 4: &c.). This ends in the rejection of the dispersion, and closes the door at Acts 28: 25, 26.

Acts 28: 25, 26. *The Dispensational Boundary*

B The later Pauline epistles.	*The kingdom in abeyance.* — "Not yet" (Heb. 2: 8). The revelation of the Mystery (Eph. 3: 1—9). The hope (Titus 2: 13; Col. 3: 4; Phil. 3: 14, 20, 21).
A The Revelation. "The day of vengeance of our God".	*The second advent.* — The coming of the Son of man in great glory. The establishing of the kingdom. "On His head many crowns".

It will be seen that for continuity of purpose we read:—

A The First Advent.
B The transitional period.
A The Second Advent.

One thing, however, which we must impress upon every reader is this, that the Old Testament record is incomplete. There must be found somewhere the conclusion of this marvellous theme, and that conclusion is found in the writings of the New Testament.

So far as things pertaining to the redemptive purposes for the earth and the nations are concerned, the New Testament, like the Old, is divided into three sections, while an additional section, containing the revelation of the Mystery, makes four in all.

The member "*B*", so far as the general plan of the Old and New Testaments is concerned, can be removed without being missed; it forms an independent revelation of the heavenly aspect of the purpose of redemption, connected with that period designated, "Before the overthrow of the world". For the time being, however, we will consider the section referring to the kingdom on earth, and then we shall be the better able to appreciate the special truth contained in the later writings of the Apostle Paul. Omitting the later epistles of Paul, we find that the Old Testament and the New have one subject, viz., the millennial kingdom, the earth restored and blessed, with Israel as the channel of blessing. We see how, in spite of all obstacles, that purpose is carried to a glorious consummation.

(1) *The Law* speaks of the preparation of the chosen people.

(2) *The Prophets* speak of the promised land, and the failure under kings and priests.

(3) *The Writings* speak of the inner reasons of that failure, but at the same time show us the hand of the Lord directing all things.

(4) *The Four Gospels* show us the Lord's Prophet, Priest, and King, and tell of His rejection.

(5) *The Acts and Epistles of that period* deal with the transitional re-offer of kingdom promises.

(6) *The Revelation* gives us the consummation of the purposes of God, leading up to the blessing of the earth and the nations in connection with Israel and Jerusalem.

It is noteworthy that we have a six-fold division by omitting the section devoted to the Mystery. By including it we have a seven-fold or perfect arrangement, suggestive of the perfection of the ultimate purposes of the God of revelation and redemption. Thus far we have scanned the book from end to end, from Genesis to Revelation; in our next chapter we shall seek to analyse the distinctive teaching of some of the books themselves. Let every reader bring all to the touchstone of the Word; let us "prove all things, and *hold fast* that which is good".

CHAPTER FIVE

The six days' creation

So far we have been considering things in their broad issues. We have seen the two great divisions which mark off the events of Scripture, viz., the *time* division, before or since the overthrow of the world; and the *place* division, in heaven and on earth. We have also seen, and shall have further proof shortly, that "the things in heaven" and "the things on earth" are related, respectively, to the two time periods before and since the overthrow. We have now to prove the next statement, which is, that the things on earth, since the overthrow, are embraced by what we have called "earthly kingdom truth", while the things in heaven, before the overthrow, are embraced by the special dispensation committed to Paul, which we have called "church truth". The examination of these two distinct sets of teaching will occupy the greater part of the remaining chapters of this book.

Matthew 25: 34 tells us that this "kingdom" was *prepared* since the overthrow of the world; accordingly we must commence our studies with the book of Genesis, and as we desire to be thorough, we will seek to lay before the reader the inception and development of this kingdom purpose, as recorded in this wonderful opening book of revealed truth. That the book of Genesis should be attacked, that its histories should be branded as myths, that its prophecies should be called puerile vagaries is only what we might expect. Satan is a real person, and God's purpose, which includes the devil's doom, is therein recorded. However, we have no need to defend either the book of Genesis or the Bible, nor have we any cause to apologise for our faith — the fact of inspiration is established to the last letter.

The book of Genesis is divided first of all into two sections, the first section being recorded in 34 verses, and the second section filling 49 chapters. The structure of the book as a whole is as follows:

A1 Gen. 1: 1-2: 3. The introduction

A2 Gen. 2: 4-50: 26. The eleven generations

These two main divisions are further sub-divided as follows:

Gen. 1: 1-2: 3. The introduction

A1 A 1: 1. "The world that then was" (2 Peter 3: 6). "*Before* the overthrow".
  B 1: 2. Its end. Disruption *(Katabole, see* chapter 2.)
 A 1: 2-31. "The heavens and the earth which are now" (2 Peter 3: 7). "*Since* the overthrow".
  B 2: 1-3. Their end. Rest (the sabbath, a pledge and type of the restitution of all things).

The introduction is thus taken up with the six days' creation and the seventh days' rest. The next verse (2: 4) commences the second section. Eleven times over do we read the words "the generations", and these will be found to be God's own division; hence we must ignore, except for reference, man-made chapters.

Gen. 2: 4-50: 26. The eleven "generations"

<table>
<tr><td>A2 C E The heavens and the earth (2: 4—4: 26).
F Adam (5: 1—6: 8).
G Noah (6: 9-9: 29).
H The sons of Noah (10: 1—11: 9).
I Shem (11: 10-26).</td><td>Preparation of the nations. 70 in number (chapter 10.).</td></tr>
<tr><td>D Terah (11: 27—25: 11).</td><td>The link between the nations and the great nation.</td></tr>
<tr><td>C E Ishmael (25: 12-18).
F Isaac (25: 19—35: 29).
G Esau (36: 1-8).
H The sons of Esau (36: 9-43).
I Jacob (37: 2—50: 26).</td><td>Preparation for the great nation. 70 souls (Exod. 1: 5). Hence literality of Deut. 32: 8.</td></tr>
</table>

Here we have God's perfect arrangement, before which all the attempts of man must give place. It is remarkable, to say the least, that the father of the faithful, the elect vessel who is chosen as the progenitor of the great nation, Abraham, does not figure in this list; we do not read, "these are the generations of Abraham". If man had arranged this structure he would certainly have given a prominent place in it to Abraham, and possibly have omitted such as Ishmael and Esau. We are not, however, dealing with man's book, but with God's, and that makes all the difference.

Before we leave this remarkable structure we want to feel sure that every reader will have grasped the witness that it bears to the subject before us, viz., *The mediatorial kingdom*. If we take the trouble to count the number of the nations originally descending from Japheth, Ham, and Shem, as recorded in Genesis 10, we shall find that there are seventy in all. After the list of the descendants of Japheth we read in verse 5, "By these were the isles of the Gentiles divided *in their lands*; every one after his tongue, after their families, *in their nations*". Following the list of the descendants of Ham we read in verse 20, "These are the sons of Ham, after their families, after their tongues, *in their countries*, and *in their nations*". Similarly after Shem's descendants we read in verses 31, 32, "These are the sons of Shem, after their families, after their tongues, *in their lands, after their nations*. These are the families of the sons of Noah, after their generations, in their nations, and by these were the nations divided in the earth after the flood".

In chapter 10: 25 we have recorded a very remarkable event. "And unto Eber were born two sons, the name of one was Peleg, for in his days was *the earth divided*". The word here translated "divided" means to "*cleave*". What does this signify? Originally, according to Genesis 1: 9, 10, the sea was gathered into one place, and the "dry" (namely, the dry land) in another. This continued to be the condition of the earth right through to the time of Peleg. If Christians would only keep these things in mind, they would not be troubled with such questions as, *Did the flood in Noah's day extend to Australia or America*? for the simple fact is that until Peleg's day there were no such places as Australia and America in the reckoning (we do not say that such places did not exist), for all that was then habitable earth was in one place; but in the days of Peleg, just as the time was approaching for the call of Abraham, mighty alterations began to be made by the Most High, continents and islands appeared, and the seventy nations were placed in their respective countries (note the above quotation "*in their lands*"), to await the advent of the royal nation, whose land and capital were of divine choice, and who were destined to be the embodiment of kingdom purposes on earth.

This is further emphasized by noting that in Exodus 1: 5 and Deuteronomy 10: 22 the number of souls that came out of the loins of Jacob, and formed the nucleus of the "great nation", is seventy. Thus the perfect order of Genesis is seen, the seventy nations answering to the seventy souls. One more observation is necessary, and that is the remarkable passage in Deuteronomy 32: 8:

> "When the Most High divided to the nations their inheritance, when He separated the sons of Adam, He set the bounds of the peoples, according to the *number* of the children of Israel".

How marvellous are the ways of God! Before even Abraham was born, the Lord knew the *number* of the souls that would find their way to that iron furnace (Egypt) — seventy, and in recognition of Israel's predestined royalty, the nations are grouped around Palestine to await the advent of the kingdom of priests. The kingdom purpose for the earth, then, is plainly visible, even at the first glance at this remarkable book, and our further studies will convince us yet more of this fact. To understand Genesis, or indeed the whole Bible, we must realize that it is the written record of a mighty purpose, a purpose including in its redemptive grace "things in heaven, and things on earth", using for the earthly sphere the instrumentality of the kingdom, primarily vested in Israel, and for the heavenly sphere, "the one body", the church of the Mystery, revealed now during the interval occasioned by the setting aside of Israel.

That Israel is intended to figure largely in this purpose is patent to the most casual reader. Genesis opens with the creation of the universe; it closes with the minute history of one man and his twelve sons. The first half of the book is compressed within eleven chapters, yet these eleven chapters cover over 2,000 years, while the remainder of the book (39 chapters) covers over 300 years. This clearly shows that Genesis has a purpose other than the satisfying of our curiosity regarding cosmogony, geology, or ethnology. Everything is subservient to the grand purpose of redemption, and the development and fruition of the primeval promise, "The seed of the woman shall bruise the serpent's head".

The first verse of Genesis 1 stands alone. It is severed from the rest of the Bible. It covers that period designated by Peter, "The world that then was". We read in 2 Peter 3: 5, 6:

> "For this they wilfully forget, that there were heavens from of old, and an earth, out of water and by means of water standing together, by the word of God, by the which, the world that then was, being flooded with water, perished; while the heavens and the earth that are now, by the same word, have been stored with fire, being kept unto the day of judgment and destruction of ungodly men".

These weighty words were the inspired answer to the scoffers, who said, "All things continue thus (or the same) from the beginning of the creation". Genesis 1: 1 is the "beginning of the creation", but that creation did not remain, it was subjected to an "overthrow"; "the earth *became* without form and void, and darkness was upon the face of the deep". Genesis 1: 2 was not understood by the "scoffers", neither will it be understood to-day except we believe the Word of God to mean what it says.

The word translated "was" in Genesis 1: 2 is translated "became" in Genesis 2: 7. "Man *became* a living soul", he was not so before. Again, "It *came to* pass" (Gen. 4: 3); "*become* a flood" (Gen. 9: 15), etc. God is not the author of confusion; He is not the author of darkness; He did not create the earth without form and void, but it *became* so. Isaiah 45: 18 distinctly declares that "He created it not *in vain*". The word is *tohu*, the very same as is translated "without form" in Genesis 1: 2. The Lord has used the words "without form and void" in another context, viz., Jeremiah 4: 23, where the whole passage speaks of *judgment*. "I beheld the earth, and, lo, it was *without form and void*; and the heavens, they had *no light*". Apart from the other occurrences of the word, this one will enable us to see that judgment is written across Genesis 1: 2.

The rendering of the Hebrew words *tohu va-bohu* by "without form and void" savours a little of the pagan legend of chaos, out of which creation is supposed to have sprung, and which veiled the truth which is recorded in Genesis 1: 2, viz., the judgment of God, and in its place gave the honours of creation to a god named *Chaos*, who is easily identified with Cush, the father of Nimrod. The proper meaning of *tohu* is "ruin" or "desolation". *Bohu* is translated better than *tohu*, for it means "emptiness", hence "void" can remain. Speaking of the overthrow of Idumoea, Isaiah 34: 11 says, "He shall stretch out upon it the line of *confusion*, and the stones (plummet) of *emptiness*". The words "confusion" and "emptiness" are *tohu* and *bohu* as in Genesis 1: 2.

We must keep well before our mind the two facts (1) that Genesis 1: 1 declares the creation of the heavens and the earth to be the direct act of God, and (2) that the earth *became a ruin*. How long it remained a ruin we do not know, but that it ever should be raised from that state of judgment, be re-fashioned and blessed tells the reader of the Word with trumpet voice that this *in itself* is an act of *grace*, that redemptive purposes begin to operate at Genesis 1: 2, and that we may expect to find that the present world and all pertaining to it will exhibit many object lessons of redeeming grace, if we have but eyes to see.

The sin which involved the heavens and the earth at the "beginning of creation" was certainly not the sin of Adam, which took place after the "overthrow" of Genesis 1: 2, and after the creation (during the six days) of the world that now is. It is imperative that we should have a clear understanding of the issues before us. Who was it that caused the fair creation to be thus involved in ruin and darkness? Why had the waters of the abyss been allowed to overflow this devoted earth? The witness of revelation and history alike confirm our belief that God did not destroy the work of His hands without adequate cause. The Scriptural teaching regarding this period is veiled, its language is involved, and we are conscious that we see but "darkly", but the vision which Scripture gives is sufficient for us to perceive that Satan, our enemy, was the prime cause of the overthrow as recorded in Genesis 1: 2. The moment we perceive that Satan and his host are involved in this earth's destinies, that moment we realize the transcendent scope of divine revelation. It lifts itself above and beyond our puny horizon and little selfishness, and we are found to be tiny and insignificant spectators and participators in a conflict waged between heaven and the unseen world, the combatants being for the most part invisible to our eyes, and beyond our ken.

Let us gather together the teaching of the Word regarding Satan. We shall be obliged at the outset to dismiss from our minds all the trifling conceptions which go to make up the devil of Christendom. Satan, before whom the archangel durst not bring a railing accusation (Jude 9), is a being possessed of marvellous powers, intelligence, and beauty. His titles include such as, "The prince of this world", and "The god of this age". He could claim, without fear of contradiction, the right to dispose to whomsoever he would the kingdoms of the world (Luke 4: 5-8). Another title is, "The prince of the power of the air", and under him are ranged those "spiritual wickednesses in heavenly places" against whom the believer of the present dispensation is exhorted to stand.

We know very little of the spiritual agencies, good and evil, by which we are surrounded. The Scriptures speak of thrones, dominions, principalities, and powers; of angels and the archangel; of world rulers, rulers of darkness, and spiritual wickednesses. Satan had access to the presence of God in the days of Job. In 1 Kings 22: 19-23 a mysterious record of spiritual interference is given, which the reader might well consider. That the Lord had given to spiritual beings delegated authority over this earth, which they failed to use aright, seems to be indicated in Psalm 82: 2. The word "mighty" in verse 1 is *El* (God), of which "gods" is the plural. Verses 6 and 7 clearly indicate that they are not mortal men, but that they shall be subjected to death as a punishment for their rebellion and disloyalty:

> "I have said, Ye are gods, and all of you are children of the Most High (*cp.* 'sons of God' in Job 1: 6; 2: 1; 38: 7), but ye shall die like men, and fall like one of the princes".

That the title "gods" is given to angels may be seen by comparing Psalm 97: 7, "Worship Him all ye *gods*", with Hebrews 1: 6, "And let all the *angels* of God worship Him". Or again, Psalm 8: 5, "A little lower than the *angels*" (Heb. *elohim* = gods), and Hebrews 2: 9, "A little lower than the *angels*". Satan and his angels had this world and its firmament (or heavens) under their authority, and in contrast to this we read in Hebrews 2: 5 with regard to the future age, "For unto the angels hath He not put in subjection the world to come". No, that is the destined prerogative of the redeemed, with their glorified Head. That Satan has his agents and representatives in the courts of the world is clear from such a passage as Daniel 10: 5, 6. The glorious being "whose loins were girded with pure gold of Uphaz", whose "body also was like the beryl, and his face as the appearance of lightning, and his eyes as lamps of fire, and his arms and his feet like in colour to polished brass, and the voice of his words like the voice of a multitude", confesses (verse 13) that he was withstood by the prince of the kingdom of Persia for twenty-one days. Michael, the archangel (here called the chief prince), came to his help, and indeed is the only one of these mighty beings who held with this angelic being in these important things. Michael is further called "your prince", and in Daniel 12: 1 he is again spoken of as "Michael . . . the great prince, which standeth for the children of thy people". There is further reference to "The prince of Grecia".

Here we have two important facts to notice. The first is that one of the principalities who owned allegiance to Satan was stationed in Persia, and another in Greece; and secondly, that Israel, unlike the nations around, had as their prince not an emissary of Satan, but the archangel Michael. This helps us to see the peculiar sacredness of the nation of Israel in the eyes of God.

Bearing in mind the references made above to the use of the word "gods" for the angelic rulers of this world, let us now turn to Ezekiel 28, a passage which contains much that is wonderful, and of the deepest interest. The first nineteen verses are occupied with an accusation against the prince of Tyre, and a lamentation over the king of Tyre. The prince of Tyre, in all his vain-glory, furnished a prophetic type of antichrist, who shall sit in the temple of God, shewing himself that he is God, and any reader having before him the Scriptures concerning the blasphemous claim of antichrist and his doom, cannot fail to see the fulness of the type.

But who is this king of Tyre? He certainly cannot be a human being, for the description would be untrue. The highest ascription of wisdom and beauty are given to him. "Thou sealest up the sum (the pattern), full of wisdom, and perfect in beauty". Throughout the whole canon of inspiration there is nowhere to be found, in a description of anyone less than God, words which exceed these just quoted. "Thou hast been in Eden, the garden of God. Every precious stone was thy covering". This seems to indicate something before

Adam's Eden; in fact, it confirms us in our belief that much of the present creation is but typical of the restitution of all things, a connecting link between the perfect heavens and earth of Genesis 1: 1, and the new heavens and earth of the future. The reference to the precious stones and gold makes one think of the new Jerusalem, the holy city.

"The service of thy tabrets and of thy pipes was prepared with (A.V. 'in') thee in the day that thou wast created". In Isaiah 14: 11 and Daniel 3 we have examples of music as the accompaniment of royalty. At Sinai, and at the return of our Lord Jesus Christ, a trumpet sounds; so with the creation of Satan, he is acclaimed king. But more, "Thou art the cherub of the anointing, that covereth, and I have set thee so". Here we seem to leave kingly terms for priestly ones, while the words, "Thou wast upon the holy mountain of God, thou hast walked up and down in the midst of the stones of fire", help to magnify this mighty being still more. Who can but see the evident parallel in Psalm 2: 6, "Yet have I set My King, upon My holy hill of Zion"? The reference to the "stones of fire" indicates nearness to the throne of God. Exodus 24: 10, 17 supply a commentary here. "They saw the God of Israel, and there was under His feet as it were a paved work of sapphire stone . . . and the sight of the glory of the Lord was like devouring fire". Everything points to the important conclusion that once in the ages past Satan enjoyed the high privilege of king and priest in relation to the earth and heavens. How was it lost? "Thou wast perfect in thy ways from the day that thou wast created, till iniquity was found in thee" (verse 15).

The word translated "merchandize" in Ezekiel 28: 16 may be allowed a rather different meaning. Merchandize in Hebrew is derived from "*rakal*" — to go about (1) in order to traffic, and (2) for the purpose of slandering. Thus we have *rakal*, a merchant, and *rakil*, slander, consequently the word *rekullah* in Ezekiel 28: 16 can mean either a going about in order to traffic, or a going about in order to slander. Scripture gives instances of Satan's slanderous reports. We find a record in Job (one of the earliest books); we find a record in Revelation (the last book), viz., Revelation 12: 10. In this last passage we read, "The accuser of our brethren is cast down", and so in Ezekiel 28: 16, "By the multitude of thy slanders . . . thou hast sinned, therefore will *I cast thee* as profane *out of* the mountain of God". "Thou hast defiled thy sanctuaries". The reference to the sanctuaries, and the word "profane", emphasize the truth already seen, that Satan had dealings with holy things. Pride was the cause of his downfall (Ezek. 28: 17 and 1 Tim. 3: 6). His final doom is terrible, yet in it we see the mercy of God, for a day is coming when in the new heavens and new earth, where curse and sin and death shall be no more, it will also be true (as in Ezek. 28: 19) concerning the fate of Satan, that "never shalt thou be any more". The priestly and kingly offices forfeited by Satan and his host are to be filled by the Lord Jesus Christ, Who as King and Priest will reign over the millennial earth, and in the ages to follow, and with matchless grace will associate His earthly and heavenly people with Himself in His throne and glory.

This is a summary of the teaching of some Scriptures concerning the one who brought about the awful judgment of Genesis 1: 2, and whose malignity is everywhere discernible in his desperate fight against the purpose and people of God. This it is that makes redemption so vast, revelation so majestic. This alone would prevent us from accepting the puny interpretation of the Apocalypse put forward by the "historic" school. To think that the "wrath of the Lamb" (Rev. 6: 16) is to be construed of some upheaval in Turkey or Asia Minor is not only absurd, but is almost blasphemous, for it degrades the divine record of the heavenly conflict to the level of a report of some mere political squabble. No, there are mightier issues before us than we suppose. Let us beware lest we belittle the wondrous plan of the ages. The six days' creation, the probation and fall of man, are but links in the chain of redeeming love. We have been apt to look upon redemption as being something subsequent to Genesis 3, whereas redemption was planned, and Christ set apart as the Lamb without blemish and without spot, "before the overthrow of the world" (1 Peter 1: 19, 20). The six days' creation was not the goal, but it was a step towards it. God never intended that the destiny of this earth, and its teeming millions, should hang upon the obedience of a creature. Strange and inexplicable as it may seem, Adam's fall was foreknown and provided for before Adam existed. We, his latest descendants, have learned for our joy that we were chosen in Christ before the overthrow of the world, that is, before our first parents were even created.

All these things shew us that we are dealing with tremendous issues. Seen in this light Israel's history ceases to be a record of a nomadic tribe having monotheistic tendencies. The history of Israel's kings ceases to be but one speck in the wider history of the nations. Israel's history, their failure, their future restoration and blessing, involve the peace of the world, the regeneration of the earth, and the deliverance of this creation from the bondage of corruption. So also is it with the church, the one Body. It is being called out during this present cessation of kingdom purposes, not merely for *our* present joy and future glory, but to bear a witness unto the principalities and powers in the heavenlies. By means of the church God is beginning to put into operation the heavenly section of His redemptive purposes, so that when Israel is again taken up, the earthly and heavenly plan will unfold itself unto its glorious consummation, that "dispensation of the fulness of the seasons, when the Lord God shall gather under one Head all things in Christ, whether they be things in heaven or on earth, even in Him" (Eph. 1: 10). O the depth of the riches, and of the wisdom, and of the knowledge of God! He makes the wrath of man to praise Him.

How wonderfully all was planned. Instead of the unbelief and rejection of Israel bringing the purpose of God to a standstill, they but provided the opportunity for the Lord to commence the heavenly section of His wondrous plan. Hence it is that "now unto the principalities and powers in heavenly places is being made known by the church" not so much the grace and love of God, but the "manifold wisdom of God". Satan and his host stand abashed, as before their wondering eyes the Lord brings to light His hidden purpose, the dispensation of the Mystery, reserved by divine foreknowledge and wisdom until this present time.

Israel have partially returned to their land, and when the Lord once again takes up the threads laid down in Acts 28, the two-fold purpose, the heavenly and the earthly, will go on together. How wonderful is the wisdom, the knowledge, the power, as well as the grace of our God. O for a faith that rests unreservedly on Him, knowing that all things work together for good to them that love God, who are the called according to His purpose.

Another feature in the transitory character of "the world that now is" is that it was made in *six* days. Six is the number of failure, of human weakness, of imperfection. The stamp of the man of sin, who is the culmination of the sin of man, is 666. At the very threshold God has emphasized the fact that this present world was not the goal before Him, but merely a step, a link. His goal is "a new heavens, and a new earth, wherein dwelleth righteousness". Once in the ages past the universe of God was clean. Sin had not reared its awful head. For His own wise yet inscrutable purpose, He permitted its entrance into the heavens, and afterwards into the earth. God is far more gracious than our orthodoxy permits. He who allowed the fall had a gracious purpose before Him. Creation is to stand no more in creature strength, but is to be finally and for ever secured by the redeeming blood and the power of Christ.

"In the beginning God created the heavens and the earth". That is the record of the sinless ages of the past. "When He shall have delivered up the kingdom to God, even the *Father* . . . that God may be all in all". This is the goal towards which everything is tending. In

Genesis 1: 1 it is God in all the mighty grandeur of *Creator*. In 1 Corinthians 15: 24 it is God in all the marvellous grace of *Father*. When that day comes there will be seen once again a clean universe; a universe having neither sin, curse, nor death, for these former things will have passed away never again to darken the creation of God. What a goal! How it helps us to patience, how it teaches us to withold our attempts to vindicate the various providences of our God. He worketh all things after the counsel of His own will. Let us be content to wait; we know Whom we have believed.

The reader will of course understand that, owing to our limited space, we cannot here attempt an exposition of Genesis. Many have pointed out the typical teaching of the six days' creation. We would just pause to emphasize the important connection of Genesis 1: 2, 3. "The Spirit of God moved . . . and God said". O that we may ever remember that in the gospel, and in every-day life, the Spirit of God moves along the lines indicated in Holy Writ. How many would have been saved from the snares of some of the so-called revivals had they but tested all by the touchstone of our faith — the Word of God.

On the sixth day God created man; Genesis 1: 26 removes man from all else that was created before him. Made of the same clay, breathing the same breath, yet differing in destiny and purpose, man is set before us as the result of a deliberate act of creation. "And God said, Let Us make man in the likeness of Our image". One thing is intended here, not two. Christ, the second person of the Trinity, was already at this time "in the *form* of God", "the *image* of the invisible God, the first-born of all creation" (Col. 1: 15). He had not then exchanged that glorious form for the "form of a servant", and the "likeness of men" (Phil. 2). It was because the creation of Adam was a pre-ordained step in the purpose of the ages that he was made in the likeness of the image of God, for Hebrews 1: 2 tells us that "through Him (Christ) God made the ages". Some assert that the "likeness of the image" was removed when man fell, but in Genesis 9: 6; 1 Corinthians 11: 7, and James 3: 9 there are unqualified references to this, which should make us ponder the subject very carefully. The purpose of man's creation is stated in the next half of the verse, "And let them have *dominion*". Sea, air, and earth were to be placed under man's dominion. Here we have the first step in the purpose of God pertaining to the earth. A dominion is equivalent to a kingdom, and a reference to Psalm 8 and Hebrews 2: 6-8 will satisfy the reader that such is the intention of the passage. God's purpose, however, is no sooner declared, than we find that Satan sets himself to attempt to thwart it. This is an essential element in the whole record of the Bible, as our studies will prove.

The section of "the generations of the heavens and the earth" include man before the fall, man tempted and fallen, and man after the fall, and extends from chapters 2: 4 to 4: 26. That man was warned against an enemy of some kind seems clear from the words of 2: 15, "And the Lord God took the man, and put him into the garden of Eden, to dress it, and to keep (*i.e.* preserve or guard) it". The word "keep" occurs again in 3: 24. Further, the man was solemnly warned as to the results of disobedience to the command to abstain from partaking of the tree of knowledge of good and evil. God is a righteous God, and even though He were not a God of love, mercy, and grace, common justice would forbid that He should threaten Adam with one punishment, and mean to punish him with another, the severity and horror of which no words can express. The Lord said, "In the day that thou eatest thereof thou shalt surely die". The majority of interpreters tell us that God did not mean merely physical death, but spiritual death, and also the second death, which according to them is not death at all, but a state of conscious agony and torment for ever and ever. Could anything be more monstrous? Let us rather stand together with God who *says* what He *means*.

The penalty with which Adam was threatened was physical death; not a natural, but an inflicted death, and it was to take place on the very day that he transgressed. He was to be cut off as unworthy of life, without opportunity of repentance, without privilege of descendants. The question as to whether he really endured the penalty will be considered presently. Before the sad account of man's fall is given, a beautiful passage occurs wherein the woman, the helpmeet, is made and presented to the man. True marriage is one of the few gleams of paradise that have come through to this blighted earth. The home life is a divine object lesson of God's ultimate purpose. The marriage of the Lamb, we read, takes place at the end of the ages; it is no wonder then that Satan has ever sought to destroy the sacredness of the marriage bond. Polygamy, adultery, and uncleanness have ever accompanied the "doctrines of demons".

There is a typical meaning in the relationship between man and wife which it is important to remember. The relationship between Jehovah and Israel is given in these terms. Take, for instance, the passage in Jeremiah 31: 31, 32; it speaks of the time when under the new covenant Israel will be blessed in their land, and the Lord refers to their disobedience and ingratitude under the old covenant, using the marriage bond as an illustration, "Although I was an husband unto them". Israel's defection is described as a wife's disloyalty. "Surely, as a wife treacherously departeth from her husband, so have ye dealt treacherously with Me, O house of Israel, saith the Lord" (Jer. 3: 20).

Terrible words are spoken by the Lord when describing the nature of Israel's sin:

> "Thou hast played the whore with the Assyrians, because thou wast insatiable ... Thou hast not been as an harlot, in that thou scornest hire, but as a wife that committeth adultery, which taketh strangers instead of her husband" (Ezek. 16: 28-34).

The beautiful words of Isaiah 54: 4-8, speaking of Israel's restoration, will come to the minds of many:

> "Thou shalt not remember the reproach of thy widowhood any more. For thy Maker is thy husband, the Lord of hosts is His name; and thy Kinsman-redeemer (*cp.* Boaz and Ruth) the Holy One of Israel; the God of the whole earth shall He be called. For the Lord hath called thee as a woman forsaken and grieved in spirit, and a wife of youth, when thou wast refused, saith thy God. For a small moment have I forsaken thee, but with great mercies will I gather thee".

Again, in Hosea 2: 16-20 we read:

> "And it shall be at that day, saith the Lord, that thou shalt call me *Ishi* (my husband) ... and I will betroth thee unto Me in righteousness, and in judgment, and in loving kindness, and in mercies; I will even betroth thee unto Me in faithfulness".

Not only the "people", but also the "land", is included in the beautiful marriage figure:

> "Thou shalt no more be termed Forsaken, neither shall thy land any more be termed Desolate, but thou shalt be called *Hephzibah* (My delight is in her), and thy land *Beulah* (married). For the Lord delighteth in thee, and thy land shall be married" (Isa. 62: 4, 5).

The verses following speak of the future restoration of Jerusalem, in which Jerusalem shall be made "a praise in the earth", and so we are not surprised to find that not only the *people* and the *land*, but also the *city*, are referred to under the figure of marriage:

> "Come hither, I will show thee the bride, the Lamb's wife. And he carried me away in spirit to a great and high mountain, and shewed me *that great city*, the holy Jerusalem, descending out of heaven from God, having the glory of God ... it had twelve gates ... and names written thereon, which are the names of the twelve tribes of the children of Israel ... and twelve foundations, and in them the names of the twelve apostles of the Lamb" (Rev. 21: 9-14).

Thus the three key words of Israel's history, "the *people*, the *land*, and the *city*" (*see e.g.*, Daniel's prayer and Gabriel's prophecy in Dan. 9), are each in turn referred to under the figure of marriage. The mountain of Revelation 21 with its city (the bride) is seen in Isaiah 2, while in Isaiah 4: 5 we read, "Upon all the glory shall be a defence", or better, a marriage canopy. It will be seen that this is quite in keeping with the purpose of God's redeeming grace, that the great type of His relationship with Israel should be seen at the beginning. The introduction of polygamy, divorce, adultery, etc., were all the attempts of the evil one to thwart the purpose of God, and were overruled by the Lord to provide object lessons and types of Israel's failure. Nevertheless, "As it was at the beginning" is to be realized when Revelation 21 is fulfilled.

Not only was Eve a type of Israel, but we also read that "Adam was a type of the coming One" (Rom. 5: 14). That he was not the true and destined head is seen by reading 1 Corinthians 15: 45-49. "The first man Adam became a living soul, the last Adam a life-giving spirit . . . The first man is of the earth, earthy; the second man is the Lord from heaven". Here Adam *as created*, not as fallen, is in view. Christ is spoken of in contrast as the *last* Adam, the *second* Man, and the Lord from *heaven*. All men that have been born since Adam are passed over. Adam was the type of Christ in his federal headship, in his dominion, and in his marriage. The garden in Eden was also typical of what the earth will be when redemption is applied to it (*cp*. Rev. 22: 1, 2). Notice that it is not the garden *of* Eden, but a garden planted eastward *in* Eden. Here was an enclosure of special beauty in a surrounding country which merited the name "Eden", or "Pleasure". In this enclosed garden Adam met and communed with God. There was the tree of life. It was the first earthly pattern of the heavenly reality, afterwards more minutely detailed in Exodus in the Tabernacle. The garden, the surrounding Eden, and the world, stand in the same relationship to the heavenly pattern as the holiest of all, the holy place, and the court of the Jewish Tabernacle. Not only the garden, but the whole six days' creation was intensely typical.

The order of the creation is full of suggestive teaching which has been observed by many, but few seem to have realized that the creation of "the heavens and the earth which are now" was a type on a grand scale. The heavens were set with two great light bearers, the sun and the moon, whose purpose was to divide the day from the night, and were, moreover, for signs (*oth* = things to come, Jer. 10: 2), and seasons (*moed* = appointed seasons), and for days, and years. These are the primary purposes of the two luminaries, to give light upon the earth is added afterwards. Now just as we have thought more of the sun and moon in their secondary capacity, so have we with regard to the whole creation. The primary purpose of the six days' creation was to give an exhibition of redemption.

During these six days the Lord created everything which we now see around us (Gen. 2: 1). He purposely placed animals which should hereafter serve as types of "clean" and of "unclean" things. The lion, the tiger, the wolf, and the serpent were created much as they are seen to-day. The fall of man did not produce an evolution in the animal world. At creation the lion had his claws, the wolf his fangs, the serpent his venom, the eagle his talons, for Genesis 3 was foreknown. The pests that beset the fruit grower, the agriculturist, the cattle rearer were all created during the six days. These creatures, harmful as they are, yet exhibit the same marvellous handiwork as do the friends of man.

Day and night even are only temporary, for a time is coming when it shall be true that there shall be "no night" there. The sea also is here for a typical purpose, for the same is written concerning the sea as the night, "I saw no more sea". Day and night, as well as the sea, we know to be part of the six days' creation, and are typical of a state wherein evil is found, and which will not pass from this scene until redemption be an accomplished fact. The fig, vine and olive are types of Israel's threefold condition. The bramble is typical of the Gentile (*see* Judg. 9: 7-16). The lamb typified the foreordained Redeemer in His sacrificial work (1 Pet 1: 19); the lion also the Redeemer in His triumph (Rev. 5: 5). The serpent, the dragon, the roaring lion, frogs, locusts, and other unclean things and beasts of prey were types of Satan and his agents. All nature is full of this one grand object lesson, providing the Lord Jesus, the apostles, and prophets with abundant illustration (*cp.* the clean and the unclean, the wheat and the tares, the sheep and the goats, the saved and the lost). The one epistle of James contains more allusions to nature than the whole of the epistles of Paul, particularly his later ones. The later epistles deal with the heavenly side of truth, the earthly types being less apposite.

To perceive the typical, shadowy, temporal character of this world, with its evident cry for redemption, to hear the groans of creation, to look ahead for "that day" are helps in the understanding of Scripture not to be underestimated, and they form a light which sheds its illuminating rays upon much that is difficult and obscure. Thus Genesis 2 leads us to the final words concerning the man and his wife, "they were not ashamed". How long will this state of innocence last? Will Adam and Eve refrain from eating of the fruit of the tree of knowledge of good and evil? The crisis is hastened by the advent of an outside temptation, an element which was not mentioned in the charge given to Adam in chapter 2. As this constitutes a subject of the very greatest importance, we will defer its consideration till the next chapter.

CHAPTER SIX

The temptation and the fall

Genesis 3 records the turning point in the history of man. Its effects are with us to this day, and will continue until the new heavens and the new earth take the place of this sin-stained universe. While many have laboured to show the position and failure of man, as set forth in this chapter, few seem to have grasped the importance of the momentous fact therein recorded — the first appearance on the page of Scripture, and in the world that now is, of the arch-enemy of God and man — Satan.

One of the items of evidence that demands recognition is the witness of Bible numerics. It is a remarkable fact that the number 13 is the brand that is stamped upon the person and agencies of Satan, and is also the numerical factor of Genesis 3. The Hebrew word *Satan* = 364 (13 × 28). The number 28 is suggestive. Genesis 1: 1 in the Hebrew contains 7 words and 28 letters. 28 = 4 × 7, or creation perfect. 13 is the number of rebellion (Gen. 14: 4), hence Satan in Hebrew = rebellion in God's perfect creation.

In the Greek expression we have 13 raised to the superlative, the height of rebellion being seen in the Greek explanation of that old serpent "who is called the Devil, and Satan" (Rev. 12: 9) = 2,197 (13 × 13 × 13). Further, the Greek words "dragon" and "serpent" are multiples of 13. So also are the titles "murderer", "tempter", and "fowler" in the Hebrew. The whole of the chapter (Gen. 3) is a multiple of 13 (13 × 6,491). The opening words, "The serpent was more subtil than any beast of the field", have the numerical value of 1,521 (13 × 13 × 9). In contrast to this the numerics of verses 15 and 16, wherein is recorded the great primeval promise, and the woman's connection with the promised Seed, are 8,512 (8,000 + 8 × 8 × 8), where 8, the dominical number, the number of the name "Jesus", and the number of resurrection, is the great factor. These numerics are simple facts; can we doubt their divine arrangement? We will not multiply instances of the connection of 13 with Satan, but will pass on to consider the teaching of Genesis 3.

The first actor in the scene is "the serpent". Throughout the varied and widespread ramifications of paganism, the serpent is a prominent and constant figure, and it requires more than the mere fascination of the reptile to account for this phenomenon of pagan worship. Genesis 3 supplies the answer. The serpent was the medium of Satan. There are many who speak as though the serpent was the tempter, but this is not so. Chapter 20 verse 2 of Revelation, the book which contains answers to Genesis in so many ways, speaks of "the old serpent" as "the Devil and Satan". When the Lord Jesus was on earth Satan himself tempted Him, and by analogy one would be led to see that the tempter of the first man was none other than Satan himself. That Satan should use the body of a serpent is in strict harmony with what we know to-day of the use of *mediums* in spiritistic séances. The reason for his choice is given in the first verse. "The serpent was more subtil (or more wise, as the word means) than any beast of the field which the Lord God had made." The comparison with "any living creature of the field" suggests that a literal serpent is in view. Throughout the record, the serpent, and Satan behind it, are to be kept before the mind.

The words "upon thy belly shalt thou go" mean exactly what the words express as addressed to the serpent itself, and the utmost degradation as applied to Satan (*cp.* Psalm 44: 25). The word translated serpent in Genesis 3: 1 is *nachash*, meaning "a shining one", but always bearing the added sense of bewitchment, fascination, and enchantment, for the verb *nachash* (to divine) carries this meaning in its occurrences (*see* Gen. 30: 27; 44: 5, 15; Lev. 19: 26; Deut. 18: 10; 2 Kings 17: 17; 21: 6, and 2 Chron. 33: 6).

Genesis 3. (The purpose in germ)

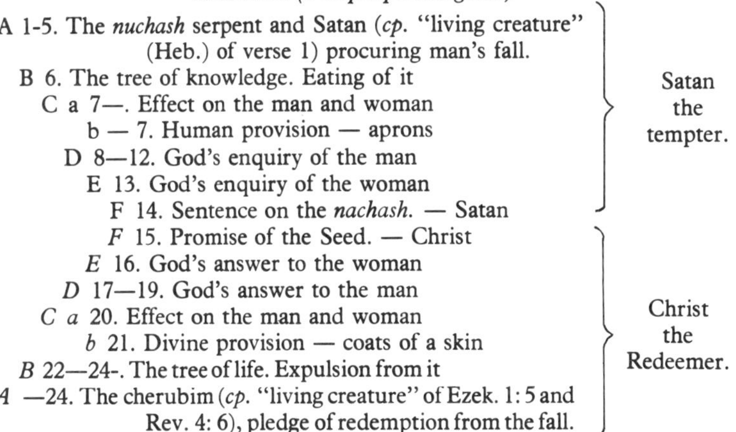

A 1-5. The *nuchash* serpent and Satan (*cp.* "living creature" (Heb.) of verse 1) procuring man's fall.
B 6. The tree of knowledge. Eating of it
C a 7—. Effect on the man and woman
b — 7. Human provision — aprons
D 8—12. God's enquiry of the man
E 13. God's enquiry of the woman
F 14. Sentence on the *nachash*. — Satan
F 15. Promise of the Seed. — Christ
E 16. God's answer to the woman
D 17—19. God's answer to the man
C a 20. Effect on the man and woman
b 21. Divine provision — coats of a skin
B 22—24-. The tree of life. Expulsion from it
A —24. The cherubim (*cp.* "living creature" of Ezek. 1: 5 and Rev. 4: 6), pledge of redemption from the fall.

Satan the tempter. (A–F)

Christ the Redeemer. (*F*–*A*)

The structure of Genesis 3 places in prominent contrast the *nachash*, or serpent, at the commencement of the chapter, and the cherubim at the close. We shall find that the cherubim are, like Satan, supernatural beings, and that they, too, are intimately connected with animal forms — the man, the lion, the ox, and the eagle. The structure of the passage is as shown on page 77.

The prominent members of a structure of this kind are the first and last, and the central two, the emphasis thus being laid upon the serpent, the Seed, and the cherubim. The first half of the structure commences with the serpent procuring man's fall, and ends with the serpent being sentenced by God. The second section commences with the promised Deliverer, the Seed, and ends with the pledge of redemption, the cherubim. Thus Genesis 3 divides into two sections, the first, beginning and ending with the serpent, being entirely occupied with the temptation, fall, and shame of man; the second, beginning with Christ and ending with the cherubim, is entirely connected with the promise and pledge of redemption.

The arrangement of the parts of this chapter is eloquent beyond words. See how the two trees are placed in correspondence, and also the aprons of leaves, and the coats of a skin; how full of teaching is this divine structural plan. The central section is the climax of the passage. We look in vain for Adam and Eve, so far as their sin or doom is concerned. What do we find? We find the two great elements of divine revelation revolving around two persons — Christ and Satan. The conflict in the Scriptures is not primarily between God and man, but between God's purpose in Christ, and Satan. Man is a desperate sinner, utterly fallen and depraved, but we do not forget that to a large extent he is the dupe of the father of lies. The true foci of Genesis 3 are "the sentence upon the *nachash*", and "the promise of the Seed of the woman". Let us learn from the Lord, and leave behind anything of our theology that interferes with a ready acceptance of the truth.

The serpent did not come to Eve and say, "What a wonderful paradise this is! How beautiful the trees and the flowers". No, he omitted all that a grateful heart should remember, and said, "Can it be that God hath said, Ye shall not eat of *every* tree of the garden". It was not a question, it was an insinuation. Why did he address the woman? We may not know. We have no reason to believe that woman was then "the weaker vessel", although it is a remarkable fact that women figure largely in the spiritistic movements, and hysterical religious revivals that break out from time to time. It may be that Satan laid his plan to involve both the man and the woman. If Adam had been first tempted, Eve would have acted under his direction, and have been shielded by his responsibility. Howsoever it may have been, the deep-laid plan was terribly successful. Most readers are fully aware of the threefold mistake of Eve. She committed the sins of omission, addition, and alteration of the Word of God. She omitted the gracious word "freely" (*cp*. 3: 2 and 2: 16); she added the extra prohibition, "neither shall ye touch it" (*cp*. 3: 3 and 2: 17); she altered the certainty of the sentence of death to a contingency, "lest ye die" (*cp*. 3: 3 and 2: 16, 17). Satan seized the opportunity, and gave a flat denial to the Word of God. His first recorded lie is, "Ye shall not surely die". This initial lie has been so instilled into the mind of man by Satan, that now paganism, philosophy, Romanism, and Protestantism repeat almost with one voice, "There is no death". "The soul is immortal".

It is not the purpose of this volume to discuss the question of the immortality of the soul, but the writer would here take the opportunity of testifying that he has studied the Scriptures with this question before him, and has become convinced that man does not possess an immortal soul, and that immortality is the gift of God alone. No one can read the record of the expulsion from Eden (Gen. 3: 22-24) with an unbiassed mind, without seeing that the Lord definitely drove out Adam and Eve to prevent them from partaking of the tree of life, and living for ever. No, His plan was far more gracious; not an immortal sinner — far from it — but immortality and eternal life through the redemption of Christ, that is His plan.

The inevitable consequences of sin follow in the wake of Eve's disobedience. She gave to Adam with her, and he did eat. Immediately a change took place (quite what it was we do not know); shame took the place of innocency, the armour of light had been eclipsed, and they took the fast-fading leaves of a fig tree to cover their nakedness. The voice of the Lord struck terror instead of joyful anticipation; the reign of sin had commenced. The guilty pair stand before the Lord. Adam is first addressed as being the head. He is asked to give a reason for his disobedience, and he does so.

We would here enter a protest against that time-worn exegesis which indulges in the unseemly pleasantry as to the man blaming the woman, and the woman blaming the serpent. Men have invented all manner of plausible reasons as to why Adam ate the forbidden fruit. He gives the reason in plain words, "The woman whom Thou gavest to be with me, she gave me of the tree, and I did eat". Adam was not deceived; he went into the transgression with eyes open to the consequences. Some motive of sufficient strength must be found for such an act, and we suggest it is here provided. Husbands now, with the marks of the fall everywhere evident about them, are enjoined to "love their wives, even as Christ loved the church, and gave Himself for it". We cannot comprehend the purity and strength of affection that united together this man and woman when marriage was indeed "made in heaven". The woman had succumbed to the wiles of the tempter, and we suggest that Adam's affection for his wife outweighed his sense of loyalty to God, and rather than she should enter the darkness alone, he ate of the fruit and shared it, also its consequences, with her. We do not seek to make Adam a hero. He disobeyed God, he showed weakness, he fell, but we see in his action a foreshadowing of that unsullied love of Christ, Who voluntarily entered this world of sin to bear that sin away by the sacrifice of Himself.

The Lord does not misunderstand Adam, and He turns at once to the woman, saying, "What is this that thou hast done?" The woman's answer is not less true than Adam's, "The *serpent beguiled* me, and I did eat". This is repeated in 2 Corinthians 11: 3, "As the *serpent beguiled* Eve through his subtilty", and emphasized in 1 Timothy 2: 14, "Adam was not deceived, but the woman, being *deceived*, was in the transgression". Adam was not deceived; he was not entrapped by the lying promises, or the denials of God's truth, but Eve was. Eve may have been culpable for allowing herself to be led into temptation, but the Scripture asserts that she was deceived. All can see that there is a great difference between wilful disobedience, and disobedience as a result of deception.

Again, the Lord does not question the truthfulness of this confession, but turns to the serpent, and utters the words of condemnation. The first part of the curse has reference to both the literal serpent, and to Satan; the second part (verse 15) has exclusive reference to Satan, and the promised Seed. We submit to the student of Scripture that in this central member of Genesis 3 we have the germ of Biblical history, doctrine, and prophecy. The enmity between Satan's seed, and the Seed of the woman, is sustained until we reach the closing chapters of Revelation.

Satan's fall is the great fact to be remembered in Genesis 1, and Satan's enmity is the central fact of Genesis 3. Adam is not the central figure by any means. There is deep significance in the words of verse 15 relating to the two seeds. If we admit, as we must, that the Seed of the woman refers to one — that is, Christ, we must also allow that primarily, if not exclusively, the seed of the serpent refers to one — antichrist. Let it be remembered that antichrist is the son of perdition, and that he will claim to be the Messiah. If he does this he will have to be able to point to a virgin birth, and we believe that spiritism is fast preparing the way for the advent of this monster of iniquity. Antichrist is the grand aim of Satan, even as Christ is the centre of the purposes of God. Satan, as the god of this age, is ever seeking worshippers, and as the prince of this world he seeks a throne. He once offered the kingdoms of this world, and the glory of them, for one act of worship, but was refused (Matt. 4). A day is approaching, however, when he will, in antichrist, receive the world's worship, and the world's throne for a brief period before his end comes (Rev. 13).

The temptation of Genesis 3 was directed against the purpose of God. God had given man the forfeited dominion of Satan, so far as this earth was concerned. Against this first step in kingdom purposes Satan directed his attacks. The sin that had led to his own fall — pride, aspiration to be like God, and an overweening belief in his natural independent immortality (*see* Ezek. 28: 17, and Psalm 82: 6, 7) — he uses as the bait to deceive the woman.

We now ask the reader's careful attention, as we are about to advance that which goes in direct opposition to practically the universal interpretation of the next verses. In *The Companion Bible*, the treasure house from which we have taken the majority of the structures found in this book, verses 16 and 17 are entitled, "God's sentence on the woman", and "God's sentence on the man". In our representation and structure we have altered the word "sentence" to "answer". We are conscious that "answer" is not the best word, but we definitely wanted to avoid the word "sentence". The verses come in that section which is stamped with redemption, and not with judgment. Most emphatically, verses 14 and 15 give the *sentence* upon the serpent and Satan, but in verses 16-19 the sentence threatened in 2: 17 never falls. The divine penalty was, "in the day that thou eatest thereof thou shalt surely die".

Three questions present themselves. What was the penalty? Did it fall? If not, why not? The idea of reading into the solemn words of Genesis 2: 17 the involved deaths (physical, moral, spiritual, and eternal), with the contradictory tradition that eternal *death* means eternal *life* in misery, is the outcome of believing that man is inherently immortal. It is awful to think that believers can allow themselves to imagine that God could have in store for man such a terrible penalty, without going to the most painstaking care of making Adam understand the nature of the sentence hanging over him. We are not left to our own conjectures, however. Take the words "surely die".

How does Scripture use them elsewhere? In Numbers 26: 65 we read, "They shall *surely die* in the wilderness". In Numbers 14: 29 we have the fulfilment of the sentence, and the interpretation of the words, "Your *carcases shall fall* in this wilderness". Again, come to Genesis itself. What did Abimelech understand by the words "surely die" in Genesis 20: 7, "Restore the man his wife . . . he shall pray for thee, and thou *shalt live*, and if thou restore her not, know thou that thou shalt *surely die*, thou and all that are thine"? "Shalt live" is in contrast to "surely die". Will they who contend for physical, moral, spiritual, and eternal death grant that in answer to Abraham's prayer God granted Abimelech physical, moral, spiritual, and eternal *life*? If not, why not? The passage is transparent; physical death as an *inflicted penalty* is the only thing meant. It was no penalty to Abimelech to be told that "surely die" meant the long process of natural decay, neither was the death of Adam 930 years after the fulfilment of the penalty which threatened death *in the day* that he transgressed. The reader is directed for further Scripture evidence to 1 Samuel 22: 16; 1 Kings 2: 37, 42, 46.

The penalty threatened in Genesis 2 was the immediate withdrawal of life, as forfeited, the cutting off from all that life involved, and to them it included the denial of offspring, for whose begetting and birth both the man and the woman were most marvellously designed. We answer the first question then, that according to the usage of the words of Scripture, the penalty was the immediate infliction of physical death. The next question is, Did this penalty fall? We might answer it by asking, Did the sinning man and.woman die according to the terms of the penalty? The answer must be, No! The guilty man and woman, standing before the Lord God, had heard the doom pronounced upon the serpent and his seed, but in that very doom they caught the first words of hope for themselves. The serpent should meet its end at the hands of the "Seed of the woman". How could death be inflicted if the woman was to have children? With all the sorrow that is connected with the words of God to Eve in verse 16, there is hope, there is an extension of life.

Verse 16 gives the terms of the great reprieve. Its final words speak of life and hope. "I will greatly multiply thy sorrow, and thy conception; in sorrow shalt thou bring forth children, and thy desire shall be subject to thy husband, and he shall rule over thee". That is the pronouncement of God. If any reader believes that the penalty threatened in Genesis 2 was not mitigated, and that it did fall, he must make verse 16 square with his definition of "dying, thou shalt die". Instead of death we have life, and Adam, looking upon the woman who was thus addressed, called her "Eve", that is, "Life-spring", showing that he believed God.

The words also of the Lord to Adam do not open with the sentence of death. A change is to come over the ground, even as over the physical constitution of the woman. The ground should be cursed, and sorrow should be a continual guest at his table, but again the passage rings with hope, "In sorrow shalt thou eat of it all the days of thy *life*!". Thorns, thistles, and sweat of face were changed conditions truly, but again we ask, Is this the fulfilment of the sentence of Genesis 2? Some may say, but death is mentioned at the close, Adam was to return to the dust. This is quite true. The man, expelled from the garden, without access to the tree of life, and thrown upon his own creature-hood, must under the very circumstances of the case finally pass away. Death was introduced among men by Adam (Rom. 5: 12; 1 Cor. 15: 21), and as a result of sin. All this is true, but this is something quite different from the immediate infliction of death, which was the original penalty.

We have not to ask, If the penalty did not fall, how can we avoid the conclusion that God broke His word? Again let us not be hasty; let us ask ourselves a question. We have sinned, have we not? And the wages of sin is death? Shall we ever receive those wages? If we are believers we can answer, No! Why not? Because of the redemption that is in Christ Jesus. Just in the same way do we answer the question concerning Adam and Eve. The penalty was not mitigated: it was stayed only because of the Lamb of God. Hence, *immediately* that the Lord finished speaking to Adam and Eve, He showed them, by the slaying of the innocent animal to provide them with a covering, that they stood sheltered beneath the atonement of the promised Deliverer. They were expelled from the tree of life, they forfeited all claim to immortality, and that being so, must sooner or later die, but they went out of the garden in Eden with hope in their hearts, with the sight of the sacrifice before their eyes, and with the symbol of redemption covering their nakedness.

One more consideration must conclude this chapter. Here in Genesis 3 we have an exhibition of the truth, repeated again and again down the ages, that Satan often over-reaches himself, and that the Lord takes the wise in their own craftiness. In the original terms of Genesis 2: 16, 17 nothing is said concerning outside temptation. The only thing before Adam was the unprovoked disobedience of a very simple commandment. We can conceive that, had the man and woman been left alone, they would have continued in innocency for any length of time. The initial cause of the disobedience was an outside temptation. A fallen being of marvellous wisdom plays upon the feelings of a woman who was no match for him in anything but in the safety of her innocence, and according to the warrant of Scripture she was deceived before she disobeyed. We are not seeking to excuse sin, far from it, we only seek to show how the enemy thwarted his own object. Man had been placed in dominion. Satan knew that this was but a step to his own downfall, and to prevent the success of this purpose he laid his plans. He tempted the man and the woman to their undoing, but by the very fact of *temptation* introduced another factor into the case, which actually overruled his own enmity, and brought into operation the mediatorial office of Christ, thus shutting men up to the Lord Jesus as their only hope. If the Lord had meted out the penalty to Adam and Eve, Satan would have succeeded in preventing the line of descendants which sprang from them, and thus have frustrated the advent of the promised Seed.

Satan's attempt to thwart the Lord was frustrated, and in the words of the Lord not only to the serpent, but also to the man and woman, he heard his own doom, and marked the irresistibility of the purpose of Him Who worketh all things after the counsel of His Own will.

Before concluding this chapter we must give a few words in explanation of the cherubim. The Scriptures speak of them as "*The* cherubim", as though the readers of Genesis were familiar with their form. Literally rendered, Genesis 3: 24 is "And He caused the cherubim *to tabernacle* at the east of the garden in Eden". Ezekiel 1: 10 gives a description of "four living creatures". He tells us that they had "the face of a man, and the face of a lion on the right side; and they four had the face of an ox on the left side, and they four had the face of an eagle". A similar vision occurs in Ezekiel 10, and this time we are definitely told that the cherubim were the living creatures seen in Ezekiel 1. This link helps us to associate them with the "living creatures", wrongly translated "beasts", in Revelation 4: 6, Authorised Version. The Revised Version renders the word accurately. They are to be distinguished from angels, for we read in Revelation 7: 11 that "all the angels stood round about the throne, and about the elders, and the four living creatures".

The elders are four-and-twenty in number, they sit upon thrones, and wear crowns of gold (Rev. 4: 4). In 1 Chronicles 24: 1-19 we read of the twenty-four courses of the priests. This division, and the similar division of the Levites, is recognised in Nehemiah 12: 24 as having been made by "the commandment of David the man of God". It appears that the twenty-four elders are representative of the nation of Israel, while the cherubim are pledges of a redeemed creation. If we examine Revelation 4, 5 and 6 we shall find that the theme is a redeemed creation and a redeemed Israel:

> "Thou art worthy, O Lord, to receive glory, honour, and power, for Thou hast *created* all things, and for Thy pleasure they are and were *created*" (Rev. 4: 11).
>
> "And when He had taken the book, the four living creatures, and the four-and-twenty elders fell down before the Lamb . . . and they sung a new song, saying, Thou art worthy to take the book, and to open the seals thereof, for Thou wast slain, and hast made a

redemption to God by Thy blood out of every tribe, and tongue, and people, and nation, and didst make them unto our God a kingdom of priests, and they shall reign on the earth" (Rev. 5: 8-10).

"And every creature which is in heaven, and on the earth, and under the earth, and such as are in the sea, and all that are in them heard I saying, Blessing, and honour, and glory, and power be unto Him that sitteth upon the throne, and unto the Lamb for ever and ever. And the four living creatures continued saying, Amen! And the four-and-twenty elders fell down and worshipped Him that liveth for ever and ever" (Rev. 5: 8-14).

The number of the cherubim (four) connects them with the earth. In the Revelation we have "*four* quarters of the earth"; "*four* corners of the earth"; and "*four* winds of the earth". "All creation" is described under four heads in Revelation 5: 13. The human race is summed up as "tribe, tongue, people, and nation" (Rev. 5: 9). Six tribes of living beings were created to inhabit the earth. Fish, fowl, cattle, beast, creeping thing, and man. The first five were placed under the dominion of Adam. When Adam named the animals, three kinds only are mentioned, viz., "cattle, fowl of the air, and beast of the field"; the fish and the creeping things are omitted. They are not specifically mentioned in Noah's covenant (Gen. 9: 9, 10): "I will establish My covenant with you, and your seed after you, and with every living creature that is with you, of the *fowl*, of the *cattle*, and of every *beast* of the earth with you, from all that go out of the ark, to every beast of the earth". We suggest that creeping things were outside the covenant. So also at the garden in Eden, the cherubim symbolized the redemption of these three tribes of creation, with man their head. The man, the ox, the lion, and the eagle were seen by Israel's high priest upon the mercy seat, immediately below the glory of the Lord. Thus it is not difficult to put together these things, and see that before God there are continual remembrancers of His covenant with the earth, and with Israel, and that it is for the fulfilment of this that the "whole creation groans, waiting".

Numbers 2 furnishes an interesting link between the redemptive pledge seen in the cherubim, and its relation to the nation of Israel. "Every man of the children of Israel shall pitch by his own standard, with the ensign of their father's house". This ensign is said to be one of the twelve signs of the Zodiac, and the four points of the compass, E., S., W., N., following the course of the sun, were represented by the cherubic signs, viz., lion, man, bull, eagle. The arrangement according to the Scriptures is given below, and the "twelve signs" as given in the Targum of Jonathan.

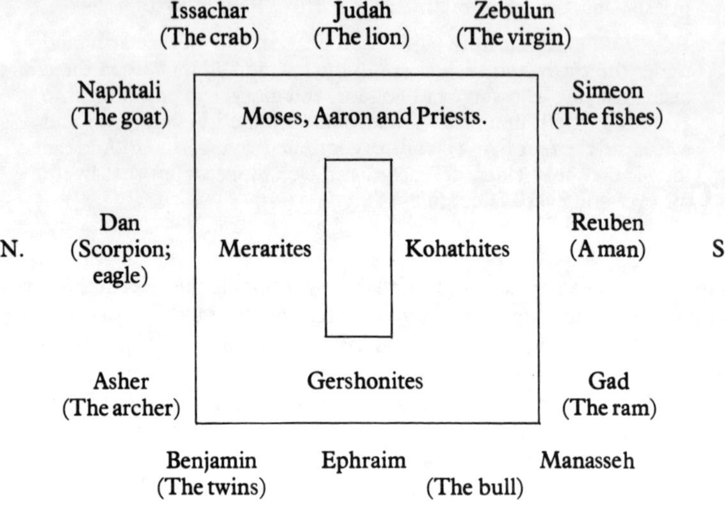
E.
Issachar
(The crab)
Judah
(The lion)
Zebulun
(The virgin)
Naphtali
(The goat)
Moses, Aaron and Priests.
Simeon
(The fishes)
N.
Dan
(Scorpion; eagle)
Merarites
Kohathites
Reuben
(A man)
S.
Asher
(The archer)
Gershonites
Gad
(The ram)
Benjamin
(The twins)
Ephraim
Manasseh
(The bull)
W.

CHAPTER SEVEN

The divine purpose and satanic opposition thereto

In the foregoing chapter we considered the record of Satan's opposition to the purposes of God, and the commencement of redemptive energies in relation to man, which immediately followed. Dominion had been given to man, the earthly kingdom had been inaugurated, but now the crown has fallen, the curse has settled down upon the creation placed under the hand of man, and henceforth "the whole creation groaneth and travaileth in pain, waiting for redemption" (Rom. 8). We shall be obliged to pass in rapid review the remainder of the book of Genesis, though the temptation to linger is indeed great.

The opposition of Satan is seen in the murder of Abel, for Cain was "of that wicked one", "the manslayer from the beginning" (1 John 3: 12; John 8: 44). Seth was appointed in the stead of Abel, "whom Cain slew", and so became the first link in the chain that should finally end in the birth of the promised Seed. The way God dealt with Cain is quite different from what we might have expected. The leniency, nay, the protection promised, suggests that once again the instigation of the tempter may have been very evident to the Lord.

Cain's descendants apparently seek to palliate the curse. The wanderer is the first to build a city, and his sons seek to hide with the veneer of civilization, music, and art the evidences of the fall. Some have had a difficulty about Cain's wife, and the land of Nod. Most misquote the Bible, and increase the difficulty. The Bible does not say that Cain went into the land of Nod and "took unto himself a wife"; it simply tells us that when Cain reached the land of Nod he "knew his wife", consequently he must have taken her with him. Further, the land of Nod was so named after the vagabond, "the land of wandering", for the word translated vagabond is *Nud*, just as Luz was renamed Bethel as a result of Jacob's dream. Scripture does not tell us how many daughters were born to Adam and Eve (Gen. 5: 4), the main purpose of the book being ever kept in view, viz., to show the plan and progress of redemption centred in the promised Seed of the woman, and also the increasing opposition of the evil one.

At first sight we have in Genesis 5 a rather uninteresting list of names, but it will be found to yield its teaching to prayerful study. The line of descent is given from Adam to Noah, and then, in chapter 6, it appears that the record concerning the "sons of God" synchronizes with the time of Noah. Two facts will, however, show us that Genesis 6: 1-3 refers back to the early history of Adam himself. First we must rectify the translation. The word "men" in verses 1 and 2, and "man" in verse 3, are in each case (Heb.) *Ha-adham* = the man Adam. To translate "the man Adam" by "men" is wrong. It is the name of the man Adam and his wife. The word "them" refers to the man and his wife also, exactly as in 5: 2. The next thing to notice is that important aid to interpretation — the structure. It will be remembered that chapter 5: 1 and chapter 6: 9 commence new sections, each starting with one of the "generations", consequently 5: 1 — 6: 8 is one complete part. Let us examine its arrangement:

The book of the generations of Adam

Gen. 5: 1—6: 8

A 5: 1, 2. Unfallen Adam; a "son of God" (Luke 3: 38)
 B 5: 3-5. Fallen Adam, and his years. The total 930, and the first 130
  C 5: 6-27. The progeny of Adam, and their deaths
   D 5: 28-32. Noah, and his promise of "comfort"

} The next step in the purpose of redemption after Genesis 3.

A 6: 1, 2. The fallen angels; "sons of God"
 B 6: 3. Fallen Adam, and his years. The total 930, and the last 120
  C 6: 4-7. The progeny of the fallen angels, and their threatened destruction
   D 6: 8. Noah, and his possession of "grace".

} Satan's next attempt to thwart the coming of the "Seed".

Every reader will see the perfect correspondence exhibited in the arrangement of the words. The fact that the structure goes back upon itself tells us that in chapter 5 we have the chronology up to Noah, and then the Scriptures tell us in 6: 1-8 what happened during that time.

The title "son of God" is given to Adam (Luke 3: 38), and Christ (Luke 1: 35). Those "in Christ", who have the new nature which is by the direct creation of God (2 Cor. 5: 17; Eph. 2: 10), are called "sons of God" (John 1: 12; Rom. 8: 14, 15; 1 John 3: 1). Those called "sons of God" in Genesis 6 are *angels*, and in every other place in the Old Testament where the expression is used "angels" are referred to, for these were a direct creation of God (Job 1: 6; 2: 1; 38: 7; Psalm 82: 1; 89: 6; Dan. 3: 25 [no article, *see also* verse 28]). The Septuagint version (Alexandrian) translates "the sons of God" in Genesis 6 by the word "angels". Jude 6 declares that there was a fall among the angels, and that their fall had some such character as is indicated in Genesis 6: 1-3 is seen in the same verse. They "left their own habitation" (*oiketerion*). This word occurs only once again, viz., in 2 Corinthians 5: 2, where it means the *resurrection body*. Jude 7 tells us further of the nature of the sin: "in like manner" to the subsequent sins of Sodom and Gomorrah.

The time of this irruption of fallen angels is given as "in the days of Noah" (1 Peter 3: 20; 2 Peter 2: 4, 5). The progeny were the "nephilim" or "fallen ones", monsters of flesh and iniquity, and their destruction necessitated the flood. Genesis 6 tells us that there were nephilim in the earth in those days; and also, *after that* (that is, after the flood) there was a second irruption, this time not universal, but local, for Satan had learned that the promised Seed was to come through the line of Shem.

The corruption was so great before the flood that it is written, "Noah was a just man, and *uncontaminated* among his *contemporaries*" (Gen. 6: 9). Enoch, the seventh from Adam, was a prophet. One prophecy is recorded in Jude 14, another in the name that he gave to his son Methuselah. The name means, "when he is dead it shall be sent". Methuselah lived 969 years, and a simple calculation will show the reader that the flood came immediately after his death. We shall have occasion to refer to the translation of Enoch later. Methuselah's son, Lamech, was also a prophet, for he called his son's name "Noah", which means "rest". The reason for thus naming him is given. "This same shall comfort us (or give us rest) concerning our work and toil of our hands, because of the ground which the Lord hath cursed" (Gen. 5: 29). Noah's parents had not forgotten the fact of the curse, and they had a prophetic vision of rest by means of the ark, and its typical redemption.

The generations of Noah occupy 6: 9 — 9: 29, and are taken up with the building of the ark, the flood, and the going forth from the ark to begin anew. Chapter 9: 1-7 echoes 1: 28-31. Satan had nearly prevented the development of the primeval promise, nearly — for but eight souls were brought through the flood. The covenant symbolized by the cherubim is again brought prominently forward; "And I, behold, I establish My covenant with you, and with your seed after you, and with every living creature that is with you, of the fowl (*cp.* the eagle, in cherubim), of the cattle (*cp.* ox), and of every beast of the field (*cp.* the lion)" (Gen. 9: 9, 10). The dominion forfeited by Adam is in measure passed on to Noah, and his family (*see* Gen. 9: 2, 5, 6), but not so fully and absolutely as was originally intended for man. Just as we found that the "book of the generations of Adam" extended from 5: 1 — 6: 8, so the next section "the generations of the sons of Noah" extends from 10: 1 — 11: 9; and just as 6: 1-8 gives an insight into the character of the times, and Satan's opposition during the period of chapter 5, so chapter 11: 1-9 records the next attempt on the part of the adversary to upset the *divine purpose*.

We have already pointed out (chapter 5) that Genesis 10 gives the apportioning of the seventy nations in relation to the great nation, whose progenitor was soon to be called forth. The arrangement of these nations, being a part of the *divine plan* (*see* Deut. 32: 8), called forth an attempt to frustrate it by the evil one. One of the sons of Ham was Cush, who was the father of Nimrod. The name Nimrod is from the Hebrew *marad* = to rebel. Wherein did his rebellion consist? Genesis 10: 10 supplies the answer. "The beginning of his *kingdom* was Babel". Nothing further is said about this city, its character, and its purpose, until the genealogy is finished, and then, in chapter 11: 1-9, we are shown the hand of Satan once again lifted up against the Lord, and His purpose. It was the divine intention that the nations should be scattered (Gen. 10: 25; Deut. 32: 8), but Babel was founded by a people whose intentions were to oppose the purpose of God, for they said:

> "Go to, let us build a *city*, and a tower, whose top with the heavens (i.e., the signs of the Zodiac as in the ancient temples of Denderah and Esnéh in Egypt), and let us make us a name (the word 'name' is 'Shem' — let us usurp the destined blessing of Shem), lest we be *scattered* abroad upon the face of the whole earth".

We know the result; the Lord confounded their language, and "so the Lord *scattered* them abroad from thence upon the face of all the earth". Two interesting items demand a moment's attention; the materials with which the tower was built, and the words "whose top with the heavens". First, the material with which the tower was built; "they had brick for stone". Centuries after in the land of Shinar, Nebuchadnezzar, king of Babylon, saw in a vision an image composed of metal, but having for feet iron and pottery. While he looked he saw a stone, cut out of the mountain without hands, strike this image, smash it to powder, and occupy its place. That stone represented the kingdom of the Messiah; the image with the feet of pottery represented the world powers under Satan's dominion. Here, in the same plain of Shinar, Satan fixed the site of his city, a city whose name and enmity should last until revelation should be finished, a city associated with rebellion and opposition to the people of Israel. The brick was of course burnt clay (11: 3) answering to the pottery in Daniel. The brick was a substitute for or a counterfeit of stone, in other words, the kingdom of Nimrod founded at Babel was but another attempt to forestall God's purpose relating to Israel and His city Jerusalem.

The expression, "whose top with the heavens", is of the utmost importance. The words, "may reach", are simply added by the Authorised Version to help them to make sense. From earliest times we read of "stargazers", "astrologers", and "monthly prognosticators". These men were those who had learned something of the secrets that lay behind the confused and twisted legends of Paganism. Jehovah refers to the "twelve signs" (Job 38: 31, 32, R.V. margin). Psalm 19 shews us that God has two books of revelation. The one was the book written in the heavens. The message of this book became corrupted, and the beginning of its corruption is traced to Babel. The other book is the written Scriptures, and again Satan has done all that he can to destroy, corrupt, and distort its message. The structure of Psalm 19 exhibits these two books thus:

A 1-4-. The heavens B -4-6. In them, the sun	God (the name used in this section)
A 7-10. The Scriptures *B* 11-14. In them, Thy servant.	The Lord (the name used in this section).

Josephus tells us that the astronomy of the "twelve signs" was invented by Adam, Seth, and Enoch. The Babylonian "creation tablets" refer to them, so also does Greek mythology. For over 2,500 years the world was without any *written* Scripture, but the hope of Genesis 3: 15, and its promise of triumph over the serpent, was kept alive in the minds of men by the "book of the heavens". There is nothing in the grouping of the stars to suggest men, crowns, serpents, fishes, &c.; they were but aids to memory. Where does the story begin, we may ask? The signs are arranged in a circle, and the usual commencement is at the sign Aries (the ram). The Scriptural witness seems to demand that the story of the Zodiac shall start at the Virgin, and end with the Lion. The Editor of *The Companion Bible* suggests that the "Riddle of the Sphinx" is connected with this problem. The word "sphinx", is from the Greek *sphingo* (to bind closely together). The Sphinx is a figure with the head of a *woman*, and the body of a *lion*. In the Zodiac of Esnéh a sphinx is placed between the signs of Virgo and Leo. If the story of the Zodiac has relation to Genesis 3: 15, we may expect that the "Seed of the woman" will be mentioned. If this be so, the sign of the Virgin seems to be the opening chapter. If we denominate "The Virgin" as the first, "Leo", the lion, will be the last chapter of the heavenly witness. We cannot spare space to give all that has been discovered of the teaching of the book of the twelve signs, but we transcribe a portion from Appendix 12 of *The Companion Bible*, to which we would refer the reader for more details:

(1) Virgo (the Virgin)
(His first coming)

(1) *Coma* (The desired). The woman and child, the desired of all nations (in the most ancient Zodiacs).
(2) *Centaurus* (with two natures). The despised sin-offering.
(3) *Bootes.* The coming One with branch.

Here we have the "sign" of the Virgin, with its three constellations. The Hebrew and Arabic names of the stars contained in the constellations are full of truth, and eloquent in their teaching. These stars were all named by God (Psalm 147: 4). Most of their names have been lost, but over 100 are preserved by the Arabic and Hebrew, and are in use to-day.

Virgo (The Virgin). Here we have the star *Al Zimach.* Hebrew *Zemach,* the branch. Isaiah 4: 2; Jeremiah 23: 5, 6; Zechariah 3: 8; 6: 12.

Coma. The desired (Hag. 2: 7). Numbers 24: 17. (Egyptian *Shesnu* = the desired son).

Centaurus, Al Beze, the despised (Isa. 53: 3).

Bootes (Heb. *bo,* to come). Psalm 96: 13. Hebrew *Arcturus* (Job 9: 9 = He cometh). Egyptian = *Smat,* one who rules.

This is the evidence of the first sign with its constellations in the Zodiac. We give the last sign with its constellations and stars. It will be found that just as the sign *Virgo* takes us to Genesis 3, so *Leo,* the lion, takes us to Revelation:

(12) Leo (The Lion)
(Messiah's consummated triumph)

(1) *Hydra.* The old serpent destroyed.
(2) *Crater.* The cup of wrath poured out.
(3) *Corvus.* The birds of prey devouring.

In the Zodiac of Denderah (Egypt) this sign is called *Pi Mentikeon* = the pouring out (of divine wrath). The Syriac name is *Aryo* = the rending lion. The Arabic, *Al Asad* = the lion leaping forth as a flame. The brightest star is *Regulus* = treading under foot. The next is *Denebola* = the Judge or Lord Who cometh.

Hydra. He is abhorred. One star has the name *Minchar al Sugia* = the piercing of the deceiver.

Crater. The cup (Psalm 75: 8; 11: 6; Rev. 14: 10; 16: 19). The constellation has *13 stars.*

Corvus. The raven. There are nine stars. Nine = judgment. The brightest star is *Chiba* = accursed.

Thus ends the story of the heavens. This is the story they tell forth. This is the "speech" they "utter". This is the "knowledge" they "shew forth". There is no articulate speech or voice, and no words are heard, but their sayings have gone out into all the world (Psalm 19: 1-6).

What is true of the first and last of the twelve signs is true of all the others. They exhibit one continuous theme, the plan and purpose of redemption. Their central figures are the central figures of Genesis 3, the Seed of the woman, and the serpent. The twelve signs had reference also to that people destined to be the channel of redemption to this earth, the nation from whom should spring the "Lion of the tribe of Judah", viz., Israel (*cp.* page 86). Twelve, the number of the Zodiac, is the number of Israel. In Genesis 37: 9 eleven stars (or constellations, as the word may mean), with the sun and moon, bow down to Joseph's star. When we perceive the testimony of the twelve signs, we can understand the attempt of Satan either to destory or alter their meaning. The confusion of tongues supplied the opportunity, and paganism sprang into being, not by slow evolution, but by the direct institution of Satan.

History tells us that Nimrod had a wife named Semiramis, and reveals that Nimrod and his wife were afterwards worshipped under the title of "the mother and child". Their names varied according to the countries whither the "scattered" nations with their "confounded" tongues went. Thus in Egypt we find *Isis* and *Osiris*. Now *Osiris* was the son of *Isis*, yet he has the strange title "the husband of the mother". This anomaly is explained when we see that *fact* (Nimrod and his wife) and *fiction* (that these were "the mother and the child" of prophecy) were blended together.

Again, in India we find *Isi* and *Iswara*. *Iswara* is both husband and infant. In Asia we have *Cybele* and *Derius*. In Rome we have *Fortuna* and the boy *Jupiter*. In Greece, *Ceres* and *babe*. Even in China we have *Shing Moo*, the mother with her child, having a "glory" in the orthodox Babylonian and Roman Catholic style. Semiramis was worshipped as the "goddess mother". Her son was also called Tammuz (Ezek. 8: 14) and Bacchus. The weeping connected with Tammuz may be seen reflected in the name Bacchus (readers may have in mind "The valley of Baca, or weeping").

History informs us that a certain king *Ninus*, king of the Assyrians, first carried on war with his neighbours. This identifies Ninus with Nimrod (Gen. 10: 9-11). Now Ninus was the son of Bel, the confounder. Nimrod was the son of Cush, and Cush and Bel are linked together. Cush was the original prophet of idolatry. The Scriptures bear witness to these fragments of truth, *see* Isaiah 46: 1, "Bel boweth down, Nebo (prophet) stoopeth". The titles Nebo = prophet, and Hermes or Mercury = interpreter, are another example of this word-twisting. It is connected with the word *peresh*, which means "to interpret", but it really refers to the "division" in the days of Peleg (*cp. peres* — "divided" in Dan. 5: 28).

The "confusion of tongues" enabled Satan to spread his false teaching with ease. Bacchus, to the ordinary person, was the god of wine. To the initiated he was Bar-Cush = the son of Cush, *i.e.*, Nimrod. So with the Saxon name for Christendom's "devil" Zernebogus. Divided into its parts it ceases to be a Saxon deity; it reveals Nimrod, Satan's first antichrist. Zer-Nebo-Gus = "The seed of the prophet Cush".

What does the garden of *Hesperides* mean in Greek? Nothing; it is Hebrew transliterated, and means in that language, "The garden of the fruit tree" = paradise. The golden apples and the serpent are easily accounted for.

We have all heard of Vulcan and his hammer. Jeremiah 50: 23 speaks of Babylon under the figure, "How is the hammer of the whole earth cut asunder and broken". Now the Greek name for Vulcan is *Hephaistos*, a word which conveys little or no meaning. If we read Genesis 11: 9, the word presents itself in the Hebrew word "scatter" (*hephaitsam*). Cush or Chaos is the scatterer, the confounder, the hammer of the whole earth. Idolatry sought to turn this (by playing upon the words) to mean "the interpreter", "the prophet". We must refrain. The strange ideas involved in such mixtures as "the husband of the mother", naturally led to the most obscene rites, and Babylon became the mother of *all* the harlot abominations of the earth.

Here is the origin and purpose of idolatry, a carefully laid plan to turn the hopes of the people away from the promised Seed to Satan and his agents; to mutilate and confuse the witness of the heavenly signs, and so prevent men from perceiving in the serpent their vindictive but doomed enemy. What Satan experimented with Nimrod, he blasphemously attempted with our Lord (Matt. 4: 8, 9), and will successfully, though but for a short season, accomplish through antichrist (Rev. 13: 1-18).

After this brief record in Genesis 11: 1-9 we have the generations of Shem. Shem was the chosen vessel through whom the Seed should come. Shem's generations were given with those of Japhet and Ham in chapter 10, but they are repeated and amplified here. In chapter 10 the descendants of Peleg are not given, but those of his brother Joktan are. Here in chapter 11 Peleg's descendants are given, but Joktan's are omitted. It is noteworthy, in passing, that Joktan was the 13th from

Shem, that he had 13 sons, that the numerical value of their 13 names is 13 × 212, and that his own name (Joktan) is 169 in value, which is 13 × 13. The number of rebellion is therefore stamped upon this man, and his descendants.

If we take the descendants of Shem as recorded in Genesis 11: 10-32, we find 16 in number (8 × 2), and also that the numerical value of the names from Shem to Abram is 3,568 (8 × 446), and from Nahor to Iscah is 1,264 (8 × 158). Thus the number of abundance and of resurrection is linked to the line of the promised Seed. These things are not trifles, they are facts, and their presence and witness must not be explained away.

At Genesis 11: 27 we reach the structural centre of the book. Not only the centre of Genesis, however, for Abraham comes about halfway between creation and Christ. Eleven chapters suffice for the first half, the second half occupies nine hundred and eighteen. This fact, of itself, is a witness to the peculiar purpose of the Bible. Terah is like a watershed. Away on the one hand the generations stretch back through the nations to Adam, and on the other hand stretch forward through Abraham to the nucleus of the "great nation", Israel. Terah is the link between the nations, and *the* nation. With Terah we leave the nations and their histories, and book after book lies before us dealing with one people, one nation (Israel), omitting all reference to the rise and fall of other nations, excepting where they come into touch with this peculiar people. In Genesis 12: 1-3 we have the call and sevenfold blessing of Abraham:

> "Now the Lord had said unto Abram, Get thee out of thy country, and from thy father's house, unto a land that I will show thee.
>
> (1) And I will make of *thee* a great nation,
> (2) And I will bless *thee*,
> (3) And make *thy* name great,
> (4) And *thou* shalt be a blessing,
> (5) And I will bless them that bless *thee*,
> (6) And curse them that curse *thee*,
> (7) And in *thee* shall all families of the earth be blessed.
>
> So Abram departed, as the Lord had spoken unto him".

Here we have the first of eight separate promises or covenants which Jehovah made with Abraham. Seven were made before Isaac was offered up on the mountain, and the eighth after his typical resurrection. Another remarkable feature is that each covenant blessing is stamped with the character of its numerical significance. Thus one signifies sovereignty; two signifies difference (either agreement or opposition); three is representative of resurrection; four is the number for the world; five denotes grace; six is the number of man; seven spiritual perfection; and eight resurrection. The eight covenants are in the following order:

(1) The great nation (Gen. 12: 1-3).
(2) The Seed. Redemption ("altar") (Gen. 12: 7).
(3) The land ("to thee" — in resurrection) (Gen. 13: 14-17).
(4) The boundaries of the land; 400 years; 4th generation (Gen. 15: 13-21).
(5) Grace, the changed name. The added letter "h" = 5 (Gen. 17: 1-22).
(6) The flesh a failure (Gen. 18: 9-15).
(7) Isaac, not Ishmael. Spiritual (Gen. 21: 12).
(8) Blessing in resurrection (Gen. 22: 15-18).

How perfect, how full is the treasure-house of divine wisdom! Two passages of Scripture demand notice while we look at Genesis 12; one is Hebrews 11: 8-10:

> "By faith Abraham, when he was called to go out into a place which he should after receive for an inheritance, obeyed, and he went out, not knowing whither he went . . . he looked for a city which hath the foundations, whose builder and maker is God".

The other passage is Acts 7: 2-4:

> "The God of glory appeared unto our father Abraham, *when* he was in Mesopotamia, *before* he dwelt in Haran, and said unto him, Get thee out of thy country, and from thy kindred, and come into the land which I shall shew thee. *Then* came he out of the land of the Chaldeans, and dwelt in Haran, and from thence, *when* his father was dead, he removed him into this land wherein ye now dwell".

By reading these two passages together, we see that the words "the Lord had said", of Genesis 12: 1, were spoken some time previous to the complete obedience on the part of Abram. Now "Abram was 75 years of age when he departed out of Haran". Some have estimated that Abram was 50 years old when the first call came to him in Chaldea. That there was some interval between the two is noticeable, for 12: 5 speaks of "substance" and "souls" gotten there. Abram lingers at Haran until his father dies. We do not mention this merely for the sake of quibbling over dates, we have far more serious business before us. Compare the two statements made in Genesis 11: 31 and Genesis 12: 5:

"They went forth out of Ur of the Chaldees, to go into the land of Canaan; *and they came unto Haran, and dwelt there*".

"And they went forth to go into the land of Canaan, *and into the land of Canaan they came*".

What had the enemy been doing during this time? Had he retired from the opposition, or did he take advantage of the halt at Haran to again seek to frustrate the divine purpose? for it was a revealed fact, and known to Satan, that Abram had been chosen to be the father of a great nation. The kingdom forfeited by Adam, and the whole race in him, was now to be vested in a peculiarly chosen and separated people, and the promised Seed should come through one of that nation. A special land also was picked out for them, and to this land Abram journeys. He left Ur of the Chaldees to go into the land of Canaan, but stopped on the frontier until his father had died. The evil one took advantage of this delay.

We have seen how in Genesis 6 he corrupted the whole human race, with the exception of Noah; that was because he had no clue as to which of the many branches descending from Seth the promised seed would come from. We also read in Genesis 6: 4 that there were Nephilim (the evil progeny of the fallen angels) *after* the flood. These were the people called "the Canaanites"; hence immediately following Genesis 12: 5 we read, "And Abram passed through the land . . . and the Canaanite was then (already) in the land". The flood was the divine instrument of destruction used against the first outbreak; the sword of Israel was to be the instrument used against the progeny of the second irruption, the Canaanites. They are called *Anakim* (Numb. 13: 33), and *Rephaim*.

It will be remembered how these giants, with their cities "walled up to heaven", terrified the spies (Numb. 13: 28). Og, king of Bashan, is described in Deuteronomy 3: 11, and his death is attributed to the "mercy" of God (Psalm 136: 20-22), his land being given as an heritage to the rightful people, Israel. The interested reader can find a great deal of information about the Canaanites by referring to Genesis 14: 5; 15: 18-21; Exodus 3: 8-17; 23: 23; Deuteronomy 7; 20: 17; Joshua 3: 10; 12: 8; 13: 13; 15: 63; 16: 10; 17: 18; Judges 1: 19, 20, 28, 29, 30-36; 2: 1-5 and 3: 1-7. They are spoken of as *Rephaim* in many places, which the Authorised Version obscures by rendering "dead", "deceased", or "giants" (Job 26: 5; Psalm 138: 10; Proverbs 2: 18; 9: 18; 21: 16; Isaiah 14: 9; 26: 14-19). The name *Rephaim* is retained in Genesis 14: 5; 15: 20; Joshua 17: 15 (marg.); 2 Samuel 5: 18, 22; 23: 13; 1 Chronicles 11: 15; 14: 9; 20: 4 (marg.); Isaiah 17: 5. *Nephilim* is rendered "giants" in Genesis

6: 4 and Numbers 13: 33; and *Gibbor* in Job 16: 14 (*cp* "mighty men"). *See* the Revised Version in many of these passages.

Thus the purpose of God and the opposition of Satan continue throughout the record. The incident recorded in Genesis 12: 11-20 was another attempt to frustrate the promise of verse 7, viz., to currupt the line of the promised Seed. The repetition of a similar attempt just before the birth of Isaac (Gen. 22: 1-18) only emphasizes the malignity and persistency of purpose which actuated the evil one in this singular attack upon Sarah. Lot's choice of Sodom is another over-ruled snare, for had Abram chosen this locality, there would have been more likelihood of accomplishing his downfall.

The people of Sodom were "wicked exceedingly" (*see* 2 Peter 2: 6, 7; Jude 7). The name Sodom occurs 39 times in the Old Testament (13 × 3), and 10 times in the New Testament (Revised Version). Isaiah 13: 19; Jeremiah 50: 40, and Revelation 11: 8 connect Sodom with Babylon, and apostate Jerusalem. Its destruction is an example (Jude 7), yet in Matthew 10: 15; 11: 23, 24, and Luke 10: 12 (in harmony with Ezek. 16: 48) the Judge of all the earth speaks of the punishment upon Sodom as being "more tolerable" than that of Capernaum, and "that generation". Deuteronomy 23: 17 (*see* margin) uses the name in connection with both male and female, and reveals the snare spread for Abram, and the corrupting of the stream. Ever unclean, ever seeking to pollute, the trail of the serpent is visible everywhere.

Abram, strengthened by Melchisedek, the "priest of the Most High God" (*cp.* Numb. 24: 16-18; Deut. 32: 8; Luke 1: 76, where the title is related to the earth and the kingdom), refuses to accept "from a thread even to a shoe latchet" from the king of Sodom, and just as after Lot's choice of Sodom, when the Lord immediately showed Abram that, after all, he (Abram) had by far the better portion (Gen. 13: 14-18), so here, for immediately following this grand refusal of the spoils, the "Word of the Lord (*i.e.*, the same as in John 1: 1 and 14) came unto Abram in a vision, saying, Fear not, Abram, I am thy shield, and thy exceeding great reward".

The reply of Abram in Genesis 15: 2 has often been quoted as meaning the very opposite to that which Abram intended. His reply meant, "Thou hast already loaded me with blessings, what can any addition to these avail, seeing that mine heir will be, after all, Eliezer of Damascus?". The Lord then makes clear to him that the seed promised in 12: 7 was to be his very own son (15: 4), and Abram "believed in the Lord, and He counted it to him for righteousness" (15: 6). In 15: 13, 14 Abram is told of the sojourning and servitude of his seed, and of their final triumphant exodus. The reason for the long period of 400 years is given in verse 16 "for the iniquity of the Amorites is not yet full". Israel were to be the scourge in the hand of the Lord against these corrupted nations. The weakness of the flesh is seen operating in Genesis 16. Hagar is driven into the wilderness, and being met by the angel of the Lord called the well revealed to her *Beer-lahai-roi* — "the well of the *living and visible One*" (the second Person in the Trinity).

"When Abram was 99 years of age" the Lord appeared unto him, and said, "I am *El Shaddai* (God all-sufficient), walk before Me and be thou perfect" (Gen. 17: 1). The word "perfect" is the same as that used of Noah, who was uncontaminated by the evil of his contemporaries (Gen. 6: 9), and doubtless refers to much the same thing. Then follows the covenant wherein Abram is re-named Abraham. This covenant, like the first call in Genesis 12, contains seven promises, viz.:

(1) *I will* make My covenant between Me and thee, and
(2) *I will* multiply thee exceedingly, and
(3) *I will* make thee exceeding fruitful, and
(4) *I will* make nations of thee, and kings shall come out of thee, and
(5) *I will* establish My covenant between Me and thee, and thy seed after thee in their generations for an everlasting covenant, to be a God unto thee (*cp.* Heb. 11), and to thy seed after thee, and
(6) *I will* give unto thee, and to thy seed after thee, the land wherein thou art a stranger (Heb. 11), all the land of Canaan, for an everlasting possession, and
(7) *I will* be their God.

Here we have the unconditional covenant made with Abraham which cannot fail of fulfilment. No stipulations are made, the sevenfold *I will* of God all-sufficient is enough. The day is coming when every jot and tittle shall be fulfilled.

Once again the wonderful harmony of the Word is seen. Each item has within it the significance of its number in the list. The first (one) is God alone. This is the testimony of Galatians 3: 20. There was no second contracting party, whose failure would spoil the covenant — "*I will make*". So in number two we have the multiplication of seed; in three, fruitfulness (*cp.* Gen. 1: 9-13); in four we have the nations and kings pertaining to earthly dominion; in five we have the emphasis on grace. In this is emphasized the same truth as is conveyed by the adding of the letter "h" (which stands for 5) to Abram's name. Number six introduces the Canaanites; and seven, God all in all. What need have we to prove the inspiration of the Scriptures by argument? The Bible speaks for itself if we will but allow its voice to be heard.

Following immediately upon this unconditional covenant, God speaks to Abraham about another of quite a different kind. The covenant of circumcision is spoken of as a "sign" and a "seal" in Romans 4; it was something that man had to do; its omission involved punishment; it was a conditional covenant entirely distinct from the one before. Note the different language: "*Thou* shalt keep", and lest there should be any uncertainty the Lord says, "*This* is My covenant which *ye* shall keep". It was a "token" of the covenant already made; it was a covenant which could be broken (verse 14). Both this, and the covenant at Sinai, must be ever distinguished from that "everlasting covenant" ordered in all things and sure.

In due course, after long trial of faith, Isaac is born. Doubtless we have all pondered that wonderful passage (Gen. 22) wherein the faith of Abraham was so tried, and where the sacrifice and resurrection of Abraham's Seed (Christ) was so marvellously typified. We see how careful Abraham is that Isaac should not marry any of the daughters of the "Canaanites", and perhaps we begin to see the reason more clearly than before. We must pass over the beautiful story of Rebekah, and the quiet life of Isaac, and take up the thread at the birth of his two sons Esau and Jacob.

Genesis 25: 19 introduces the eighth "generation" of Genesis. Even the order of these generations conveys teaching to us. Noah's generation is the third (resurrection). "The sons of Noah" give the fourth (their descendants formed the nations of the earth). Shem is fifth (he found "grace"). Terah (whose name means "delay") is sixth, a picture of the flesh hindering the believer (*cp.* Gen. 12: 1). Why Ishmael should be seventh is a question we cannot as yet answer. Isaac, being eighth, emphasizes the connection the promise has with resurrection and regeneration.

Isaac was 40 years of age when he married Rebekah, and although through him the promised Seed was to come, years roll by, and his wife remains barren. Isaac does not follow his father in taking another wife, but "intreated the Lord for his wife". The word "intreated" is very beautiful; it carries the idea of "opening or expanding". Isaac "opened" his heart, and the Lord "opened" His hand, and "Rebekah his wife conceived". She too acts in the same way, for when "the children struggled together", she "went to inquire of the Lord". It is important for us to note the Lord's answer: "Two *nations* are in thy womb, and two manner of *people* . . . the elder shall serve the younger".

Romans 9, 10 and 11 form the *dispensational* section of that epistle, a portion which we shall have to study presently. In chapter 9 the apostle referring to this says, "When Rebecca also had conceived by one, by our father Isaac (for the children being not yet born, neither having done any good or evil, that the *purpose* of God according to *election* might stand, not of works, but of Him that calleth); it was said unto her, The elder shall serve the younger" (Rom. 9: 10-12). The choice of Jacob was for no reason outside the *purpose* — the theme of the book. This purpose is clearly stated in Genesis 25: 23 in the word "nation". The promise to Abram was "I will make of thee a great *nation*". Isaac now had the son born who should be the father of that *nation*. Here we see that the primeval promise concerning the "Seed of the woman" is interlinked with the Abrahamic covenant concerning the nation — "of whom, as concerning the flesh, Christ came, Who is over all, God blessed for ever" (Rom. 9: 5).

Jacob and his mother made a profound mistake, however, in this connection. They knew what God had promised, and they believed it; but they tried to help God work it out, and by so doing evidenced their sin and folly. The first step was the capture of the birthright from Esau. True, he was "a profane person, and despised his birthright" (Heb. 12: 16, and Gen. 25: 34). God had nowhere said, however, that the covenanted blessing of Abraham and Isaac went by way of the firstborn or the birthright; indeed, he had overturned this many times before. Abel, not Cain; Shem, not Japheth; Abram, not Haran; Isaac, not Ishmael; the younger, not the elder, and yet Jacob schemes for the birthright! In chapter 27, we have the record of a despicable action. Jacob and his mother so far forget the Lord's power and purpose as to descend to one of the meanest acts recorded in Scripture, the deception of an old and apparently dying father and husband. Jacob so far succeeds as to hear the words:

> "God give thee of the dew of heaven, and the fatness of the earth, and plenty of corn and wine. Let people serve thee, and nations bow down to thee; be lord over thy brethren, and let thy mother's sons bow down to thee. Cursed be every one that curseth thee, and blessed be he that blesseth thee" (Gen. 27: 28, 29).

The agitation of Isaac at the entry of Esau, and his words recorded in Genesis 27: 32-35, show clearly that the blessing given to Jacob is not the one referred to in Hebrews 11: 20, for there we read, "*By faith* Isaac blessed Jacob and Esau concerning things to come". No amount of argument can make the act of Isaac recorded in Genesis 27 an act of faith, neither was God bound in the slightest degree to ratify the blessing thus deceitfully obtained. The words "plenty of corn and wine" must have echoed ironically in Jacob's ears as his sons went down to Egypt to buy corn to prevent starvation. The true Abrahamic blessing, the blessing which Jacob sought so diligently though so despicably, was given freely and "by faith" when the Lord's time came. Esau's marriage with the daughters of Heth was such a cause of vexation to Rebekah, that she urged Isaac to send Jacob to her old home, as Abraham had done before, in order that he might obtain a wife of his own people (Gen. 27:46). This was entirely in harmony with the purpose of God:

> "And Isaac called Jacob, and blessed him, and charged him, and said unto him, Thou shalt not take a wife of the daughters of Canaan . . . and
>
> (1) *El Shaddai* (Gen. 17: 1) bless thee, and
> (2) Make thee fruitful, and
> (3) Multiply thee,
> (4) That thou mayest be a multitude of people; and
> (5) Give the *blessing of Abraham* to thee, and
> (6) To thy seed with thee, that
> (7) Thou mayest inherit the land wherein thou art a stranger, which God gave unto Abraham" (Gen. 28: 1-4).

Here we have *the blessing of Abraham*; here we have the *seed*, the *land*, and the *people*. The covenant blessing with Abraham had little "corn and wine" in it. These patriarchs "dwelt in tents", and confessed themselves "strangers and pilgrims on the earth".

We have drawn no lessons so far, but we cannot refrain from a word to believers here. Let us never adopt Jacob's policy; let us remember that in Ephesians 1, where we have the opening chapter of the epistles of the Mystery, the key thought is "blessing according to purpose". Jacob received no confirmation from God of the blessing received by stealth, but when resting on his journey, with a stone for a pillow, the Lord appeared and confirmed the blessing of Genesis 28: 3, 4:

> "I am the Lord God of Abraham thy father, and the God of Isaac: the *land* whereon thou liest, to thee will I give it, and to thy *seed*, and thy seed shall be as the dust of the earth, and thou shalt spread abroad to the west, and to the east, and to the north, and to the south; and in thee, and in thy Seed, shall all the families of the earth be blessed. And, behold, I am with thee, and will keep thee in all places whither thou goest, and will bring thee again to this land; for I will not leave thee, until I have done that which I have spoken to thee of" (Gen. 28: 13-15).

Words cannot more plainly indicate that the *land and people* of Israel are those here spoken of. No amount of *spiritualizing* can ever alter these facts. The resurrection of Abraham, Isaac, and Jacob, and the restoration of Israel to their land, must take place if God is to keep

His word. What passages of interest lie between this 28th chapter and the end of Genesis! The marriage troubles, and family troubles of this man have struck a chord of sympathy in many a heart, but our purpose will not allow us to linger over them.

Twelve sons, the nucleus of the great nation, are born to Jacob. "I am God, the God of thy father, fear not to go down into Egypt, for I will *there* make of thee a *great nation*" (Gen. 46: 3). Jacob's heart is torn by the loss of Joseph and Rachel, by the sin of Reuben, and the rape of Dinah. The history of this man Jacob has made him a fit type of the "wandering tribes of weary feet". His descendants are not called Abrahamites, or Isaacites; they are known as Israelites, and the tribes of Jacob. It is Jacob that goes down into Egypt with his family; it is a redeemed nation that goes out, under the shelter of the passover lamb, through the Red Sea into the wilderness.

We must pass quickly by their wanderings in the wilderness, the Tabernacle with its wonderful typology, their failure in the land under the Judges, and take up the thread of their history where yet one more feature is added to the purpose of God. Starting with the promised *seed*, its development embraced a peculiar *nation*, and a special *land* , and we now arrive at that period when there is added a covenant concerning a *king*, and the choice of a *city*.

CHAPTER EIGHT

The consummation of the earthly purpose in the King and the kingdom

The reader may wonder why the period associated with the name of Moses is given so small a space in this volume, for we shall proceed almost at once to the next development of the purpose of God, viz., *the King* and *the kingdom*. We have sought to emphasize the *unconditional* character of the covenant made with Abraham, and repeated to Isaac and Jacob.

The Mosaic legislation, the giving of the law from Sinai, and the assumption of responsibility by Israel in their reply, "All that the Lord hath spoken we will do" (Exod. 24: 7), are parenthetical to the great purpose. The land *promised* to Abraham, and the land *possessed* by Israel during the past are not co-extensive. The possession of the full extent of territory and dominion awaits the fulfilment of the "covenant ordered in all things and sure". A reference to Galatians 3 will help us to see that the dispensation of law was transitional and preparatory, and its failure or success in no wise affected the oath and promise given 430 years before Sinai.

> "Brethren, I speak after the manner of men; Though it be but a man's covenant, yet if it be *confirmed*, no man *setteth aside* or *addeth* thereto. Now to Abraham and his Seed were the promises made. He saith not, And to seeds, as of many; but as of one, And to thy Seed, which is Christ. And this I say, that the covenant, that was *confirmed* before of God in Christ, the law, which was 430 years after, cannot *disannul*, that it should make the promise of *none effect*. For if the inheritance be by law, it is no longer of promise, but God gave it to Abraham by promise (as a free gift in grace, *charisomai*)" (Gal. 3: 15-18).

Here it is made abundantly clear that the covenant with Abraham, and the covenant at Sinai, must be kept clearly apart. The Sinaitic covenant has been in operation, with its inevitable results; the Abrahamic is yet future. The reader may say, Why then the law? We can best answer by further quoting from Galatians 3, "It was added because of the transgressions". The Abrahamic covenant took no account of man's failure. Nothing was asked of Abraham, Isaac, or Jacob, all was promised and confirmed. The law was introduced "as a pedagogue unto Christ", and when Christ came then its mission ceased.

The law contained many precious types of redemption, atonement, forgiveness, and justification, all of which will be fully realized by Israel under the New Covenant. The law was enforced "till the Seed should come to whom the promise was made". It was not an "everlasting covenant" in the same way as that promised to Abraham. The two covenants are further contrasted by the fact that a mediator was employed at Sinai, but God alone took all responsibility with Abraham (*cp.* "*I* will" in Gen. 17). This is the meaning of that much-disputed verse (Gal. 3: 20), about which so much that is unprofitable has been written. Where there is a mediator, there are two parties, and when one of those contracting parties is fallen man, failure and instability is a certainty. The "promise to Abraham" rested upon a firmer foundation:

> "For when God made promise to Abraham, because He could swear by no greater, He sware by Himself . . . Wherein God, willing more abundantly to show unto the heirs of the promise the unchangeableness of His counsel, confirmed it by an *oath*" (Heb. 6: 13-17).

Verse 20 connects this with "Jesus, made an High Priest for ever after the order of Melchizedek". The Aaronic priesthood was entirely different in its calling and purpose from that of Melchizedek. Christ is nowhere said to be the fulfiller of the Aaronic priesthood, for that is not connected with the unconditional promise, but with the conditional law.

Summarizing the intervening books therefore, we find the beginning of Exodus is occupied with two main features, (1) Bondage, and (2) Freedom. The later portion is occupied with another pair of important items, (1) the giving of the law, and (2) the making of the Tabernacle. Leviticus is taken up with the offerings, the priesthood, the fasts and feasts, each and every one being typical. Numbers covers the period of the wandering in the wilderness (*Bemidbar*, which is the Hebrew title). Like Exodus and Leviticus it contains types of Christ, (1) the bread of life (11: 7-9); (2) the water of life (20: 11); (3) the serpent lifted up (21: 9) and (4) the coming Star out of Jacob (24: 17). Deuteronomy contains ten addresses by Moses to Israel, given upon the verge of the promised land before his death. In "The song of Moses" (Deut. 32: 1-43) we have a prophetic outline of Israel's history, so wonderfully complete that we cannot do better than point out its main features before we enter upon the consideration of the Davidic covenant.

Structure of Deuteronomy 32: 1-43

A 1-6. Call to hear, and the reason. The publishing of Jehovah's name. Perfect work, and righteous ways
 B 7-14. The goodness of Jehovah to Israel (Period. Pentateuch)
  C 15-19. Israel's evil return; their pride; forsaking God (Period. Historical books)
   D 20. Divine reflections on period while Israel is "*Lo-ammi*" (not my people). (Period. Minor Prophets, especially Hosea)
    E 21. Jehovah's provocation by and of Israel (Rom. 11:11). (Period. Acts)
    E 22-25. Jehovah's threatening of judgment on Israel (Period. The great tribulation)
   D 26-33. Divine reflections on period while Israel is scattered (Period. Hosea)
  C 34-38. Jehovah's merciful return to Israel; their helplessness; His not forsaking them (Period. Future history)
 B 39-42. The judgment of Jehovah upon His enemies (Period. "Day of the Lord". Apocalypse)
A 43. Call to rejoice, and the reason. Vengeance on enemies; mercy for "land" and "people" (Fulfilment of the "Purpose of the ages").

We would particularly ask our reader *not* to be satisfied with this *skeleton.* Skeletons are necessary, but not attractive. Read Deuteronomy 32: 1-43 itself, and the underlying structure suggested above will be of help. To be satisfied with the structure alone is neither creditable to the student nor honouring to the Word.

That the omission of the Mosaic economy from the main line of God's purpose is in harmony with the Word may be seen by examining the opening words of Matthew 1, "The book of the generation of Jesus Christ, Son of David, Son of Abraham". Verse 17 says, "So all the generations from Abraham to David are fourteen generations; and from David until the carrying away into Babylon are fourteen generations; and from the carrying away into Babylon unto Christ are fourteen generations". Thus we see David is the next link in the chain of purpose, and the Mosaic period is passed over.

The books entitled 1st and 2nd Samuel, which are regarded as one book in the Hebrew canon, have as their main theme the ending of the rule under the judges, and the beginning of the rule under the kings.

These kings are two in number, Saul and David. David's kingdom is recorded as first divided, and afterwards united. This may be exhibited to the eye as follows:

Rule under the judges. 1 Samuel 1:1-7:17

A 1:1—4:1-. The provocation of Israel
  B 4:—7:2-. Subjection by Philistines
A 7:—2-6. The repentance of Israel
  B 7:7-17. Deliverance from Philistines.

This leads on to the demand for a king, and the remaining portion of the book deals with the rule of the kings (1 Sam. 8: 1 to 2 Sam. 24: 25). Saul occupies the first section and David the second.

King Saul. 1 Samuel 8:1 to 2 Samuel 1:27

A 1 Sam. 8:1—12:25. Choice of Saul
  B 1 Sam. 13:1—15:35. Provocation of Saul. Rejection threatened.
A 1 Sam. 16:1—27:4. Choice of David
  B 1 Sam. 27:5—2 Sam. 1:27. Provocation of Saul.
  Rejection carried out.

Thus Scripture records the rise and fall of Israel's choice, and immediately following David is represented as enquiring of the Lord, saying, "Shall I go up to the cities of Judah?". And the Lord said unto him, "Go up". And David said, "Whither shall I go up?" And He said, "Unto Hebron". "And the men of Judah came and anointed David king over the house of Judah". Thus we are brought a step nearer to the important passage which records the covenant connecting David with Abraham and the promised Seed. The remaining portion of the book is divided thus:

King David. 2 Samuel 2:1—24:25

A1 2 Sam. 2:1—4:12. Kingdom divided.
A2 2 Sam. 5:1—24:25. Kingdom united.

After a series of trials and conflicts (in which we can trace the enemy's endeavour to prevent David becoming king over all Israel, raising "Ish-bosheth" = "a man of shame" to the throne of Israel), David is triumphant, and ascends the throne of a united kingdom. "And they anointed David king over Israel". The first act of David as king over all Israel is the attempt to bring into subjection *Jerusalem*. A portion was gained named Zion. Here we have the final link in the chain; the *seed*, the *nation*, the *land*, the *king*, and the *city*. The true King (i.e. Christ) will unite in Himself the office of priest, even as He did that of prophet (as David did in type). These added to the above list give us the *seven* links in this perfect purpose. David was conscious of the fact that he was blessed not for his own sake, but by reason of the outworking of this wondrous plan:

> "And David perceived that the Lord had established him king over Israel, and that He had exalted his kingdom for His people Israel's sake" (2 Sam. 5: 12).

We now approach the central feature of this man's history (6: 1-7: 29), the ark of the Lord, the house of the Lord, and the covenant of the Lord with David, and his Seed. The ark is brought to the "city of David", and after the rejoicings have ended, the thoughts of David run on to the contemplation of building a house of God "exceeding magnifical". This provided the moment for the Lord to confirm the *throne* to the Seed of David by an *unconditional covenant*:

> "And it came to pass, when the king sat in his house, and the Lord had given him rest round about from all his enemies; that the king said unto Nathan the prophet, See now, I dwell in a house of cedar, but the ark of God dwelleth within curtains. And Nathan said to the king, Go, do all that is in thine heart, for the Lord is with thee" (2 Sam. 7: 1-3).

The answer of Nathan proved to be merely his opinion, for the Lord sends a different message (verse 5), "And it came to pass that night". All the Hebrew manuscripts have a *hiatus* after these words, making a solemn pause, and pointing back to the corresponding night of Genesis 15: 12-17, thus connecting the two links in the great unconditional covenants. In answer to the words of David, the Lord replies:

> "Also the Lord telleth thee that He will make thee an house . . . thine house and thy kingdom shall be established for ever before thee (some Codices with Sept. and Syr. read 'before me'); thy throne shall be established for ever" (2 Sam. 7: 11-16).

David is overcome with the sense of this abounding grace, and confesses that it is purely an unconditional covenant in the words of verse 21, "For Thy word's sake, and according to Thine own heart, hast Thou done all these great things, to make Thy servant know them". (In verse 19 the Hebrew leads the thought on to Psalm 8, the

Psalm of the Messiah, "And is this the law of the man?" *i.e.*, the man of Psalm 8: 5, 6). David is overwhelmed with the thought that Messiah is destined to come through him. David also saw in this covenant the confirmation of Israel as the great nation. "And what one nation in the earth is like Thy people, even like Israel, whom God went to redeem for a people to Himself . . . For Thou has confirmed to Thyself Thy people Israel to be a people unto Thee for ever, and Thou, Lord, art become their God" (verses 23, 24). "And I will be their God" was the last clause of the covenant with Abraham. David sees here that this will be fulfilled when the *king*, who is also Abraham's *Seed*, reigns (Matt. 1: 1, David . . . Abraham). In 2 Samuel 23 there are recorded the "last words of David". In them occurs one verse (verse 5) which needs a little retranslation. It should read:

> "For is not my house through God?
> For He hath made with me an everlasting covenant, ordered in all things and sure.
> For this (covenant) is all my salvation, and all my desire,
> For shall He not cause it to prosper?"

"Although", "for", and "yet" (A.V.) are all the same in the Hebrew here; therefore it will be seen that once again we must leap over centuries to take up the next link in the chain of purpose. Soon the marks of failure and human instability began to appear, and the glories of the reign of Solomon are eclipsed by his love of foreign women, some of them Canaanites. This involved the nation in idolatry, and idolatry of such a kind that it cannot be described. The snare of the "strange" woman, so many times emphasized in *Proverbs*, has reference to this solemn failure (*see* also Deut. 17: 17). It is a remarkable fact that the proverbs written for the guidance of Solomon repeatedly warn him against the strange woman, but the proverbs written by Solomon never mention this his peculiar weakness. Truly man at his best estate is altogether vanity. Solomon was succeeded by Rehoboam, whose ill-advised words were over-ruled to bring about the rending of the kingdom foretold in 1 Kings 11: 27-31. It is pathetic, if such a term may be allowed, to read in this same chapter:

> "Behold, I will rend the kingdom out of the hand of Solomon, and will give ten tribes to thee. But he shall have one tribe for My servant *David's* sake, and for *Jerusalem's* sake, the *City* which I have chosen out of all the tribes of Israel" (1 Kings 11: 31, 32).
>
> "So Israel rebelled against the house of David unto this day" (1 Kings 12: 19).

From this point onwards we have the chequered history of Judah (the two tribes), and of Israel (the ten tribes).* The lapse of the nation into idolatry, and its connection with the "outlandish women" (Neh. 13: 26), are indications that Satan was still busy seeking to thwart the divine purpose. The channel for the promised Seed was now narrowed down to one family and one tribe — the tribe of Judah, the family of Jesse, and the house of David; hence we may expect that the attack of the evil one would be made against the royal house and line. Israel had been completely seduced by Jezebel into idolatry, and the marriage of Athaliah, her daughter, to Jehoram, the son of Jehoshaphat, seems to have been a part of Satan's design to effect the corruption of the house of Judah. The outcome of events were used by Satan, who almost blotted out the line of David. Jehoram, king of Judah, began by killing his brethren (2 Chron. 21: 4); the Arabians slew all his sons save the youngest, called Ahaziah (2 Chron. 22: 1), Azariah, or Jehoahaz (2 Chron. 21: 17); and Athaliah slew all the sons of Ahaziah (2 Kings 11: 1; 2 Chron. 22: 10), or thought that she had, but the infant Joash was rescued. This child was hidden for six years in the temple. Upon this one life hung the promise made to Adam, Eve, Abraham, Isaac, Jacob, and David. One life (how frail a link), yet over all was One whose purpose stands fast. The darkness that came in, even in the days of Solomon, settled in ever deepening gloom, until:

> "In the ninth year of Hoshea, the king of Assyria took Samaria, and carried Israel away into Assyria . . . For they served idols . . . and worshipped all the host of heaven, and served Baal . . . Therefore the Lord was very angry with Israel, and removed them out of His sight; there was none left but the tribe of Judah only" (2 Kings 17: 6-18).

Thus ends the sad history of the ten tribes. But what of Judah? Alas! they too were soon to follow in the way of desolation. During the reign of Hezekiah, Judah seemed to turn to the Lord, but Manasseh who followed:

> "Built again the high places which Hezekiah his father had destroyed, and he reared up altars for Baal . . . and he built altars in the house of the Lord, of which the Lord said, In Jerusalem will I put

---

* We do not intend to enter into the discussion concerning the "lost" ten tribes, other than to say that our studies of the Scriptures have convinced us that the teaching known as "Anglo-Israelism" is an error of a serious kind. The terms *Israel* and *Judah* certainly are used to indicate the two parts of the divided nation, but this is not by any means universally the case, nor must it be taken as a canon of interpretation.

> My Name . . . and Manasseh seduced them to do more evil than did the nations whom the Lord destroyed before the children of Israel" (2 Kings 21: 1-18).

This sealed the doom of Judah; the Lord threatened that He would "wipe Jerusalem as a man wipeth a dish, wiping it, and turning it upside down, and I will forsake the remnant of Mine inheritance, and deliver them into the hand of their enemies, and they shall become a prey and a spoil to all their enemies" (verse 14). In the days of Jehoiakim, Nebuchadnezzar king of Babylon appears on the page of Scripture, and the kingdom of Judah hastens to its ignominious close. The treasures of that glorious temple were carried away to Babylon, and all Jerusalem save the poorest, and all the princes, and all the mighty men of valour, even 10,000 captives, and all the craftsmen and smiths, Jehoiachin and the king's mother, the king's wives, his officers, "and the mighty of the land carried he into captivity from Jerusalem to Babylon" (2 Kings 24: 13-16). Zedekiah's rebellion brought about the sack of the city. The sons of Zedekiah were slain before his eyes, and then his own eyes were put out, and he, being bound in fetters of brass, was carried to Babylon. The house of the Lord, the king's house, and every great man's house was burnt with fire; the walls of Jerusalem were broken down, and the place left a wreck. "So Judah was carried away out of their land". Thus ended the kingdom of Judah, even as Jeremiah had foretold (Jer. 20: 4-6).

For 70 years the captives languish in exile, and then according to the "Word of the Lord spoken by the mouth of Jeremiah", Cyrus, the king of Persia, made a proclamation concerning the re-building of the house of the Lord at Jerusalem, and gave permission to any who desired it to return to the city of their fathers. The book of Ezra records the re-building of the temple, and the book of Nehemiah details the re-building of the walls of the city. The remnant that returned formed the people whose descendants are found in the land as recorded in the opening chapters of the New Testament.

Now just as we found that when Adam fell the Lord introduced the promise of the Seed (Gen. 3); when the nations rebelled the Lord introduced His purpose in the great nation, and when the people made choice of their king the Lord introduced the next link — the king after His own heart — so even at the carrying away of Zedekiah a word is given that, while it gives no hope of man in himself, turns the hearts of those who will heed the Word to the coming Seed and King:

> "And thou profane lawless prince of Israel, whose day is come, when iniquity shall have an end, thus saith the Lord God; Remove the mitre, and take off the crown: this shall be no more the same; exalt

the low, abase the high. I will *overturn, overturn, overturn it;* this shall be no more, until He come whose *right* it is, and I will give it Him" (Ezek. 21: 25-27).

Thus does the Lord describe the character of the people and the times that should intervene until "He come whose right it is".

We must once again pass over much that is of great interest. Nehemiah, Ezra, Esther, and Malachi are books full to overflowing. When considering the future of Israel we shall have to come back to Daniel, Joel, Zechariah, etc., but our course is set, and the next consideration before us is the *Gospel of Matthew* and the *Acts of the Apostles*.

One incident recorded in Zechariah 6: 9-13 has reference to the passage already quoted from Ezekiel 21, and links up this period with Matthew 1. The question may have been asked among the returned remnant, Were the crown and mitre to be restored? Were they to look upon Joshua and Zerubbabel as the rightful successors? The Lord directs them to make crowns of silver and gold, and to say:

"Behold the man Whose name is the *Branch*; and *He shall* grow up out of His place, and *He shall* build the temple of the Lord . . . and *He shall* bear the glory, and *shall* sit and rule upon His throne, and *He shall* be a priest upon His throne; and the counsel of peace *shall* be between them both".

The proclamation being given, the crowns are placed as a memorial in the temple. The name *Branch* would be already understood as being a Messianic title. Thus the looked-for king was to be also priest. This pointed the hearer to David's prophecy in Psalms 110 and 2. "The Lord hath sworn, and will not repent, Thou art a priest for ever after the order of Melchisedek". Melchisedek, beside being *priest*, was also "*king* of Salem". "Yet have I set My King upon My holy hill of Zion". Matthew's Gospel opens with the genealogy and birth of Him "Who is born king of the Jews". This accordingly is the subject of the following chapter.

CHAPTER NINE

The testimony of the Gospel according to Matthew

In our last chapter we left the consideration of Israel's history, and the progress of the purpose of the earthly kingdom, at the period immediately following the return of the captivity from Babylonian exile. We are apt, by reason of custom, to forget that the Gospel of Matthew is a direct continuation of Old Testament history. We open the New Testament feeling that we are starting something new. Undoubtedly there are many new and wonderful truths brought to light, but the dispensation, people, land, and city are the same that we had in Malachi. Look at the opening words of Matthew's Gospel:

> "The book of the generation of Jesus Christ, Son of David, Son of Abraham".

Nothing can be clearer than that we are to have in this Gospel something bearing very strictly upon the special covenants that form the foci of the Hebrew Scriptures. Nor is this all. We see standing out as beacons four great promises, alike in that they are unconditional, and consequently can never fail, and alike in that they speak of the promised Seed. These four covenants or promises the reader will recognise as those made to *Eve* (Gen. 3: 15), to *Abraham* (Gen. 12), to *David* (2 Sam. 7: 8-17), and to the *regenerated nation*, "the new covenant" (Jer. 31: 31-34).

An examination of Matthew 1 shows us that these covenants are before us in the "book of the generation of Jesus Christ". He is the Seed of David, the Seed of Abraham, and the Seed of the woman ("Lo, a virgin", etc.). A threefold division of the genealogy is given in Matthew 1: 17, each cycle of time being opened with one aspect of the unconditional covenant:

(1) From Abraham to David (Gen. 12: 1-3). The *nation* and *land*
(2) From David to Babylon (2 Sam. 7: 8-17). The *throne* and *city*
(3) From Babylon to Christ (Jer. 31: 31-34). The *new covenant*.

Furthermore, these periods are marked by different administrations, and by special personal attacks of Satan.

From Abraham to David was characterised by *patriarchal* rule; from David to Babylon by *kingly* rule; while from Babylon to Christ, and on to the nation's end, *priestly* rule obtained. During the age of innocence Satan enters as the serpent. During the patriarchal age (Abraham to David) Satan attempts to thwart the purpose of the Lord by means of the Canaanite, Abimelech, and Pharaoh, while the attack on Job is typical of his attitude throughout the ages. During the monarchy Satan tempts David (1 Chron. 21: 1), and after the exile from Babylon Satan seeks to resist the Lord's purpose in the restoration of Jerusalem, and the priesthood of Israel (Zech. 3). Each period indicated in Matthew 1: 17 commences with an unconditional covenant, and ends in unmitigated ruin. At the close of each period Israel is found under the yoke of heathen conquerors, Philistines, Babylonians, Romans.

What will be the outcome of this momentous period? At last was born the One Who was the promised Seed of the woman, the promised Seed of Abraham, the promised Seed of David, and the promised Mediator of the New Covenant. Alas, history repeated itself with terrible exactness. Israel's rejection of their Messiah and King was followed by awful judgments, and Israel was banished for a period, still unfinished, whose length surpasses all other periods of their captivity and exile. Should the reader be yet unconvinced of the exclusively Jewish mission of the Lord Jesus, we quote three passages of Scripture; two, His own words concerning the scope of His ministry, and the third, the inspired words of Paul in describing its purpose:

> "These twelve Jesus sent forth, and commanded them, saying, Go *not* into the way of the Gentiles, and into any city of the Samaritans enter ye *not, but* go rather to *the lost sheep of the house of Israel*" (Matt. 10: 5, 6).
>
> "I am *not* sent *but* unto *the lost sheep of the house of Israel*" (Matt. 15: 24).
>
> "Now I say that Jesus Christ was a minister of the *circumcision* for the truth of God, to confirm the *promises* made unto the *fathers*" (Rom. 15: 8).

Here words cannot tell us more plainly the purpose and scope of the Saviour's earthly mission. Negatively, it was *not* to Gentiles or Samaritans. Positively, it was to the people of Israel, and to confirm the promises made unto the fathers. In Him were centred the covenants and promises that had been made to the fathers, to confirm and fulfil them being the object of His mission. Of course, with a complete Bible before us, *we* can see that *much more* than this was to be accomplished by His coming. Away back before the covenant with Abraham was the promise of the Redeemer (Gen. 3: 15) this portion, however, is not developed until Israel has heard the gospel of the kingdom, and rejected the King, and then and not till then does He speak of His suffering and death. Gentiles too were to share in the blessings of redeeming grace, but this must not be *read into* the Gospel of Matthew. We have been so anxious that the *church* should be early found in the New Testament, that we have spoiled the clear witness of this Gospel in its gathering up of the covenants and promises made to the fathers, and centralizing them in Christ.

One further word and we pass on to the consideration of the Gospel of Matthew as a whole. We have seen that the three periods of Israel's history given in Matthew 1:17 each ended in failure, and were each visited by Satan. Hence, when the Lord Jesus entered on His ministry He had to face the same kind of temptations that overcame the faith of the people of old. Matthew's record of the temptation in chapter 4 varies from that given by Luke. There is no "discrepancy", all is by design and of purpose. The first temptation of the Lord is connected with food and the wilderness. The first famine mentioned in Scripture occurs in Genesis 12: 10, *immediately* after the record of the covenant made with Abram. The famine drove Abram into *Egypt*, and caused him to tell lies. Later, the nation cried out for food, and in heart turned back to the flesh pots of Egypt. It is significant that the first temptation also (Gen. 3), was connected with "that which was good for food". In Deuteronomy 8: 3 we read, "He suffered thee to hunger . . . that He might make thee know that man *doth not live by bread alone, but by every word that proceedeth out of the mouth of the Lord* doth man live". Israel failed to learn this lesson, but the Lord Jesus, "tempted in all points" as His people, triumphed over the enemy, quoting this very verse in His reply.

The second temptation was connected with the Temple, and tempting God. During the period of Judah's kings, the times of distress and peril either sent men like Hezekiah (in his faith) to God in prayer, or like Hezekiah (in his fear) to rob the temple treasures to buy off the enemy. Again the Saviour triumphed by the patient waiting that is the outcome of perfect trust. From Babylon to the birth of Christ, Israel had nothing before them but to hope for the long-promised kingdom. They grew weary of waiting, the fact that they were a conquered people, instead of the ruling nation, galled them more than the chains of Babylon. Hope in God's Messiah gave place to hope in the successive world rulers. Would the Roman Emperor fulfil the promise? Could they expect help from Herod? Should they seek freedom by unfaithfulness? We know, alas, that once again Israel failed, but not so the Lord Jesus. Satan offers Him the very kingdoms that He came to receive, but He will not take them from the hand of the enemy. He awaits the Father's good pleasure.

Before investigating its message further, let us now look at the Gospel as a whole. The book is divided into two sections, each section commencing with the voice from heaven, and ending with a confession on earth. It is further marked off by two passages of time in the words, "from that time Jesus began" etc. We set this simple arrangement before the eye as follows:

The Gospel of Matthew

A Matt. 1:1-3:12. Preparation.
   B Matt. 3:16, 17. Voice from heaven. "My beloved son".
      Matt. 4:17. Time. "From that time forth".
      C Matt. 16:16. Peter's confession. "Thou art the Christ, the Son of the living God".
   B Matt. 16:21 Time. "From that time forth".
      Matt. 17:5. Voice out of cloud. "My beloved Son".
      C Matt. 27:54. Centurion's confession. "Truly this was the Son of God".
A Matt. 28. Conclusion.

This simple structure emphasizes the two-fold message of the Gospel, and also the fact that Abraham's Seed, David's Heir, and the Virgin's Son was the Son of God. The time divisions of Matthew are as follows:

> "*From that time Jesus began* to preach, and say, Repent, for the kingdom of the heavens is at hand" (4: 17).
>
> "*From that time forth began Jesus* to shew unto His disciples, how that He must go unto Jerusalem, and suffer many things of the elders and chief priests and scribes, and be killed, and be raised again the third day" (16: 21).

If Scripture declares, as it does, that the subject of the death and resurrection of Christ was not mentioned by Him until the moment of Matthew 16: 21, how can the "gospel of the kingdom of the heavens", which formed the theme of the earlier ministry, be identical with the gospel of the epistles? Confessedly, *we* have no gospel at all if the redemption and resurrection be taken from it (1 Cor. 15: 3,4), yet the gospel of the kingdom does not stress redemption but repentance. This tells us plainly that the gospel of the kingdom as proclaimed to Israel is to be separated completely from the gospel of salvation as proclaimed to Jews and Gentiles in after times. The one has to do with the setting up of a kingdom, the other with forgiveness and life.

What is this "good news of the kingdom of the heavens"? Again Scripture is eloquent, if we will but heed. Mark tells us in chapter 1: 14, 15 that "Jesus came preaching the gospel of the kingdom of God (Matthew alone uses the expression 'the kingdom of the heavens'), and saying". Here, surely, we shall have a definite statement as to what that gospel or good news was. It had nothing whatever in it about "justification", "sanctification", and all that goes to make the gospel of the grace of God now. The inspired explanation is

"The time is fulfilled, and the kingdom of God hath drawn nigh, repent and believe the glad message"

Again words cannot be plainer. The three items of the gospel are patent to all. The *time* had run its course, the promises to the fathers were on the eve of their fulfilment. Those promises centred in the King and the kingdom; the King was here, and His subjects were called upon to repent, and believe this glad message. This gospel had two facts as the bases of exhortation, (1) the time was fulfilled, and (2) the King was here, therefore repent and believe. That both time and Person had arrived Matthew makes abundantly clear in Matthew 2. The Magi from the East (who had retained the message of the heavenly signs) saw the star which told them that the King was born upon Whom hung the destiny not only of Israel, but of the whole creation. They followed the star and enquired, "Where is He that is born King of the Jews?" The royal and priestly gifts of gold, frankincense, and myrrh tell us clearly that these men knew what they were doing when they set out to follow the star that had arisen. Before His birth it was announced, "The Lord God shall give unto Him the throne of His father David, and He shall reign over the house of Jacob for ever and of His kingdom there shall be no end" (Luke 1: 32, 33). The Lord Jesus was born at Bethlehem, and as King of the Jews He died at Calvary (Matt. 28: 37). It is therefore a matter beyond dispute that the primary title of the Lord Jesus in the New Testament is "King".

Turning to the next chapter we find four quotations from the old Testament that are full of teaching. They have been summarized very ably as follows:

Matthew 2: 6. Homage and hatred. *Bethlehem* (Micah 5: 2).
Matthew 2: 14, 15. Exile and exodus. *Egypt* (Hosea 11: 1).
Matthew 2: 17, 18. Sorrow and song. *Ramah* (Jer. 31: 15).
Matthew 2: 23. Meanness and majesty. *Nazareth* (*spoken* by the Prophets).

Micah in his message speaks out against the misrule of the kings, and looks forward to the coming of the true Ruler. Hosea denounces Israel's backsliding, and anticipates the time of their restoration, as from an exile in Egypt. Jeremiah 31: 15 is followed by the consolation of verse 16, "Refrain . . . from weeping and thine eyes from tears . . . they shall come again from the land of the enemy, there is hope in thine end, saith the Lord, that thy children shall come again to their own border". This is ratified a few verses lower down by the New Covenant (verses 31-37). The final quotation is not from any one passage, but is the united testimony of the prophets that Christ should be "despised and rejected".

Coming now to a consideration of the main purpose of the book, we shall find that three discourses of the Lord Jesus are singled out from all else in this Gospel, and a due appreciation of their place and testimony will help us considerably in understanding the whole book. They are

(1) The *Sermon on the Mount.*
(2) The *Parables* (the mysteries of the kingdom of heaven).
(3) The *Prophecy on the Mount of Olives.*

The Sermon on the Mount opens with the words, "And seeing the multitudes, He went up into a mountain, and when He was set, His disciples came unto Him; and He opened His mouth and *taught* them" (5: 1, 2). It ends with the words of 7: 28, 29, "And it came to pass, when Jesus had ended these sayings, the people were astonished at His doctrine, for He *taught* them as one having *authority*, and not as the Scribes" (*cp,* "But *I* say unto you"). The emphasis is upon His authoritative teaching. Matthew 13 opens thus, "The same day went Jesus out of the house, and sat by the sea side . . . and He spake many things unto them in *parables*". It finishes with the words of verse 53, "And it came to pass, that when Jesus had finished these *parables*, He departed thence". Here it is not authority nor teaching, but parables that are emphasized. Now most of us were brought up to believe that a parable was an earthly story with a heavenly meaning, and that the purpose of a parable was to make the gospel easy, so easy that Sunday school teachers continually use them in their lessons to the little ones. This is a serious mistake. Listen to the Lord's answer to the disciples' enquiry, "Why speakest Thou unto them in parables?" He answered and said unto them:

> "Because it is given unto *you* to know the mysteries of the kingdom of heaven, but to *them* it is not given . . . Therefore speak I to *them* in parables, because *they* seeing see not, and hearing *they* hear

not, neither do *they* understand, and in *them* is fulfilled the saying of Isaiah . . . but blessed are *your* eyes, for they see, and *your* ears, for they hear" (Matt. 13: 11-16).

Parables were used because the kingdom was rejected, and the secrets of the kingdom were not for all, but for the chosen few. The prophecy on Olivet opens with the words, "And as He sat upon the Mount of Olives, the disciples came unto Him privately, saying, Tell us when shall these things be? and what shall be the sign of Thy coming, and the end of the age?" (Matt. 24: 3). It ends with the solemn words of Matthew 26: 1, 2, "And it came to pass, when Jesus had finished all these sayings, He said unto His disciples, Ye know that after two days is the feast of the passover, and the Son of man is betrayed to be crucified". The first and last discourses were given upon a mountain. The first, before the kingdom was rejected, dealt with its laws for its entry and characteristics, the third, after the kingdom was rejected, and the King about to be crucified, dealt with the future coming in power and glory to take the kingdom and reign. The central one deals with the intervening period which extends up to the time when Israel was cut off from being a nation, and takes up the thread again when the Lord once again deals with them, after the present dispensation has run its course. They harmonize thus:

A Matt. 5-7.	On a mountain. *(Past).*	Precept.	The kingdom explained.
B Matt. 13.	Out of the house *(Past and future, but not present).*	Parable.	The kingdom rejected.
A Matt. 24, 25.	On a mountain. *(Future).*	Prophecy.	The kingdom anticipated.

The Sermon on the Mount has been taken by many as being God's mind and will for believers to-day, whereas it should be viewed in connection with the time, people, and dispensation then in operation, and should not be dissociated from the "promises made unto the fathers". The King gives the laws for the entry into His kingdom in the opening words known as "The Beatitudes". The reader should compare the blessings here with those which he will find in Ephesians, Philippians, and Colossians, viz., "spiritual blessings in heavenly places". Chapter 6 deals with:

A Matt. 6:1-4. Almsgiving
  B Matt. 6:5-15. Prayer with single eye
    C Matt. 6:16-18. Fasting
A Matt. 6:19-21. Treasure
  B Matt. 6:22-24. Service with single eye
    C Matt. 6:25-34. Anxiety over food and clothing.

Chapter 7 concludes with its warnings concerning "judging", "false prophets", and the illustration of the two houses, the one built upon a rock, and the other upon the sand. This ends the section devoted to the Saviour's teaching. The next portion is more directly connected with His Person. So we have:

A Matt. 5-7. The words of Christ *(Precept)*.
B Matt. 8-16:20. The Person of Christ (Lord, Son of man, Son of God, Messiah)
B Matt. 16:21-23:39. The work of Christ (Suffering and death)
A Matt. 24-26:1. The words of Christ *(Prophecy)*.

The section 8-16: 20 records many wonderful miracles, and upon examination it will be found that these miracles are arranged in groups. In 8: 1-15 we have:

Leper healed
Centurion's servant healed } The body. — The Law.
Peter's wife's mother healed

"He healed all that were sick"(Matt. 8: 16). O.T. reference: Isa. 53: 4, "He bare our sicknesses".

In 8: 23—9: 13 we have:

The storm. — The wind and sea obey Him
The demons. — Cast out } Spiritual. — Sin.
Sins. — Forgiven

"They that be whole need not a physician, but they that are sick" (Matt. 9:12) O.T. reference: Hosea 6: 6, "Mercy not sacrifice" (ritual).

Again in Matthew 9: 18-38 we have:

Ruler's daughter.......... Raised from dead ("12 years", Mark 5:42)
The woman................. Healed ("12 years", Matt. 9:20) } Death, etc.
The Blind.................. Receive sight
The Demons................ Cast out

"And Jesus went about all the cities and villages . . .
(1) Preaching the gospel of the kingdom, and
(2) Healing every sickness and every disease among the people" (Matt. 9: 35).

It will be observed that each set of miracles is followed by a reference to healing or bearing sickness. It is important to notice this close connection between the miracles of healing, and the gospel of the kingdom. Where we find the one, we find the other; where one ends, there ends the other.

Up till this juncture the miracles and preaching had been the work and witness of the Lord alone. In chapter 10, we find the Lord calling unto Himself:

> "Twelve disciples, and He gave them power over unclean spirits, to cast them out, and to heal all manner of sickness, and all manner of disease . . . These twelve Jesus sent forth, and commanded them, saying, Go not into the way of the Gentiles, and into any city of the Samaritans enter ye not, but go rather to the lost sheep of the house of Israel. And as ye go, preach, saying, *The kingdom of heaven hath drawn nigh. Heal the sick, cleanse the lepers, raise the dead, cast out demons*" (Matt. 10: 1-8).

Here the evidence is overwhelming in support of the vital connection between the gospel of the kingdom and the miraculous gifts. These miracles we find in the *Acts of the Apostles*; they continue right on to the *last chapter* (Acts 28: 1-9), and then *suddenly cease*! We must keep this in mind when we examine the Acts and the Epistles written during, and after, the period covered by that book. To see the connection of these miracles with the proclamation of the kingdom gives point to the words of Christ in chapter 11. John Baptist had been sent before His face to prepare the way. Separated by God from birth for his special mission, he lived alone in the wilderness awaiting the signal. At length the time arrived, and there rang out a cry which for a while thrilled the whole population, "Repent, for the kingdom of heaven hath drawn nigh!" and which brought "Jerusalem, and all Judaea, and the region round about Jordan" to hear his burning eloquence, and to be baptised of him in Jordan.

John had said, "He that cometh after me is mightier than I". He had seen heaven opened, and had heard the voice of God, saying "This is My beloved Son, in whom I am well pleased". Time went on, and John for his faithfulness is cast into prison, to suffer all the agonies of bodily pain and tortured feelings. Had he made a mistake? Was it all a dream? Why was it that the kingdom was not set up? So John sent two of his disciples, who said, "Art Thou He that should come, or do we look for another?" For answer the Lord replied:

> "Go and show John again those things which ye do hear and see; the blind receive their sight, the lame walk, the lepers are cleansed, and the deaf hear, the dead are raised up, and the poor have the gospel preached unto them, and blessed is he whosoever shall not be offended in Me" (Matt. 11: 4-6).

If the reader will turn to Isaiah 29: 18, 19; 35: 5, 6; and 42: 1-7, he will see how this answer would tend to confirm the faith of John.

Everything was being done by the Saviour according to the word and will of God, but *unbelief* was bringing this witness of the kingdom to a close; for a little further on in Matthew 11: 20, we read that He began to "upbraid the cities wherein most of His mighty works were done, because they *repented* not". It is evident that if the mighty works were rejected, the good news that the kingdom of the heavens had drawn nigh would be rejected also, and consequently the cry "Repent" would go unheeded.

The Lord Jesus knew that this opposition was to be over-ruled to the accomplishing of God's ultimate purpose, and with the words, "Even so, Father, for so it seemed good in Thy sight", He awaits the end. It soon comes, for in chapter 12 we reach a climax. There He is seen as greater than the *Temple* (verse 6), greater than the *prophet* Jonah (verse 41), greater than the *king* Solomon (verse 42), and in all three capacities He is rejected. The reason for this rejection is given in verses 43-45. The captivity at Babylon had cured the Jews of external idolatry, and they were like a room "empty, swept, and garnished". They were, however, possessed by a spirit more evil than that of their idolatrous fathers; "the last state is worse than the first", for in rejecting their Messiah they reached the culminating point of their iniquity. This leads to Matthew 13, where we have a series of parables which speak of "The mysteries (or secrets) of the kingdom of the heavens". Up till this point nothing had been secret, all had been open, but now the Saviour is about to reveal to the hearing ear, and seeing eye, that the rejection of the message and the King was foreknown, and the efforts of the Apostles would meet with a like fate, and that not until the end, when the Lord makes bare His arm, and brings about the deliverance of Israel, would the gospel of the kingdom be received. This is the burden of the parable of the Sower.

This parable has been beclouded, tortured, and twisted, until it is hardly recognizable. It constitutes a resource for the wearied Sunday school teacher, it provides a sermon for the harvest festival, it is made to teach the most widely differing doctrines, but its real meaning is lost sight of. This of its setting! The chosen nation to whom the Lord had come, with every credential, with the glad message that at last the earthly kingdom was at hand, had rejected both the good news and the King. To think that after being rejected as Prophet, Priest, and King (chapter 12), the Lord should indulge in platitudes and sermonizing is to say the least improbable. We should expect something very much to the point, and we get it in Matthew 13. The parable presents to view the sower with the seed. The interpretation (13: 19) tells us that this seed is "The word of the *kingdom*". The sower sows His seed over four different kinds of ground. The wayside, stony places, thorns, and good ground. The seed on the wayside was devoured by the birds, the seed on the stony places, having no depth, was scorched. The seed among thorns was soon choked, but the seed on good ground brought forth fruit, some an hundredfold, some sixtyfold, and some thirtyfold.

The wayside hearer is explained in verse 19. The first statement is that he *understandeth not* the word of the kingdom (*cp.* 13: 13-15), and that the wicked one (Satan, Mark 4: 15; the devil, Luke 8: 12) catcheth the seed away which was sown in the heart. The one who is represented by the stony ground is one who hears the word, and rejoices for a while, but when tribulation or persecution arises because of the word, he is offended and falls. The thorny ground represents the one who is overburdened with the care of the world, and the deceitfulness of riches which choke the word. The good ground indicates those who hear the word, and *understand it* (*cp.* Dan. 11: 33-35). Now the parable has direct reference to the kingdom of the heavens; it is the first word of the secrets of the kingdom of the heavens. The Lord portrays with graphic touch the course of this gospel. His own ministry, so far, had been like sowing seed by the wayside; Satan had taken advantage of the lack of understanding, and had snatched the seed away, and while in individual cases each of the four grounds would constantly recur, yet in the main those who succeeded the Lord (*e.g.*, the apostles during "Acts",) would find their ministry much like that depicted in the next two types.

In considering the teaching of this parable, we must bear in mind the way in which the "seed" *i.e.*, the Word, becomes identified with the hearer himself. Note such passages as, "This is *he* that was sown by the wayside"; "And *he* that was sown among thorns, this is *he that heareth* the word". When the application of this parable is made to those who reject the word, the word is likened to the seed, and the hearers to the ground. When the application is made to a child of the kingdom, the seed represents both the word and the believer, and the ground then represents the environment in which he is placed. A characteristic example of this double reference may be seen in the case of Peter and Judas. Satan had dealings with each, but Peter is likened to wheat being sifted. Peter denied the Lord with oaths and curses; Judas betrayed Him. Peter went out and wept bitterly; Judas went out and hanged himself. Peter was a child of the kingdom, and for a while the thorns overcame him; Judas never was a child of the kingdom (John 6: 70, 71), he was the thorny ground itself, or, as in the next parable, one of the enemy's tares sown among the true wheat.

The four sowings of the kingdom seed are as follows*:

John Baptist.	Wayside hearers.	"They seeing, see not, neither do they understand".
The Lord Jesus, the Twelve, and the Seventy.	Stony ground hearers.	"Nothing but leaves . . . it withered away".
Peter and the Twelve during the "Acts".	Thorny ground hearers.	"No fruit to perfection" (Heb. 6). "Riches, pleasures, the lust of other things".
The final witness (Matt. 24:14).	Good ground hearers (the heart of the new Covenant).	"The honest and good heart." "Some hundred-fold".

If one will but look at the Acts of the Apostles and note the character of those who "believed" and who went back under persecution (noting also Heb. 6, etc.), he will find that the stony ground and the thorns give the history of the gospel of the kingdom up to the end of the Acts. Confessedly, the last "good ground" is not a picture of the present time, but it is the last and future stage of this gospel preaching. When the Lord returns and sends out His messengers once more, then the Word will be received by those who will have been "made ready" (Luke 1: 17 and Mal. 4: 5, 6), and then will they understand it. These parables are the secret history of the kingdom of the heavens, having nothing whatever to do with the history of Christendom, or the present time.

A careful reading of Matthew 13 reveals not seven, but eight parables, and we present them in their structure and order, hoping thus to make their meaning clearer to our readers.

The correspondence is fairly self-explanatory. A and *A* contrast broadcast sowing with distributing treasure and food to one class only — those in the house. In B and *B* the parallelism is obvious, and extends to details. Read the parables, and their interpretations together. In C and *C* the one tree and the one pearl are the most difficult to understand. D and *D* contrast the *hid* leaven with the *hid* treasure.

---

* For fuller notes on the parables see *The Berean Expositor,* Vol. 2/3, same Author and Publisher.

Structure of Matthew 13.

A 1—9. The *sower.* The sowing of seed into four kinds of ground.
 a They (Israel) did *not* understand.
B 24—30. The *tares.* Good and bad together. Separated at the harvest (the end of the age); the bad are cast into a furnace of fire, there shall be wailing and gnashing of teeth.
C 31, 32. The *mustard tree.* One tree.
D 33. The *leaven.* Hid in three measures of meal.

} The first four parables spoken outside the house to great multitudes.

D 44. The *treasure.* Hid in a field.
C 45, 46. *Goodly pearls.* One pearl.
B 47—50. The *drag net.* Good and bad together. Separated at the end of the age; the bad are cast into a furnace of fire, there shall be wailing and gnashing of teeth.
 a They (disciples) *did* understand.
A 51, 52. The *scribe.* The treasure opened to those in the house.

} The last four parables spoken inside the house to the disciples.

The four spoken outside may be taken together thus:

A. *Sower. Three* bad grounds
 B *Tares.* "Both *grew* until harvest". } Earth.
 B Mustard tree. "When it is *grown*". }
A Leaven. Three leavened measures.

Those spoken inside may be also taken together thus:

A Treasure in field
 B Pearls. } Sea
 B Fish. }
A Treasure in house.

The outside aspect has the appearance of failure. The inside teaching reveals God's hidden purpose in the remnant according to the election of grace. Thus it will be seen that we have the history of the kingdom from an outer and inner standpoint during its temporary rejection. The first four parables speak largely of failure, Satan and his agents figuring in each of them, while the last of the first four parables shows us "the whole (of the measures of meal) leavened". All look forward to the harvest, which is the "end of the age" (verse 39). A brief review of the state of the times as depicted in the book of the Revelation will abundantly confirm this description of the "time of the end".

The second set of four gives the development from the divine standpoint. Satan's woman (Rev. 2: 20; 17; 19: 2) will corrupt the testimony of the kingdom to such an extent that thousands will accept antichrist as their messiah. She has "hidden" her *leaven*, but the Lord also has "hidden" His *treasure*. The pearl, too, is connected with redeemed Israel (Rev. 21: 12, 21), and is a fit emblem of those who have "come through the great tribulation", for pearls as we know are the product of suffering. The parallel between the "tares" (13:24), and the "net" (13:47) is emphasized by the exactly similar words used in the explanation in verses 41, 42, and 49, 50. The fact that the harvest is spoken of as being "the end of the age" links Matthew 13 with Matthew 24: 3: "What shall be the sign of Thy coming, and of the *end of the age*?" An examination of this chapter shows that it deals exclusively with events that are still future, the period of the great tribulation, and the coming of Christ, the present dispensation being entirely ignored.

There is a passage from the Old Testament quoted in Matthew 13: 14, 15, viz., Isaiah 6: 9, 10, which in this connection is so important that we propose passing over it now, finishing our review of Matthew in this chapter, and devoting the next to the important dispensational bearing of the passage in its several occurrences.

Chapter 17 as we have already noted occupies a place in the second division of Matthew parallel to the end of chapter 3. What is the meaning of the Transfiguration? It is the solemn investiture of the *Priest*. As King, the Lord Jesus has been rejected. Over the Transfiguration we may write the words of Hebrews 2: 8, 9, "But *now* we see *not yet* all things put under Him, but we see Jesus, made a little lower than the angels, because of the suffering of death, crowned with glory and honour". Peter, who was one of the three chosen to witness this wonderful sight, declares in 2 Peter 1: 16, "We have not followed cunningly devised fables, when we made known unto you the power and coming of our Lord Jesus Christ, but were eye-witnesses of His majesty; for He received from God the Father honour and glory". We notice the repetition of the words "honour and glory". That they pertain to kingship is evident (*see* Psalm 8), but that they pertain to priesthood is not so evident to all.

Hebrews 5: 4, 5 uses the two words with regard to the priesthood, and emphasizes the fact that Christ did not assume this honour of Himself, but that the Father gave it to Him; and further, in Exodus 28: 2 the Septuagint translates the words "glory and beauty" by the very same words that are translated "glory and honour" in 2 Peter. This links the Transfiguration with the passage in Exodus 28. Aaron is arrayed in the garments of glory and honour, "that he may minister unto Me in the priest's office" (verses 1, 2). The rejection of Christ as King led to the next step in the divine plan. Prophecy had said, "He shall be a *priest* upon His *throne*", and had declared, "Thou art a priest for ever after the order of Melchisedek" (king of righteousness). God's *king* must be God's *priest*. The rejection of Israel was their responsibility, but it was foreseen and overruled as a means to the end. The priesthood of Christ, following His rejection as King, is the theme of the epistle to the Hebrews.

If the early chapters of Matthew set forth the Lord Jesus as King, and the next section as Priest, the discourse of Matthew 24 and 25 shows Christ as the true Prophet. We have seen that we may expect a parallel between Matthew 13 and Matthew 24 and 25 by the fact that both have reference to the "end of the age". The opening verses of the chapters are similar. After the rejection of Matthew 12 we read, "The same day went Jesus out of the house, and sat by the sea side" (13: 1). This had particular reference to His kingship. Matthew 23 has much in it to do with the religious leaders, the Scribes and Pharisees, and 24 commences with the words, "And Jesus went out and departed from the temple".

When the disciples heard His words concerning the overthrow of the Temple, they connected them with the "end of the age", and the "coming of the Lord", as is evident from their question in verse 3. They had to learn what many Christians have failed to perceive, that there would be a break, and a period of unmarked time must elapse before "the end". Nothing is here revealed as to what shall fill the interval, that being reserved for the writings of the Apostle Paul. Note the words of verse 6, "*The end is not yet*", and verse 8, "All these are the *beginning* of sorrows". Verse 13 speaks of those who endure to the *end*, and as over eighteen centuries have rolled by since Matthew 24 was uttered, it is evident that those spoken of in verse 13 refer to some living in the future, and can be easily identified with the "overcomers" in Revelation 2 and 3. The present interval is omitted. The "gospel of the *kingdom*" is to be published once again, and "*then shall the end come*" (verse 14).

The Lord refers to the abomination of desolation spoken of by Daniel the prophet, and the great tribulation, which is again referred to in the book of the Revelation. This tribulation is a dividing mark in the discourse. Space will not allow a detailed exposition of these wonderful chapters, but we set out their arrangement, hoping that the reader will be stimulated to examine them for himself:

The first part (Matt. 24:4-28).

Events up to the great tribulation.

A 4-6-. Events *heard.* "Ye shall *hear* of wars", etc.
  B -6-. Direction. "Be not troubled"
    C -6. Reason. "For all these things must be"
      D 7, 8. The beginning of sorrows or birthpangs
        E 9-14. Following events. "Then"
A 15-. Events *seen.* "When ye therefore shall *see*", etc.
  B -15-20. Direction. "Understand"
    C 21. Reason. "For then shall be great tribulation"
      D 22. The shortening of sorrows
        E 23-28. Following events. "Then".

The second part (Matt. 24:29-25:46).

Events after the great tribulation.

F a 24:29, 30. The Son of man coming in clouds of heaven
    b 31. The gathering of the "elect" (Israel)
      G c 32-41. Parables. Fig tree and Noah
          d 42-44. Warning. "Watch therefore"
            e 45-51. Servants (general)
      G *c* 25:1-12. Parables. Ten virgins
            d 13. Warning. "Watch therefore"
              e 14-30. Servants (special)
F *a* 31. The Son of man sitting on the throne of His glory
    b 32-46. The gathering of the "nations" (Gentiles).

It will be seen that the parable of the ten virgins is in the heart of the prophecy which refers to that which takes place "after the great tribulation". It has nothing whatever to do with the church (except by application), or the time present. The parable starts with the word "then", which indicates that "when" the great tribulation has passed, "then" the state of affairs will be as described in chapter 25. The link between the prophecy and the book of the Revelation is found by comparing Matthew 24 with Revelation 6, 7. We place the passages together under their respective heads:

FIRST SEAL

I saw a white horse ... conquering (Rev. 6:1, 2).	Many shall say, I am the Messiah (Matt. 24:4, 5).

SECOND SEAL

Take peace from the earth ... kill one another (Rev. 6:4).	Wars ... kingdom against kingdom (Matt. 24:6, 7-).

THIRD SEAL

Black horse. Famine prices (Rev. 6:5, 6).	There shall be famines (Matt. 24:-7-).

FOURTH SEAL

Pale horse . . . his name was death (Rev. 6:8).	Pestilences (Matt. 24:-7).

FIFTH SEAL

The souls of the slain . . . wait till the others are martyred (Rev. 6:9-11).	They shall kill you . . . great tribulation (Matt. 24:8-28).

SIXTH SEAL

Sun as sackcloth, moon as blood. Wrath (Rev. 6:12-17).	Sun darkened. Moon not giving light. The coming of the Son of man (Matt. 24:29, 30).
The sealing of the twelve thousand of the twelve tribes (Rev. 7).	All tribes of the land mourn. The elect gathered (Matt. 24:30, 31).

Perhaps a word or two may be of help in connection with the *sheep* and the *goats*. The time of the judgment mentioned there is "When the Son of man *shall come in His glory*, and all the holy angels with Him, then shall He sit upon the throne of His glory". The place of this judgment is given us in Joel 3: 2: "I will also gather all *nations* . . . into the valley of Jehoshaphat, and will plead with them there for My people, and for My heritage Israel, whom they have scattered among the nations, and parted my land". The title of Christ, *Son of man*, associates Him with Israel and the earth, but this title is *never* used in His relation to the church or the heavenly places. This judgment has for its object "the gathering out of all things that offend", just like the "tares", and the "bad fish" of Matthew 13 preparatory to the setting up of the kingdom.

Matthew 26: 1 finishes "these sayings", and we have seen that Matthew gives us three links in the chain of divine purpose: (1) the Sermon on the Mount, enunciating the character and laws for the entry of the kingdom. This is rejected, and is followed by (2) the parables of the mysteries of the kingdom of the heavens, which deal with the failure that would apparently follow the preaching of the gospel of the kingdom, and (3) the prophecy on the Mount of Olives referring to the future time when the kingdom should no longer be "offered" and "rejected", but when the righteous king comes "in power and great glory" to rule and reign. The remainder of the Gospel of Matthew deals with those memorable days — the last supper, the betrayal, the death, burial, and glorious resurrection. The Seed of the woman has bruised the serpent's head. The first promise has been wonderfully fulfilled.

It must be evident to the reader that the Gospel of Matthew has nothing in it in any way like what we know as "church" teaching. When we come later to compare the epistles of Paul, we believe that this will be seen even more clearly. We cannot spare time to consider each of the four Gospels, but we give a suggestion regarding them which links them on to the witness of the cherubim, focussing the hope of creation as well as of Israel on the Lord Jesus Christ.

Matthew.	*The King.*	The *Branch* (Jer. 23:5).	Genealogy: Abraham and David.	*Lion.*
Mark.	*The Servant.*	The *Branch* (Zech. 3:8).	A servant needs no genealogy.	*Ox.*
Luke.	*The Man.*	The *Branch* (Zech. 6:12).	Genealogy to Adam.	*Man.*
John.	*Jehovah.*	The *Branch* (Isa. 4:2; cp 40:9).	God can have no genealogy.	*Eagle.*

In the next chapter we shall deal with the quotation of Isaiah 6: 9, 10, and its dispensational bearing.

CHAPTER TEN

The cumulative fulfilment of Isaiah 6, showing that Acts 28 and not Acts 2 marks the commencement of this dispensation

In almost every department of Bible study errors have been formulated, and perpetuated, by reason of the persistency on the part of students to omit consideration of the context.

Let it be accepted as a golden rule for the study of the Word of God that one cannot have too much of the context in the study of any passage. Thus Isaiah 6 must not only be studied in its relation to the surrounding *chapters*, but it must be studied in relation to the rest of the whole *book*. Nor is this all, Isaiah itself receives light by its position in the canon of Scripture. A reference to page 53 will show that Isaiah's prophecy immediately follows the book of Kings, wherein is recorded the failure and rejection of the kings of Israel and Judah. The book as a whole may be considered thus:

A 1-5. Exhortations; reprehensory and prophetic
  B 6. The *voice* from the temple. Dispersion
    C 7-12. History and prophecy (Ahaz)
      D 13-27. Burdens alternated with Jehovah's blessing
      D 28-35. Woes alternated with Jehovah's glories
    C 36-39. History and prophecy (Hezekiah)
  B 40:1-11. The *voice* from the wilderness. Gathering
A 40:12-46. Exhortations; promissory and prophetic.

Chapter 6 is now seen to be related to chapter 40. In the one we have the *voice* which pronounces the nation's doom and its dispersion, in the other the *voice* which tells of its gathering and blessing.

Turning our attention to Isaiah 6, we find that Isaiah was commissioned to "go and tell *this people*". Who are this people? They are the same as those referred to in Isaiah 1: 3, "The ox knoweth his owner, and the ass his master's crib, but *Israel* doth not know, *My people* doth not consider". There are connections to be noted between Isaiah 1 and Isaiah 6 in the words used.

Isaiah 1.	*Isaiah 6.*
"Consider" (verse 3)	"Understand" (same word) (verses 9, 10)
"Your land desolate" (verse 7)	"The land utterly desolate" (verse 11)
"They have forsaken the Lord" (verse 4)	"A great forsaking in the land" (verse 12)

The *people* is Israel; the *land* is Palestine. In Isaiah 6: 11 Isaiah asks "How long?" He was told of desolation, and a remnant according to election, but did not know how long. This was revealed by Paul in his last epistle written before Acts 28 (*see* page 29), viz., Romans 11: 25, 26: " . . . blindness in part hath happened unto Israel, *until* the fulness of the Gentiles be come in, and so all Israel shall be saved" (*see also* Luke 21: 24).

We have already referred to the exclusively Jewish ministry of the Lord as indicated in Matthew 10: 5, 6, and 15: 24. In both chapters the Gentiles are excluded. Matthew 13 comes in between these two passages, and therefore "this people" of Matthew 13: 15 is none other than Israel, and it is a perversion of God's truth to whittle away these "secrets of the kingdom of heaven" upon some fanciful allusions to the career of Christendom and church history. Some have claimed the "Pearl" parable as being descriptive and predictive of their assembly or fellowship, and have generally ignored the plain fact that this is *entirely and exclusively* concerned with *Israel* and the kingdom. When will we believe that God *means* what He *says*?

Is it not significant that the recurring cry "Repent, Repent", is never heard again in this Gospel after Matthew 12: 41! The quotation of Isaiah 6 immediately follows. The word "Repent" is next heard in Acts 2, but the word is never again heard with reference to the gospel after the quotation of Isaiah 6 in Acts 28. In each case the quotation signifies that a door has been closed. In Matthew 13 the door closed upon this people in the land; in Acts 28, the door closed upon the Jews of the dispersion.

John 12: 39, 40 is the next independent quotation of Isaiah 6. Like Matthew 13, it marks an important division in the book, and follows hard upon rejection. John 1: 11: "He came to His *own*, and His *own* received Him not". John 13: 1: "Jesus . . . having loved His *own* . . . loved them to the end". John 1-12 gives a record of public ministry. John 13-20 gives the account of the Lord's private ministry among His disciples, both before and after the crucifixion. Thus in Matthew and John, Isaiah 6 is quoted at the close of a public ministry ending in rejection. This ended the testimony to the people "in the land", until after the Lord had been raised from the dead.

When the Lord Jesus was hanging upon the accursed tree, surrounded by men who seemed actuated by the devil, dying the Just for the unjust that He might bring us to God, He uttered a prayer, "Father, forgive them, for they know not what they do". This prayer, as all the words and works of the Saviour, was in perfect harmony with the Father's will; consequently it was answered, and the respite, the opportunity afforded during the Acts, was the result. There we once again hear the kingdom cry "Repent", and forgiveness is proclaimed in the name of the crucified yet risen Saviour.

Christian people have for generations regarded the Acts of the Apostles as a collection of fragments of early church history. It is practically a fundamental that The church began at Pentecost. This consensus of opinion has wrought havoc among the people of God. It has been the foundation of much of the "gifts" and "tongues" movements, "faith healing", and the many sects and splits that go to form Christendom. We unhesitatingly challenge this hoary tradition, and seek to show by the Word itself that Pentecost has nothing whatever to do with the "Body of Christ" but like Matthew and the earthly ministry of the Lord Jesus, is a continuation of the gospel of the kingdom, related to Abrahamic and Davidic promises, hopes, and people. The book is written around two ministries, and three cities, the ministries being that of Peter, the apostle of the circumcision, and that of Paul, the apostle of the uncircumcision, the cities being Jerusalem, Antioch, and Rome. The whole book has been ably set out thus:

Acts of the Apostles

A 1:1-11. a Christ is teaching concerning "the kingdom of God"
b "Wilt thou restore the kingdom to *Israel?*" } The Jew prominent.

B c 1:12-26. Peter's preparation and introduction
d 2:1-13. Peter's spiritual qualification, and enduement
e 2:14-11:26. Peter's ministry. Jerusalem, Judaea
f 12:1-23. Peter's sufferings, imprisonment, and deliverance.

B *c* 12:24, 25. Paul's preparation and introduction
d 13:1-4. Paul's spiritual qualification, and enduement
e 13:5-19:20. Paul's ministry. Antioch, and the regions beyond
f 19:21-28:24. Paul's sufferings and imprisonment

A 28:25-31. *a* Paul preaching "the kingdom of God," and teaching concerning the Lord Jesus Christ.
b Salvation of God *sent* to *Gentiles.* } The Jew set aside.

We would draw the reader's attention very particularly to the opening and closing verses of the book of the Acts, for therein lies the key to the understanding of its purpose. It opens with the Saviour instructing the Apostles concerning the kingdom of God, and in answer to their enquiry concerning the restoration of the kingdom to Israel, He bids them tarry at Jerusalem until they be endued with power from on high. Peter, to whom the keys of the kingdom were given, opens the door for the repentant Israelite, the Proselyte, the Samaritan, the Ethiopian, and the Gentile to enter the kingdom of the heavens. Paul, in Acts 28, closes the door of the kingdom of the heavens, and opens the door of the present dispensation, the church of the Mystery, and there in this final passage Isaiah 6 is again quoted for the last time.

Before we consider the last quotation from Isaiah 6, let us run through the book of the Acts to note the course of events which led to the setting aside of Israel, and the kingdom. God has placed the key to many of the books of the Bible at the entrance. It is so with the Acts. The first eleven verses give the object of the book. We may ask, "Does this book of the Acts commence some new phase of teaching, or is it a continuation of the gospel narrative? Is it the first chapter in church history, or the last chapter in Israel's probation? Is it the commencement of a new era, or the close of an old one?" Let the writer tell us:

> "The former treatise have I made, O Theophilus, of all that Jesus *began* both to do and teach, until the day in which He was taken up after that He, through the Holy Ghost, had given commandment unto the apostles whom He had chosen".

Acts then is a *continuation* and not a commencement. The reader will remember Matthew 4: 17, "From that time Jesus *began* to preach, saying, Repent, for the kingdom of heaven is at hand". What He began, the apostles continue in the power of the Holy Spirit (Acts 2: 38; 3: 19; 5: 31; 11: 18, etc.). The Gospels record the proclamation of the kingdom while the king was *on earth*; in Acts the proclamation is *continued* by the Apostles, the king being, however, *in heaven*.

The words "after ... He had given commandment" referred, among other things, to the "power from on high" (1: 8). This is the burden of the opening verses of Hebrews 2. Hebrews 1: 1, 2 tells us of the days of old when Jehovah spake to Israel, Whom they refused, and of the period covered by the Gospels, when the Lord Jesus, the Son, spoke to this same people, and was rejected. Hebrews 2: 3, 4 refers to the period of the Acts where the Spirit bears His witness, and is again refused. Thus Father (O.T.), Son (Gospels), and Spirit (Acts) have alike testified to this kingdom truth, and have alike been refused. This filled up the measure of Israel's iniquity, and for a time they are put aside. The words of Hebrews 2: 3, 4 are:

> "How shall we escape, if we neglect so great salvation, which at the first *began* to be spoken by the Lord, and was confirmed unto us by them that heard, God also bearing witness, both with signs and wonder, and with divers miracles, and gifts of Holy Spirit (power from on high), according to His will?"

The Lord Jesus *began* His ministry, preaching the gospel of the kingdom of heaven among the lost sheep of the house of Israel, and accompanied that witness with miracles and signs. The Apostles continued this ministry among the *same* people, and accompanied with the *same* signs. Many of those who believe the tradition that "the church began at Pentecost" have the temerity to punctuate the Acts with *their* statements that the Apostles were mistaken here, or that Peter was prejudiced there; they never seem to imagine that a system of teaching which demands such unwarranted aspersions *may itself* be a huge mistake, not merely "here" and "there", but throughout.

The question of the disciples in Acts 1: 6 was the direct outcome of forty days' instruction. The Lord does not correct any "error": He indeed tells them that "times and seasons" were not for them to know. This answered the "time" question, "Wilt Thou at this *time*", but the remainder of the question — "restore the kingdom to Israel" is confirmed rather than otherwise. They were told to tarry at Jerusalem, and that after they had received power they were to be His witnesses. What that witness was we shall see when we consider Acts 2.

Another link with Israel, the Davidic throne, and Abrahamic covenants is the connection made by the Lord between "John's baptism", and the "baptism with holy spirit" at Pentecost, which connection is remembered in the subsequent appointment of Matthias (Acts 1: 21, 22). The disciples' question in 1: 6 shows us that they understood the Scriptures better than their would-be judges. Their illumination was doubtless due to the forty days' teaching of our Lord. Isaiah 32: 13-15 says, "Upon the land of My people shall come up thorns and briers . . . until the Spirit be poured upon us from on high". The mention of the baptism of the Spirit made the disciples ask whether this Scripture (Isaiah 32) was upon the eve of fulfilment. The Lord's answer confirmed them in their faith as to the coming kingdom, but did not reveal the events which would ultimately postpone the setting up of that kingdom for nearly 2,000 years!

The final witness to the nature of the book is found in verse 11: "Ye men of Galilee, why stand ye gazing up into heaven? This same Jesus, which is taken up from you into heaven, shall so come in like manner as ye have seen Him go into heaven". Once again, they who believe that the Acts is church history, limit the "like manner" to one phase of the Lord's ascension. We have no such need. He was taken up from the Mount of Olives, and to the Mount of Olives He will return (Zech. 14: 4). What has Zechariah 14 to do with the church? His ascension was associated with clouds, so also will be His return (Dan. 7: 13; Matt. 24: 30; 1 Thess. 4: 17; Rev. 1: 7). He had ascended from a little company of Jews, and will return to a little company at the time of the end (Isa. 66: 5-15; Psalm 50: 1-6). The Acts is not the opening chapter in the church era; it is the final witness of God to Israel, and extends beyond the confines of Palestine to the Dispersion even in Rome.

The first section of Acts may be viewed as a record of three widening circles of witness, and if the "uttermost parts of the *earth*" be taken to mean the uttermost parts of the *land* (*see* the use of "*ge*", earth, land, etc.), then we can see that the command to witness in Jerusalem, Judaea, Samaria, and the uttermost parts of the land has received fulfilment.

Acts 1:12-7.	Preaching of the gospel of the kingdom.	Jerusalem.
	Transitional event. — Murder of Stephen.	
Acts 8-9:30.	Preaching of the gospel of the kingdom.	Samaria.
	Transitional event. — Call of Saul of Tarsus while "breathing out threatenings and slaughter."	
Acts 9:31-12.	Preaching to Jew and Gentile proselytes.	Uttermost parts of land.
	Transitional event. — Imprisonment of Peter and murder of James.	

Acts 1 and 2 are distinctly Jewish, but as the record continues the trend of the book Gentileward is manifested. Jerusalem is the scene of the first witness to Israel, but Rome is the last. Gradually, yet certainly, the Jew is left behind. Jerusalem is the centre of operations at the opening of the book, Antioch in the middle, and Rome at the end. The conversion of Saul took place outside the land of Israel. Each outbreak of opposition increases the widening rift, and swells the current of grace towards the nations. The Samaritans are gathered in; the "Ethiopian stretches out his hands unto God" (Psalm 68: 31; Acts 8: 27), the uncircumcised proselytes are endued with power from on high, until at last in the very metropolis of heathenism an imprisoned Jew utters the epoch-making words of Acts 28: 25-28.

The choice of Matthias to fill the vacant apostleship has been attacked by not a few, who, zealous for their traditions, not only see a "mistake" in the disciples' question of Acts 1: 6, but also in the choice of Matthias in Acts 1: 15-26. The qualification which demanded one who had companied with the rest since the beginning of the baptism of John limited the possible candidates to two. The use of the lot was of divine sanction (Josh. 14: 2; 1 Chron. 24: 5; Prov. 16: 33; 18: 18). The lot fell upon Matthias, and in accord with Proverbs 16: 33 he was recognised as the one appointed to take the place of Judas.

It is a prevalent though mistaken idea, that there was but one order of apostles. Fourteen times over it is stated that the number of Apostles as first chosen was twelve. They are designated in Revelation 21: 14, "the Apostles of the Lamb". Their peculiar position in the kingdom of the heavens is given in Matthew 19: 28, "In the regeneration, when the Son of man shall sit on the throne of His glory (*cp.* Matt. 25), ye also shall sit upon twelve thrones, judging the twelve tribes of Israel". Scripture recognises Matthias as being "one of the twelve", for 1 Cor 15: 5-8 says that after the resurrection, and before the ascension, the Lord Jesus Christ was "seen of the *twelve*", and if Judas hanged himself before the resurrection of the Lord, and Matthias was not the man of God's choice, and Paul was unconverted, who was the twelfth? In verse 8 Paul disposes of the figment that *he* instead of Matthias was the twelfth, by saying, "last of all, He was seen of me also", thus distinguishing himself from the rest.

We know the names of the twelve, and we can well believe that it would be a short-lived attempt to impersonate any one of them, yet in 2 Corinthians 11: 13 we read of some who were "deceitful workers, transforming themselves into apostles of Christ". Ephesians 4: 11 tells us that when the Saviour ascended up on high (*i.e.*, after the ascension), He gave some *apostles*, some *prophets*, etc. This new order is referred to in Ephesians 2: 20. Using the Revised Version we find under this new order of Apostles Barnabas and Paul (Acts 14: 14), Apollos (1 Cor. 4: 6-9), Epaphroditus (Phil. 2: 25 marg.), Titus (2 Cor. 8: 23), Silvanus and Timothy (1 Thess. 1: 1; 2: 6, *cp.* Acts 17). Here we have *seven named* Apostles of the new order; there may have been others, *e.g.*, Romans 16: 7.

It is evident that the term "apostle" must not be restricted to "the twelve"; it is also quite as evident that *no more* than twelve were ever connected with the kingdom; the other order was related to the church. The twelve apostles, according to the command of the Lord, tarried at Jerusalem until endued with power from on high. When the day of Pentecost arrived, the promised blessing came. The Apostles were filled with Holy Spirit, and spake with other tongues as the Spirit gave them utterance.

Pentecost had attracted "devout men from every nation under heaven" (Acts 2: 5), and these were astonished to hear in their own languages the wonderful works of God. In answer to the inquiry, "What meaneth this?" Peter stood up and addressed the men of *Judaea*, and all that were at *Jerusalem*. They were wrong to think that the Apostles were drunken; "this is that which was spoken by the prophet Joel", and Acts 2: 17-21 is a quotation from Joel 2: 28-32. The *place* is "in Mount Zion, and in Jerusalem". The *time* is "when I (the Lord) shall bring again the captivity of Judah, and Jerusalem" (Joel 2: 32, 3: 1). It will take a skilful spiritualizer to show many references to the church of the Mystery or the epistle to the Ephesians, in the book of Joel. Peter definitely refers to a passage which is related to

> The day of the Lord.
> Judah and Jerusalem, and the
> Bringing again of the captivity.

Further, the presence and power of the Holy Spirit in the Acts is spoken of in a manner similar to that of the Old Testament period, and of the future millennial kingdom; "coming upon", and "falling upon" are terms frequently used. The spirit of God was *upon* Moses, and the seventy who prophesied (Numb. 11: 25, 26). The Spirit came *upon* Balaam (Numb. 24: 2), *upon* Gideon, *upon* Saul, and *upon* David. The Spirit spoken of by Joel is poured *upon* all flesh. The Holy Ghost was *upon* Simeon in the Temple (Luke 2: 25), *upon* the Apostles (Acts 2: 3), *upon* the believers in Samaria, *upon* the household of Cornelius, and *upon* the disciples of John (Acts 19: 6). All this is evidently a continuation of the Old Testament economy. Will those who take Acts as "the first chapter in church history" make good their position even in this one particular. If not, why do they teach that the church began at Pentecost? Peter's address is to the men of Judaea, to the men of Israel, to the house of Israel, and to all that were afar off. This last phrase was a name given to those Jews who had been scattered among the nations (*see* Dan. 9: 7). Are these titles of the church?

The moment Peter perceived that they were pricked to the heart, he once again sounds the word *Repent*, unheard since the rejection of Matthew 12. Not only repent, but "be baptised"; not only be baptised, but "be baptised for the remission of sins". Let those who will have Pentecost be consistent, let them have "baptism for the remission of sins" as Peter preached it. The theme of Peter's preaching may be found in verses 30-36. The covenant concerning the *throne of David* is emphasized; "that same Jesus" whom they crucified is declared to be both Lord and Christ.

In Acts 3: 19 Peter says, "Repent ye therefore, and be *converted*". This word "converted" is the same as that used by the Lord in the quotation from Isaiah 6 in Matthew 13. Peter's question was, Would they hear, would they see, would they turn and be healed? Before their very eyes had been enacted a miracle bearing directly upon their case. The lame man who was healed was a living picture of Israel, both before and after their restoration through the Lord Jesus Christ. This miracle is the subject of further discussion in 4: 9-12. The word "heal" and the word "salvation" are words from the same Greek root. Peter declares that not only bodily healing, but "*the* salvation", "*the* healing" of Isaiah 6: 10 comes alone from the rejected yet risen Lord. The burden of Peter's ministry may be summed up in the words of Acts 3: 19-21:

> "Repent and be converted, that your sins may be blotted out, that the times of *refreshing* may come from the presence of the Lord, and He shall send Jesus Christ, which before was preached unto you, Whom the heavens must receive until the times of the *restoration* of all things, which God hath spoken by the mouth of all His holy prophets since the ages".

What this time of restoration is will be found by referring to the prophets of the Old Testament. All of them looked forward to that bright day. Moses is cited in verses 22, 23. All the prophets from Samuel, and those that followed after, have likewise foretold of these days. They are reminded of the *Abrahamic covenant* in verse 25, even as they had been reminded of the *Davidic covenant* in 2: 29-31, and of their national position and privilege. "Unto you *first* God, having raised up His Son Jesus, sent Him to bless you, in turning away every one of you from his iniquities" (3: 26). It will be seen that the two related events are hinged upon the repentance of Israel, viz:

(1) The times of refreshing from the presence of the Lord.
(2) The sending of Jesus the Messiah.

The words *re*-stitution, and *re*-freshing are parallel with the *re*-generation of Matthew 19: 28, and the *re*-storation of Acts 1: 6. The Abrahamic blessing to "all nations" (Acts 3: 25) awaits Israel's reception of the true Son of David. The "turning away every one of you from his iniquities" is an absolutely necessary prelude to a reign of righteousness, and a kingdom of priests (Rev. 1: 5, 6). This enables us to see the meaning of the words in Galatians 3: 10-14:

> "As many as are of the works of the law are under the *curse*".
> "Christ hath redeemed *us* from the *curse of the law* . . . that . . . the blessing of *Abraham* might come on the *Gentiles*, through Jesus Christ".

The Jew was the destined channel of blessing; through a redeemed and righteous Israel should flow out blessing to every family of the earth. Hence the need for the removal of the curse and stain from *them* before the times of refreshing could come. Israel did not repent, and those times are still future. The utter depravity of the Jews of Jerusalem was exhibited in the stoning of Stephen. He had told them the truth. As their fathers "moved with envy, sold Joseph", so had they treated the Lord. As their fathers said to Moses, "Who made thee ruler over us?" so had they said to the Lord. But Joseph and Moses were received "*the second time*", and so will it be with the Lord Jesus Christ.

At the stoning of Stephen the Lord laid hold of a young zealot, made him uneasy (for he "kicked against the pricks" before conversion), and finally made him a monument of sovereign grace. Saul or Paul received a two-fold commission. He tells us that the Lord said:

> "I have appeared unto thee *for this purpose*, to make thee a minister, and a witness (1) *both* of those things which thou *hast seen*, and (2) of those things in the which *I will* appear unto thee, delivering thee from the people (*i.e.*, the Jews), and from the Gentiles, unto whom now I send thee, to open their eyes, and to turn them from darkness to light, and from the authority of Satan unto God (*cp.* Col. 1.), that they may receive forgiveness of sins, and inheritance among them which are sanctified by faith that is in (into) Me" (Acts 26: 16-18).

We do not read of this commission, however, until Paul is a prisoner on the way to Rome.

In chapter 13 we have the opening verses of the second division of the Acts. Peter disappears from the scene, and Paul fills the remaining chapters. Peter's first miracle was anticipatory of Israel's restoration (Acts 3). Paul's first miracle was predictive of Israel's blindness, and Gentile blessing (Acts 13: 6-12). The words used of the Gentile deputy show that we are to contrast him with the blinded Jew. He "desired to *hear* the word of God"; "he *saw*" sufficient to bring about belief. Israel neither *heard* nor *saw*, as Isaiah 6: 10 testifies.

The opening and closing sections of Paul's ministry, as recorded in the Acts, are very suggestive. In the opening chapter (13) the Jew is smitten with blindness, and the Gentile believes. Moreover, the

Gentile's name is *Paulus*, and from this moment onwards the Apostle to the Gentiles is known by that name too. It will be seen by the following arrangement that the ministry of Paul, as connected with Jerusalem and the kingdom, was parenthetical to his real commission:

A a Acts 13:11. Judicial blindness foreshadowed
  b Acts 13: 12. A typical Gentile (Paulus) blessed
  c Acts 13, 14. Paul's independent ministry
} *Antioch.*—Not connected with the twelve.

B Acts 15-21. Paul's ministry in connection with *Jerusalem*, and the twelve.

A *a* Acts 28:25-27. Judicial blindness fulfilled
  b Acts 28:28. The Gentiles blessed
  c Acts 28:30, 31. Paul's independent ministry.
} *Rome.*—Not connected with the twelve.

Paul, in entire independence of Jerusalem or the twelve, fulfils his mission from Antioch (14: 27). From the commencement he was "separated". Peter opens the door of the kingdom to Jews first, and afterwards to Gentiles, as in the case of Cornelius. Paul returns from his mission and speaks of another door, "the door of faith opened to the Gentiles". Soon after this an incident occurred which led Paul to come into touch with Jerusalem and the twelve. "Certain came down from Judaea, and taught the brethren, and said, Except ye be circumcised after the manner of Moses, ye cannot be saved" (15: 1). The Apostle Paul, with Barnabas, after disputing the question, finally went up to Jerusalem about the subject, which was not only vexing the company of believers, but threatening the "truth of the gospel".

Galatians 2 tells us the inner history of that visit: "Then fourteen years after I went up again to Jerusalem with Barnabas, and took Titus with me also". The reason why Paul took Titus will be manifest presently. He declares that he went up according to a revelation, and not merely at the bidding of the assembly. Arriving at Jerusalem, he obtained private audience with the Apostles, and "laid before them that gospel which he preached among the Gentiles". The proof that the Apostles were convinced of his divine authority is evidenced by the case of Titus. "But neither Titus, who was with me, *being a Greek*, was compelled to be circumcised". Timothy, the son of a Jewess, was circumcised by Paul, but Titus was a Gentile, and to compel a Gentile, who was already saved and justified, to be circumcised was diametrically opposed to "that gospel which Paul preached"; it aimed a blow at "the *truth* of the gospel" (Gal. 2: 5), and consequently we see this champion of grace withstanding the council of Apostles at Jerusalem, and yielding subjection "no, not for an hour", that the truth of the gospel might continue with us.

So completely did Paul convince them of the truth of his mission, that the only thing that these leaders at Jerusalem ever "added" to him was that he should "remember the poor"! For some time Paul works in what might be termed "independent fellowship" with Jerusalem, always visiting the "Jew first" (Acts 9: 20; 13: 5, 14, 42, 44, 46; 14: 1; 17: 1, 2; 18: 4-6, 19; 19: 8, 9; 28: 17-31), yet ever turning more and more to the Gentiles. The last synagogue witness, and the last witness but one to the Jew as a people in Acts, is recorded in Acts 19: 8, 9. This is followed by the Apostle "separating the disciples", and gathering them together in the school of one Tyrannus.

After several trials Paul at length reaches Rome — a prisoner. Calling for the chief of the Jews (Acts 28: 17), he states his object, "For this cause, therefore, have I called for you, to see you, and to speak with you, because that for the *hope of Israel* I am bound with this chain" (verse 20). The hope of Israel reaches to the last chapter of Acts, yet according to traditional teaching the church began at Pentecost! The Jewish leaders appoint him a day, and "there came many unto his lodging, to whom he expounded and testified the kingdom of God, persuading them concerning *Jesus*, both out of the *law of Moses*, and out of the *prophets*, from morning till evening" (verse 23).

During this long conference, Paul would probably trace the history and development of the purpose of the earthly kingdom starting in Genesis at the introduction of evil, and the promise of the Deliverer. He would lead on to the call of Abraham, the promise of the land, and of the Seed. Coming further he would show the temporary character of the Mosaic economy, the failure of Israel under law, and would pass on to the covenant made with David. He would show by many infallible proofs that Jesus was the Messiah, the Seed of Abraham, the Seed of David, that the blessing of the earth was hanging, humanly speaking, upon the national repentance of Israel. He would bear this in mind as he took his hearers over the period covered by Matthew, and he would show how they had rejected their King. He would tell of the day of Pentecost, and the offer of pardon to the Jews in the land. He would dwell upon the murder of Stephen, and his own conversion, and he would lead them step by step to the very moment before them, when the wonderful exposition closed.

The result was that "some believed", and "some believed not". We too have tried, though very feebly, to follow the same line of argument. The reader has had in the preceding pages an exposition of the kingdom of God out of the law and prophets. O that it may be believed!

Immediately upon this division among the Jews, the Apostle quotes Isaiah 6. We might say, Why was this? If none had believed we might have understood it, but some believing creates a difficulty. The reason is this. "Some", signified that the *people as a whole* were not ready. It must be a national repentance. "Some" only proves that the attitude of the dispersion of Rome was similar to that of the Jews at Jerusalem. Acts 28 stands related to that book as Matthew 13 does to the first 12 chapters of that gospel. It is a climax, and a climax having nothing to do with the church, but with *Israel*. They repented not, they were not converted, they were not healed. Never again in the Apostle's epistles do we hear this word "converted"; like the word "repent" it belongs to Israel and the kingdom.

There is a remarkable and confirmatory fact regarding this quotation of Isaiah 6 here. It is not exactly like the Greek version of the Old Testament (the Septuagint), but it is a word for word repetition of the words of Christ in Matthew 13. It does not matter to us whether Paul did or did not see Matthew's Gospel. What is important is that this clinches the parallelism between the two passages. *What Matthew 13 was to the Jew in the land, Acts 28 was to the Jew of the dispersion.* Paul follows the quotation of Isaiah 6 with the words, "Be it known therefore unto you, that the salvation of God is *sent unto the Gentiles*, and that they will hear it". The opening verses of Acts 1 emphasize the kingdom of God in relation to Israel and Jerusalem; the closing verses set Israel aside and turn to the Gentiles apart from Israel.

That phase of the kingdom of God which is called the kingdom of the heavens, and which pertains to earthly dominion in relation to Israel and Palestine, passed off the scene for the time being, and another phase of the kingdom of God was ushered in. After this we read that Paul preached the kingdom of God, and taught those things which concern the Lord Jesus Christ. To the Jew it had been "Jesus"; to the Gentile it was the title found in the church epistles, "The Lord Jesus Christ". To the Jew it was from the law and prophets, even as Peter had declared (Acts 3: 24), but neither the law nor the prophets are mentioned with regard to the teaching of the new Gentile era.

Once the Jew had heard from Peter's lips that God had sent to them *first* (Acts 3: 26); Paul at Antioch showed that a difference had begun, for he said in the synagogue of Antioch, "Men and brethren, children of the stock of *Abraham*, and *whosoever* among you feareth God, to you (*i.e.* both together now) is the word of this salvation sent" (Acts 13: 26), but Acts 28 takes us to the solemn end, no longer to the Jew first, not even to the Jew and the Gentile, but to the Gentile "the salvation of God is sent", and a Jew can now get nothing from God on the ground of his being a Jew, but must come like the Gentile simply as a sinner, casting himself upon God's unconditional favour.

The Acts of the Apostles *is the history of a transitional dispensation*, which for clearness sake we call, "The Pentecostal dispensation", and the epistles written by Paul during that period have a great deal that is transitional in them, which must be divided off from the teaching of the present dispensation of the Mystery. Here at Acts 28 Israel ceases as a nation, and a people. Soon after this Jerusalem ceases as a city. The end has come. No longer "blessed with faithful Abraham"; we must, if blessed at all, be "blessed with all spiritual blessings in the heavenlies in Christ" (Eph. 1: 3).

I, as a saved Gentile, have no more to do with the Abrahamic covenant, and the kingdom unalterably promised to Israel, than I have to do with the law of Moses, and with circumcision. The great dispensational boundary is marked by the Holy Ghost. The tremendous importance of Isaiah 6 cannot be too fully recognized. The Jewish line stretches unbroken down the ages from prophet to prophet; crossing the gap between Malachi and Matthew, it runs on through each Gospel on through the entire length of the book of the Acts, and does not cease until Paul sets Israel aside in its closing verses.

With this ancient landmark set by God and sealed by the Holy Ghost palpable and evident, how can we tolerate the undispensational cry of "Back to Pentecost", and the unscriptural aping of miraculous gifts? Everything distinctly connected with the earthly kingdom abruptly ceases here. The hope of Israel reaches here and ceases. Here is the dividing line even of the use of words peculiar to the Jewish dispensation. *Abraham* and *Moses* are not mentioned in the Prison Epistles at all. *Repent* is never sounded. New terms, new teaching, a different sphere, and a different relationship are opened out before us in the next epistle written by Paul, viz., Ephesians. The Davidic throne is lost sight of, and Christ is seen "far above all . . . dominion . . . in heavenly places" (Eph. 1).

Acts 28 is the dividing line between the things pertaining to the earthly and heavenly spheres of the purpose of the ages. Acts 28 is the boundary line between those things which are connected with the promises made *since* the overthrow, and the promise made *before* the overthrow of the world. Israel figures pre-eminently in every book written during the period covered by Genesis to Acts 28. Israel is not reckoned during the intervening period covered by the epistles of the Mystery. Subsequent chapters will prove this to a demonstration. If we can but see this divine dispensational boundary, scales will fall from our eyes, tradition will be seen in its ugly reality, and, better than all, the peculiar blessedness of the church of the Mystery will be appreciated by us with a degree of fulness.

For further notes on the dispensational position of the Acts, the reader is referred to *The Apostle of the Reconciliation*, by the same Author and Publisher.

CHAPTER ELEVEN

The Pentecostal dispensation neither permanent nor continuous

In this chapter we shall examine the epistles of Paul written before Acts 28, and seek to show that there is much in them that pertains to the transitional dispensation which commenced at Pentecost and ended at Acts 28. We will first turn our attention to the epistle to the Romans, and consider the proposition that the Abrahamic covenant, and the millennial kingdom govern the theology of the Pauline epistles written before Acts 28.

We have seen the setting aside of Israel in the last chapter of Acts, and we may expect to find a change of dispensational dealings following such a momentous occurrence. Romans was the last epistle to be written during the Pentecostal dispensation. It contains doctrinal teaching which forms the basis of the truth for to-day, and it contains dispensational teaching which was true only for the time when it was written. The casual reader may not be aware of the many references there are in Romans and in these early epistles to the Jew. Below is given the number of the occurrences of the words "Jew", "Israel", "Israelite", and "Abraham" in the two sets of epistles:

Before Acts 28 (*Six epistles*).	*Occurs*	*After Acts 28.* (*Six epistles*).	*Occurs*
Jew	25 times	Jew	1 (neither Greek nor Jew).
Israel	14 ,,	Israel	2 (Eph. 2:12; 3:5).
Israelite	3 ,,	Israelite	nil.
Abraham	19 ,,	Abraham	,,
	61		3

So far the witness of the mere words used is directly in favour of the teaching that a dispensational change, in which Abrahamic blessings were set aside, took place at Acts 28. Notice how the words "the Jew first" come in Romans 1: 16 and 2: 10. This is exactly the position of Israel in the millennial kingdom, and harmonizes with Peter's words in Acts 3: 26. The prophets declare that Israel shall be "head and not tail", that the Gentiles shall call them "ministers of our God", while the same Gentiles will stand and feed the flocks, and be Israel's ploughmen. The sons of the stranger shall do their building, Gentile kings shall minister unto them, and the nation and kingdom which refuses to serve them shall perish (Isa. 60 and 61). So long as God recognized Israel as a nation, and Jerusalem as His city, so long this pre-eminence lasted. Nebuchadnezzar could not be "the head of gold" until both the kingdoms of Judah and Israel were removed from their land. Blessing for the Gentile during the Acts was through Israel.

We must be careful to distinguish what we might call *dispensational* teaching, and *foundational* teaching. In Romans 2: 28, 29 the Apostle says that circumcision profited if one kept the law, but failing that, circumcision was nullified, that he only "is a Jew who is so inwardly, and circumcision is of the heart in spirit, not in letter". The opponent, failing to see the difference between basic and dispensational standing, says, "What then is the *superiority* of the Jew, or what *profit* is there in circumcision?" The answer relates to the dispensational privileges of Israel, being "Much every way". So far, so good; within a few verses, however, the Apostle seems to give a contradictory answer, for in reply to the question, "Are we (Jews) *better* than they?" he replies, "No, in no wise!"

If we notice the words which follow these two statements (Rom. 3: 1 and 9), we shall see that the first considers Israel's *privileges*, while the second considers Israel's *sins*. The Gentile cannot be reckoned with the Jew in privilege; no nation has been so signally favoured since the world began, but the Jew could be on a level with the Gentile, for "both Jew and Gentile were sold under sin". Romans 9 furnishes us with another statement concerning Israel's pre-eminence. Romans 3 is in the midst of the great doctrinal section, hence Israel's dispensational blessings are passed over. Romans 9, however, is the commencement of the dispensational section, and Israel's privileges are set out in full.

Paul's peculiar "dispensation of the grace of God" to the Gentiles depended, humanly speaking, upon the foreseen defection of Israel, and had a gospel the terms of which did not commend it to Jewish exclusiveness. This laid him open to many bitter attacks. His sensitiveness is everywhere apparent. They said his gospel was of his own invention, hence the moment he mentions it in Romans 1: 1, 2 he adds, "which He had before promised by His prophets in the holy Scriptures"; so also Romans 3: 21. This accounts for the solemn introduction to Romans 9: "I have great heaviness, and continual sorrow in my heart for my brethren, my kinsmen, according to the flesh, (for I used to wish myself to be a cursed thing from Christ)". His own experiences taught him to pity rather than to chide. His own experiences, typical of Israel in each case, figure also in Romans 7, 10: 1-4, and 11: 1, 2. The next few verses of Romans 9 bear witness to the pre-eminent position of Israel.

Israel's dispensational privileges (Rom. 9:3-5)

A According to the flesh (*kata sarka*). Brethren
  B Who are Israelites (descendants of Jacob)
    C To whom the sonship.
      D Glory
        E Covenants
        E Legislation
      D Service
    C Promises
  B Whose are the fathers (Abraham, Isaac, Jacob)
A According to the flesh (*kata sarka*). The Messiah.

The blessings of Israel are bounded by the *flesh*; the blessings of the Body of Christ are spiritual (Eph. 1: 3, 4). The words "not of the Jews only, but also of the Gentiles" (Rom. 9: 24) echo the question of Romans 3: 29, "Is He the God of the Jews only?" statements which would have no point unless the Jew was in a pre-dominant position. In this dispensational section mention is made several times of a *remnant*. Although the whole nation had been addressed by Peter and Paul, only a remnant believed, which formed the nucleus of the "assembly of God" during the Pentecostal dispensation. To this remnant the Gentile believers were added, and while basically their standing in Christ was equal, dispensationally this Jewish remnant had preference.

> "Isaiah also crieth concerning Israel, Though the number of Israel be as the sand of the sea, the *remnant* shall be saved . . . Except the Lord of Hosts had left us a *Seed*, we had been as Sodom, and been made like unto Gomorrha" (Rom. 9: 27, 29).
>
> "Isaiah is very bold (Paul seemed to rejoice to find a kindred spirit), and saith, I was found of them that sought Me not,I was made manifest unto them that asked not for Me, but to Israel He saith, All day long I have stretched out My hands to a disobedient and gainsaying people" (Rom. 10: 20, 21).

This gives the state of affairs during the Pentecostal period. The Jew stubbornly rebelling, the Gentile believers gradually increasing, and the preparation for the great upheaval growing. "Israel hath not obtained that which he seeketh for (*see* Rom. 10: 1-4), but the election hath obtained it, and the rest were blinded" (hardened) (11: 7). When

Romans was written, it was true to say, "even so *now* there has been a remnant according to the election of grace" (11: 5). This is *not* true NOW, for there is no Jewish remnant. In the present dispensation the Jew is not, and the Gentile is not, either basically or dispensationally. It is this Jewish remnant that is everywhere prominent in the earlier epistles of Paul. To a large extent the Jewish remnant never left the traditions of their fathers, nor the law of Moses. Those who came under the direct ministry of Paul may have seen the truth more clearly than the others. Over twenty years after Pentecost it could be said, "Thou seest, brother, how many *myriads* of Jews there are which believe, and they are all *zealous of the law*!" (Acts 21: 20, 21). It was to these that *Hebrews* was written, seeking to show the transitional and temporary character of the law of Moses, and to emphasize the unalterable covenant made with Abraham 430 years before the law, and the blessed consummation under the New Covenant. Hebrews might have led some out to embrace the truth of the Mystery, but the Mystery itself does not form a part of its teaching.

Romans 11 tells the Gentile believer that for any share he may have in the foretaste of millennial blessings, he had it as a "wild olive grafted in contrary to nature", that the "root bare him", and not that he bare the root. He was warned concerning a possible cutting off, although comforted with the previous teaching that "nothing could separate him from the love of God in Christ Jesus our Lord" (Rom. 8). The time for the cutting down of the olive tree was seen by Paul to be approaching nearer and nearer. He tells us, however, that God's purposes are by no means thwarted. Israel shall yet be righteous, even though but a remnant believed during the transitional period:

> "For the gifts and calling of God are not subject to a change of mind; for as indeed ye were formerly not believing in God, but now have been objects of mercy, by reason of the unbelief of others (Jews), so they too have now become unbelieving, that they may also obtain mercy by reason of the mercy shown to you" (Rom. 11: 29-31).

Here is a mystery of grace and magnificent mercy beyond our wildest dreams. Truly our God *delighteth* in mercy. The Jews gave occasion for greater mercy by their unbelief; the Gentiles by their faith. The promises which we have seen in our studies are yet to be fulfilled. God hath *not* cast away His foreknown people. All Israel shall yet be saved, ungodliness shall be turned away from Jacob. "As regards the gospel, they are enemies on your (Gentiles) account, but as regards the election, *beloved because of the fathers*" (11: 28). Here are God's own words. Here are the words of the One Who is working out His mighty purpose; "blinded", "hardened", "broken off", "scattered", wanderers for centuries, yet "*beloved* because of the fathers". They were not forgotten, "for God hath shut up *all* in unbelief"? Why? Orthodoxy would say, In order to pour out upon them His wrath, but God says, "That He might show mercy upon *all*", and the "all" is the same in each case. No wonder, in such a sea of grace, the Apostle should feel out of his depth. It was beyond him, he could not trace it out, but he rejoiced in it, and added his hearty *Amen*.

> "O the depth of the riches (*riches*),
> Both of the wisdom (*wisdom*),
> And knowledge of God (*knowledge*);
> How unsearchable are His judgments (*unsearchable*),
> And his ways past finding out (*untraceable*)
> For who hath known the mind of the Lord (*knowledge*),
> Or who hath been His counsellor (*wisdom*),
> Or who first gave to Him and it shall be recompensed unto him again (*riches*)?
>
> For *of* Him, and *through* Him, and *to* Him are all things, *to* Whom be glory for ever and ever, Amen" (Rom 11:33-36).

Galatians 3 is parallel to Romans 11 so far as dispensational teaching is concerned. In Romans 11 the figure used is the olive tree, whereas in Galatians 3 Abraham is named instead. The "gospel" was proclaimed to Abraham, but the "mystery" was not. We read in

3:9. "Blessed with faithful Abraham".
3:14. "The blessing of Abraham might come on the Gentiles".
3:29. "If ye are Christ's, then are ye Abraham's seed, and heirs according to the promise".
4:26, 27. "Jerusalem which is above is free, which is the mother of us all".

Abraham, the father of many nations; Jerusalem, the mother of those who then believed. The new Jerusalem was a part of Abraham's faith (Heb. 11: 14-16); after Acts 28 the heavenly city which comes down from God out of heaven is no longer before us; we are now "citizens who have a citizenship *in heaven*" (Phil. 3: 20), and our blessings are "in the heavenlies" (Eph. 1: 3), still "in Christ", but not "with Abraham".

If the dispensational position was Abrahamic in character and millennial in hope, we shall expect to find something of this in the nature of the Second Coming of Christ in these epistles. For this we turn to 1 and 2 Thessalonians and 1 and 2 Corinthians; Romans and Galatians deal with basic and dispensational matters, but these other epistles have a good deal to tell us concerning the hope that was before the believer during the Acts of the Apostles. Peter's words in Acts 3: 19-21 give the key to the nature of this hope, and we quote it again, this time using the Revised Version:

> "Repent ye therefore, and turn to the Lord, that your sins may be blotted out, that so there may come the times of refreshing from the presence of the Lord, and that He may *send the Messiah*, Who hath been appointed for you, even *Jesus*, whom the heavens must receive until the times of *restoration* of all things, whereof God spake by the mouth of His holy prophets *since* the ages".

It was for this that the believers at Thessalonica waited. Peter had said "Repent, and turn to the Lord", and in 1 Thessalonians 1: 9, 10 we read, "Ye turned to God from idols . . . to wait for His Son from heaven". Humanly speaking, the Lord's return was hanging upon Israel's repentance, consequently until it was clear that Israel was set aside, believers could hope that this restoration and coming would take place during their own times. As 1 Thessalonians was the first epistle penned by Paul, he could quite truthfully say, "we which are alive", including himself, or he could pray that these believers might be preserved alive until that blessed event, as recorded in 1 Thessalonians 5: 23. In the 2nd epistle to the Thessalonians we have mention of the "tribulation", "anti-christ", "the day of the Lord", and "taking vengeance", all of which are as essentially connected with Israel as they are severed from the hope of the One Body.

The following arrangement of the references to the Lord's return in these epistles may be useful to the student who desires to go further into this subject. The passages in 1 Thessalonians mostly give the believers' view, whereas the 2nd epistle gives more prominence to the judgment aspect.

1 Thessalonians 1:10-5:23

A 1:10. Waiting for God's Son from heaven (Acts 3:19, 21)
  B 2:19. The servants' joy at the Lord's coming (*Our*)
    C 3:13. The Lord coming with holy ones (angels) to His people
    C 4:15, 16. The Lord coming with the archangel for His people
  B 5:2, 3. The world's sorrow at the Lord's coming (*They*)
A 5:23. Prayer that believers may be preserved until the coming of God's Son from Heaven.

2 Thessalonians 1:7-2:8

A 1:7, 8. Revealed in flaming fire taking vengeance
  B 1:10. When He shall have come to be glorified
    C 2:1. The coming of our Lord, and our gathering together unto Him
  B 2:2. The day of the Lord (when He shall come to judge)
A 2:8. Destruction with the brightness of His coming.

In 1 Corinthians 11: 26 we have the well-known words, "As often as ye eat this bread and drink this cup, ye do shew the Lord's death *till He come*". When these words were addressed to the Corinthians the special revelation of Ephesians, Philippians and Colossians was unknown. The only *coming* that was known to them was that preached by Peter (Acts 3: 19, 21), by Paul (1 Thess.), by the Lord Jesus (Matt. 24) and the Old Testament prophets. It was the "hope of Israel" right through the Pentecostal dispensation. The dividing line between the hope of Israel and the hope of the Body is in Acts 28. Before Acts 28 the *parousia* is everywhere before us, Paul never using the term afterwards in relation to the Lord Jesus at all.

To many students the word *parousia* needs no explanation, but for the sake of clearness we will say that it is a word literally meaning "presence", or "being beside", and is used in reference to the coming of the Lord in the Pentecostal period, and is synonymous with the hope of Israel. In Matthew 24 the word comes four times, viz:

> "What shall be the sign of Thy *parousia*, and of the end of the age" (verse 3).
>
> "For as the lightning cometh out of the East and shineth even unto the West, so shall also the *parousia* of the Son of man be" (verse 27).
>
> "But as the days of Noah were, so shall also the *parousia* of the Son of man be" (verse 37).
>
> "Until the flood came and took them all away, so shall also the *parousia* of the Son of man be" (verse 39).

Here we have the first four occurrences of the word *parousia* in Scripture. It is a canon of interpretation, which will stand a rigorous test, that the first occurrence of a word gives its scriptural value. If we grant this, the *parousia* is essentially stamped with the impress of the earthly kingdom. Further, "the sign of the *parousia*" is *dated* for us; at least, we know that it will not be *before* the great tribulation:

> "*Immediately after* the tribulation of those days shall the sun be darkened, and the moon shall not give her light . . . then shall appear the *sign* of the Son of man in heaven, and then shall all the tribes of the land mourn, and they shall see the Son of man coming in the clouds of heaven, with power and great glory" (Matt. 24: 29, 30).

The reader has only to refer to Acts 2: 17-21 and 3: 19-21 to see that this is identical with Pentecostal hopes. 1 Thessalonians 2: 19; 3: 13; 4: 15; 5: 23; 2 Thessalonians 2: 1, 8 are the references to this same coming in the Thessalonian epistles. 1 Thessalonians 4: 16 mentions "*the* archangel", who is *Michael*, and who is always connected with *Israel* (*cp.* Dan. 10, 12; Jude 9).

The word *parousia* is used of antichrist as well as of the Lord, for Satan travesties truth. 2 Thessalonians 2: 9: "Whose *parousia* is after the working of Satan, with all power, and signs, and lying wonders". This forges another link with Acts 2 and 3. A reference to Hebrews 2: 4 will show that the miraculous gifts of Pentecost are spoken of under the very same terms as these false miracles of satanic origin. Just as the *parousia* of the true Messiah is in direct connection with the signs and wonders of Acts 2, so the *parousia* of the false messiah will be preceded by a display of miraculous gifts also. Peter and James, who wrote to the dispersion of Israel, and not to Gentile believers, or the church of the Mystery, have several references to the *parousia*, viz., James 5: 7, 8; 2 Peter 1: 16; 3: 4-12.

The first reference in Peter links the *parousia* with the earthly kingdom, as we have already seen when considering the Transfiguration. The references in the third chapter are interesting because they refer so definitely to the special teaching of Paul's epistles. That this coming of Christ was not part of a secret hidden since the age-times is evident by the fact that "scoffers" were saying, "Where is the promise of His *parousia*?" Peter would feel this keenly, for he had declared that God would "send the Messiah". Israel had not fulfilled the conditions, however, and had been set aside. Peter confesses that he did not know how to account for this. He is quite sure that "the Lord is not slack concerning His promise" — He is still waiting for Israel to come to repentance — but to get a really full explanation Peter refers his readers to the writings of Paul. He tells them, in reference to the long delay:

> "To account the longsuffering of our Lord as salvation, even as our beloved brother Paul also, according to the wisdom given unto him, hath written unto you; as also in all his epistles, speaking in them of these things" (2 Peter 3: 15, 16).

This gap in the working out of the divine purposes with Israel is filled by the dispensation of the Mystery revealed to Paul. Of this Paul speaks in Colossians 1: 25, 26, where he speaks of the commission which "filled up the Word of God, even the Mystery". Peter *did* know the truth concerning the *parousia*, but he did *not* understand a great deal of the teaching given to Paul, yet we are asked to believe that, although the *parousia never once* figures in the epistles of the Mystery, nevertheless that is the hope of the Body of Christ! The *parousia*, mentioned again in 1 Corinthians 15: 22, 23, is connected with Isaiah 24, 25 by the words of verse 54. "When" this takes place, "then" Isaiah 25: 8, 9 will be fulfilled, but Isaiah 25 has no word about the secret hidden by God. 1 John 2: 28 is the last reference to this coming in the New Testament.

We have considered the teaching of Matthew, 2 Peter, James, 1 and 2 Thessalonians, and 1 Corinthians, Scriptures which were either written *about* and *for* the Jew, or before the dispensation of the Mystery began. We must turn to Paul's epistles written after Acts 28 if we would find his teaching *for us* about the *parousia*. We read through Ephesians, Philippians, Colossians, 1 and 2 Timothy, and Titus, but we find *no mention* of it. The Scriptures concerning the dispensation of the grace of God to the Gentiles have no place in them for the hope of Israel, the *parousia*. Chronologically 1 Corinthians 15 is the last reference that Paul makes to it, and the words "till He come" must be interpreted by this fact. The coming connected with the Lord's Supper was the *parousia*, the hope of Israel, the coming *after* the tribulation. When the hope of the earthly kingdom was set aside, everything connected therewith was set aside also. If it is to be repeated or perpetuated in the present interval, we shall find it in the Scriptures written *for us* and *about us*, otherwise we must leave it alone.

Passing from the examination of the Second Coming, we take up another important feature connected with the kingdom and with Israel, that is, "spiritual gifts". We find miraculous powers connected with the gospel of the kingdom in Matthew 10. We find miraculous powers given as a confirmation of the preaching in Acts. We find miraculous powers *right up to the last chapter of Acts*, but we do not find them in the epistles of the Mystery. In 1 Corinthians 1: 5-7 we read:

> "In everything ye are enriched by Him, in all utterance, and in all knowledge, even as the testimony of Christ was confirmed in you, so that ye come behind in no gift, waiting for the revelation of the Lord Jesus Christ".

"Utterance" and "knowledge" are explained by the word "gift" as being special in character. This enrichment by the bestowal of *gifts* was "according as the witness of Christ was *confirmed* in you". This is parallel with Mark 16: 17-20:

> "These signs shall follow ... speak with tongues ... take up serpents ... drink deadly things unhurt ... lay hands upon sick and they shall recover ... and they went forth and ... preached everywhere, the Lord working with them, and *confirming* the word with signs following".

Paul had these powers right to the end of Acts (*see* Acts 28: 3-6, 8, 9). There are many who lay their hands on the sick, and who think they speak with tongues, but we have yet to meet the one who will venture the "serpent" and the "poison" tests, yet if Matthew, Mark and Acts are truth for the time, if the miraculous gifts of 1 Corinthians 12 are still claimed, why cannot they be thus substantiated? The answer is, the claim is *false*. The cessation of gifts synchronizes with the end of the Pentecostal dispensation in Acts 28, and we are under no restraint to attempt to invent some plausible reason for their cessation, for it is explained for us by the Word.

Hebrews 2: 3, 4 bears the same witness as 1 Corinthians 1: 5-7 and Mark 16, and links these gifts to the "world to come" *i.e.*, the millennial kingdom, as is shewn by the context. The "gift of tongues" which continually comes forward in the revivals of the present day, is according to 1 Corinthians 14: 21, 22 a sign to Israel; as it is written in Isaiah 28: 11, "to provoke to jealousy" (*cp.* Rom. 10: 19; 11: 14). Israel, instead of being provoked to emulation, "resisted the Holy Spirit" (Acts 7). The blessings to the Gentiles provoked their anger, "they filled up their sins" (1 Thess. 2: 16), and were scattered, and with their scattering the "gifts" vanished also.

In 1 Corinthians 12, 13 and 14 we have instruction as to the *origin, object, use, and cessation* of spiritual gifts. Some teach that these gifts were taken from the church in chastisement, and that we should humbly seek for their return. We do believe that a terrible departure from truth marked these early days, and alas has continued, but we find no warrant for the fancied reason of the cessation of gifts. "Back to Pentecost!" "Back to 1 Corinthians 12!" are as unscriptural, undispensational, and destructive of truth as the Judaizer's cry, "Back to Moses and legalism!" No one can read 1 Corinthians 12 from the first verse onward without seeing that the whole passage deals with "spiritual gifts". Once these Corinthians were Gentiles led away with idolatry (verse 2), which is connected with *demons* (10: 19-21). Spirit influences, other than the operation of the Spirit of God, were at work, hence the need to discriminate, to "try the spirits whether they are of God". "No man speaking by the Spirit of *God* saith Jesus is anathema", and no man speaking under the influence of an evil spirit could say "Lord Jesus". This divine test is parallel with that of 1 John 4: 1-3.

After having seen that there were spiritual gifts good and bad, they were next to see that the gifts of the Spirit of God were in wonderful variety, viz.:

> "There are diversities of *gifts*, but the same *Spirit*; and there are diversities of *administrations*, but the same *Lord*; and there are diversities of *workings*, but the same *God*, Who worketh all things in all" (1 Cor. 12: 4-6).

In verses 8-11 we have a list of the "gifts of the Spirit". No other name but the "*Spirit*" occurs here. "All these energizeth that one and the self-same Spirit, dividing to every man severally as *He* will". In verse 18 we read that "*God* hath set the members each one of them in the body as it hath pleased Him"; and in verse 28, "God hath set some in the church, first apostles, secondly prophets, thirdly teachers, then miracles", etc. In verses 8-11 we have the gifts of the *Spirit*, in 18 and 28 we have some of the workings of *God*, but where are the administrations of the *Lord*?

The term "administration" is, in the original, *diakonia*, from which we get the words "deacon" and "minister". If we turn to Ephesians 4: 7-13 we shall read of the gifts of Christ, "He gave some, apostles; and some, prophets; and some, evangelists; and some, pastors and teachers". Now let us compare this with 1 Corinthians 12: 28.

1 Corinthians 12:28		*Ephesians 4:11*
Firstly.	Apostles.	Apostles.
Secondly.	Prophets.	Prophets.
Thirdly.	Teachers.	Evangelists.
		Pastors and Teachers.

The next verse in Ephesians 4 goes on to say, "for the perfecting of the saints, unto a work of ministry". "Ministry" is *diakonia*, the same word that is translated "administration" in 1 Corinthians 12. Here we have the "diversities of administrations of the one Lord" (For the use of the word *diakonia* and *diakonos, see* Phil. 1:1; 1 Tim. 3:8, 12; Eph. 6:21; Col. 1: 7, 23, 25; 4: 17; Eph. 3: 2, 9; 1 Tim. 1: 12). 2 Timothy 4: 5 says, "Do the work of an *evangelist*, the ministry (*diakonia*) that is thine fulfil". Thus we distinguish between the "gifts" of the Pentecostal period, and the present. The administrations of the Lord were not put into operation until after Acts 28. Turning back again to 1 Corinthians 12, we find that verse 12 follows the list of the Spirit's gifts with an illustration:

> "For as truly as the body is *one*, and hath *many* members, and *all* the members of the one body, being *many*, are *one* body, so also is the Christ ... for the body is not *one* member, but *many*".

Verses 15-26 give a detailed and graphic analogy between the parts of a human body, and the various diversities, yet withal unity, of the saints. We say advisedly "human body", as it is illustrative of a unity of diversities. It cannot be the "one body" of Ephesians, for that had not been revealed, neither is there in that one Body members who are "the *ear*, the *eye*, or the *nose*", all of which belong to the head; neither are some members of the body of Christ "uncomely". The opening words of 1 Corinthians 12 say nothing about the Mystery of the one Body; they say, "concerning *spiritual* gifts, brethren, I would not have you ignorant". We are to learn about "spiritual gifts", their diversity, origin and use. We have not to learn anything about that which was unrevealed. Paul, viewing the gathering at Corinth possessed of many and varied gifts, uses the illustration of the human body to teach them all to remember their place, to avoid pride, and to honour those whose gift was apparently not so great or important as their own.

Verse 27 has caused a great deal of controversy, the majority believing that this is the same as the one Body of Ephesians. The verse reads, "But ye are literally body of Christ, and members partially". It is not *the* Body; it is simply "body", the absence of the article showing us that a description (not a definition) is intended. The word "partially", or "in part", is a translation of two Greek words, *ek merous*, and they occur together nowhere else except in 1 Corinthians 13. 1 Corinthians 12 and 13 are parts of a connected argument, and we may reasonably expect that a peculiar word occurring in both chapters will bear the same meaning, and throw light upon each other. Turning to 1 Corinthians 13: 9-12:

> "For we know *in part*, and we prophecy *in part*, but when that which is perfect has come, then that which *is in part* shall be done away. When I was a child, I spake as a child, I thought as a child, I reasoned as a child; now that I am become a man, I have done away with childish things. For now we see in a mirror, enigmatically (darkly, obscurely), but then face to face; now I know *in part*, but then shall I know fully, even as also I have been fully known".

The reference to the "enigma" looks back to Numbers 12: 8, where the Septuagint uses the same word as here. The word means "to hint obscurely". 1 Corinthians 2: 6, 7 gives "hints" of the impending change, but only "perfect" or "full grown" ones, as contrasted with "babes" (1 Cor. 3: 1, and 13: 10, 11), could receive the teaching. During the Pentecostal period, while the things of Israel and the kingdom were still in evidence, the Apostle Paul could only speak of the coming dispensation in "hints" to those of a kindred spirit with himself. Referring to the much vaunted spiritual gifts, he compared them to babyhood, saying, "We know *partially*, we prophecy *partially*", but when the dispensation of babyhood gives place to "the perfect man" (Eph. 4), then that which is *partial* will be done away. The words rendered "fail", "vanish away" in verse 8, "done away" in verse 10, and "put away" in verse 11, are all the same in the original — *katargeo*. In 2 Corinthians 3: 7, 11, 13, 14 the same word is used of the

Old Covenant. In 1 Corinthians 15: 24, 26; 2 Timothy 1: 10; and Hebrews 2: 14 it is used of death. It will be seen, therefore, that it is a very strong word. The argument of chapter 13 is complete. "Gifts" are compared to "childish things", and are to be "done away". "Gifts" are termed "partial" as compared with the "fulness" of the present dispensation — "that which is perfect".

Looking back to 1 Corinthians 12: 27 we find right in the midst of a passage dealing with spiritual gifts, the words "Ye are body of Christ, and members *partially*", and further on we read that that which is *partial* is to pass away when that which is *perfect* has come. The Corinthian assembly was as babyhood is to manhood, when compared with the dispensation of the Mystery. Now we have come "to the full knowledge of the Son of God, unto a *perfect* (full grown) man, unto the measure of the stature of the *fulness* of Christ, that we may be no longer babes" (Eph. 4: 12-14). Here we have maturity, here we reach full knowledge. That which is perfect has come, and partial things vanish away. If this be so, how foolish it is for us to ignore our high calling, and while confessing that we have no gifts like those of 1 Corinthians 12, to cling still to the empty shell of that which is partial, when we might be enjoying the fulness.

Miraculous gifts were bestowed during the period when the possibility of Israel's repentance made the setting up of the millennial kingdom a possibility. Hence many "tasted of the powers of the age to come" (Heb. 6), but Acts 28 has come, and with it the present dispensation where the gifts find no place. "Back to Pentecost" is back to the *nursery*: it is the sorry spectacle of the full-grown man content with the toys and occupations of the infant. The church at Corinth was essentially associated with spiritual gifts. It is idle to claim 1 Corinthians 12: 27, while we ignore the context. In that church God set *one* order of ministry (1 Cor. 12: 28), including miraculous gifts. In the present period Christ has given *another* order (Eph. 4), with no miraculous gifts.

Up to Acts 28 Paul had the power of healing the sick; afterwards he grieves over the sickness of Epaphroditus, but does not lay his hands upon him. He *advises* Timothy what to do for his oft infirmities, for it would have been mockery to have sent a handkerchief then. Trophimus is left sick. *None* are healed by him. During the Pentecostal dispensation, a period when God stretched forth His hand to a disobedient and gainsaying people, "signs and wonders" abounded, but all that has gone now. Faith without sight, hope without sign, love without token, has taken its place. Fulness has come, and the present distinctive dispensation has been inaugurated. There are many who confuse the baptism of the Spirit as found in Acts with that of Ephesians. Acts 1: 5 and 11: 14-16 settle the meaning of the expression in the Acts.

> "They began to *speak* with other tongues" (Acts 2: 1-4).
> "Simon *saw* . . . the holy spirit was given" (Acts 8: 18).
> "They *heard* them speak with tongues" (Acts 10: 44-46).
> "They *spake* with tongues" (Acts 19: 6).

See also 1 Corinthians 12: 1-27. Is this the record of the epistles to the Ephesians, Philippians, Colossians? How much *seeing* and *hearing* is there connected with the "one baptism" of Ephesians 4? Again, consider the subject of ministry. The instructions given to the Corinthians before Acts 28 and to Timothy after Acts 28 concerning ministry are as different as can well be.

1 Corinthians	*1 Timothy and Titus*
"Every man" possessed of a spiritual gift (12:7-11). "Every one of you hath a psalm, hath a doctrine, hath a tongue, hath a revelation, hath an interpretation" (14:26). "Let the prophets speak two or three" (14:29).	"An overseer must be blameless, the husband of one wife, vigilant, sober, of good behaviour, given to hospitality, apt to teach . . . Likewise the deacons" (1 Tim 3:1-13; Titus 1:5-14).

In Corinthians it is *all* gifts; in Timothy it is *no* gifts. 1 Corinthians 12-14 is God's truth, but wrested from its true setting it is utterly useless, nay false, as a guide for ministry to-day. All this confusion comes through failing rightly to divide the Word of truth.

We conclude this chapter with a list of words, the study of which will but confirm the distinction which must be drawn between the two sets of Paul's epistles.

The epistles of Paul written before Acts 28 do not contain the truth of the Mystery of the One Body. There is much contained therein which links them to the Abrahamic covenant, and the kingdom of Israel. The Scriptures written *for us* and *about us*, which teach us our standing, our duties, our hopes, and our dispensational position, are those written after the people of Israel were set aside.

		Before Acts 28	*After Acts 28*	
		1 & 2 Thess., 1 & 2 Cor., Gal., Rom.	*Eph., Phil., Col.*	*1 & 2 Tim., Titus.*
		Times	*Times*	*Times*
Jew		25	1	—
Israel		14	2	—
Israelite		3	—	—
Abraham		19	—	—
Moses		9	—	—
To baptise		12	—	—
Baptism (*baptisma*)		1	2	—
Lord's Supper		1	—	—
The loaf in connection with the Lord's Supper		7	—	—
The cup in connection with the Lord's Supper		7	—	—
Gifts (*charisma, i.e.,* gifts of the Spirit)		9	—	2
Miracles		4	—	—
Tongues		22	—	—
Interpret, interpretation, interpreter	*As gifts*	7	—	—
Healing	*As gifts*	3	—	—
Prophesying	*As gifts*	13	—	—
Prophecy	*As gifts*	4	—	2
To circumcise		8	1	—
Circumcision		23	6	—
Parousia (of the Lord)		6	—	—

CHAPTER TWELVE

The dispensation of the Mystery

The reader will remember that we have traced the purpose of God, as pertaining to the millennial kingdom and Israel, from Genesis to the end of the Acts. We found perfect continuity existing between the close of the Old Testament, and the opening of the New. Matthew continued Malachi, and Acts continued Matthew. The time-honoured tradition that the "church" (*i.e.*, the church of the Mystery) is found in Matthew or Acts finds no warrant from Scripture. This continuity will be more apparent when we consider the fact that the Lord used different messengers, who had each one his own particular message. Hebrews 1: 1, 2 gives us the record of two such messengers:

> "God, Who at sundry times and in divers manners spake in time past unto the fathers by the prophets, hath in these last days spoken unto us by His Son".

The first messengers are the "prophets", and they "spake unto the fathers". The duration of their ministry is co-extensive with the earthly kingdom purposes. Just as the kingdom is said to have been prepared since the foundation or overthrow of the world (Matt. 25), so Luke 11: 50 speaks of the prophets as having been persecuted since the foundation or overthrow of the world. Prophets are mentioned 87 times in the four Gospels, whereas when we come to the epistles of the Mystery (Eph., Phil., Col., 1 and 2 Tim. and Titus) the word occurs but four times, once referring to the Cretan prophet, who was not a prophet of God, while the other references (which occur in Ephesians) speak not of the prophets of the Old Testament, but of the new order given by the ascended Christ (Eph. 2: 20; 4: 11).

Matthew 11: 13 tells us that "all the prophets and the law prophesied until John", and John became the forerunner of the Lord Jesus, of Whom the Apostle speaks in Hebrews 1: 2. It has already been pointed out that the Lord took up the same message as that of John the Baptist, "the prophet of the Highest" (Luke 1: 76). Both John and the Lord cried, "Repent, for the kingdom of the heavens is at hand" (Matt.

3: 2; 4: 17). Thus we see that the ministry of the Son of God was a *continuation* of the ministry of the prophets, who spake unto the fathers. This is clearly taught in Romans 15: 8, where we have the inspired statement concerning the ministry of the Son: "Now I say that Jesus Christ was a *minister of the circumcision* for the truth of God, to confirm the promises made unto the fathers". Here it will be seen that the ministry of Christ was limited to the circumcision, and that it was confirmatory in character. He came not so much to open up new truth, as to confirm the old. After the people of Israel had rejected Him in the land, and He had died and had risen again, a further witness was inaugurated by the Holy Spirit at Pentecost. This is referred to in Hebrews 2: 3, 4:

> "How shall we escape, if we neglect so great salvation; which at the first began to be spoken by the Lord, and was *confirmed* unto us by them that heard Him, God also bearing them witness, both with signs and wonders, and with divers miracles, and gifts of holy spirit (power from on high), according to His own will".

Thus the ministry of the twelve in the Acts of the Apostles, with its accompanying signs and miracles, was confirmatory of the truth as proclaimed by the Lord Jesus while on earth. The emphasis upon this one element of "confirmation" may be fully seen in Mark 16: 19, 20:

> "So then after the Lord had spoken unto them, He was received up into heaven, and sat on the right hand of God; and they went forth and preached everywhere, the Lord working with them, and *confirming* the word with signs following".

The "signs and miraculous gifts" of 1 Corinthians 12-14 were given with the same purpose, as may be seen by referring to 1 Corinthians 1: 5-7:

> "That in everything ye are enriched by Him, in all utterance, and in all knowledge; even as the testimony of Christ was *confirmed* in you. So that ye come behind in no gift, waiting for the revelation of our Lord Jesus Christ".

The Son confirmed the witness of the prophets (Rom. 15: 8). The twelve in the Acts confirmed the witness of the Son (Heb. 2: 3, 4). This was carried out by the ascended Lord, who confirmed the word with signs following (Mark 16: 19, 20), and throughout the period covered by the Acts of the Apostles individual members of the assemblies, equally with the chosen witnesses, had the testimony of Christ confirmed in them by the kingdom gifts received (1 Cor. 1: 5-7). At the end of Acts we find these gifts in operation. Paul, shipwrecked on the island of Melita, fulfils Mark 16: 18, and Acts 28: 3-6 records how the Apostle could "take up serpents". The healing of the father of Publius (verse 8) fulfilled the words "they shall lay hands on the sick, and they shall recover". In verse 20 Paul says, "for the hope of Israel I am bound with this chain". When the hope of Israel passed from view at verses 25-28, and Paul became the "prisoner of Jesus Christ for *you Gentiles*" (Eph. 3: 1), the confirmatory signs and wonders ceased. Paul did not send a handkerchief to Timothy to cure him (1 Tim. 5: 23), although this would have been sufficient during the Pentecostal period (Acts 19: 12); he did not lay hands upon Epaphroditus, although his sickness caused Paul such great sorrow.

The Lord Jesus, in His last discourse to His disciples, told them plainly that He had only given them a portion of the truth of God, and that there was truth yet to be revealed which could not then be uttered, one reason being that the Apostles could not then bear it, another being that it was truth relative to an aspect of the purpose of God other than the kingdom of the heavens, and still further, that it had relation to events which had not as yet happened. Could the gospel of Ephesians the glorious fact that the believer has "died with Christ, been buried with Him, been raised with Him, and is *seated in the heavenlies with Him*" be proclaimed until Christ Himself had died, been buried, raised, and seated at God's right hand? Thus it was that the Lord Jesus said to His disciples:

> "I have yet many things to say unto you, but ye cannot bear them now, howbeit when He, the Spirit of the truth, is come, He will guide you into all the truth, for He shall not speak from Himself, but whatsoever He shall hear, that shall He speak, and He shall show you things to come. He shall glorify Me, for He shall receive of Mine, and shall shew it unto you" (John 16: 12-14).

The Lord Jesus told them a portion of the witness of the Spirit, but omitted that special revelation of "all truth", which is now made known in the epistles of the Mystery.

> "And when He is come He will convict the world of sin, and of righteousness, and of judgment.

(1) Of sin, because they are not believing in Me.	(*Peter's* ministry).
(2) Of righteousness, because I go to My Father.	(*Paul's* first ministry during Acts).
(3) Of judgment, because the prince of this world hath been judged".	(*Future* ministry during time of antichrist).

The Lord gives no details concerning that witness of the Spirit of which He says, "He shall glorify Me"; that awaits the ministry of the Apostle Paul. This ministry is indicated in Acts 26: 16-18, where Paul, relating to king Agrippa the circumstances of his conversion, gives a fuller account of the Lord's words to him than it was expedient to record in the earlier chapters of the Acts. Now that the Apostle had finished the first half of his ministry, and is *already a prisoner on the way to Rome*, he gives an indication of the second section of his commission, which fulfils the promise of John 16: 13, 14. In answer to his enquiry, "Who art Thou, Lord?" the reply was:

> "I am Jesus, whom thou persecutest; but rise, and stand upon thy feet, for I have appeared unto thee for this purpose, to make thee a minister and a witness *both* of these things which thou *hast seen*, and of those things in the which *I will appear unto thee*; delivering thee from the people, and from the Gentiles (the Jews at Jerusalem, and the Romans), unto whom now I send thee (*apostello*).
>
> To open their eyes (Eph. 1: 18),
> To turn them from darkness to light (Col. 1: 13),
> From the authority of Satan unto God (Eph. 2: 1-3),
> That they may receive forgiveness of sins (Eph. 1:7),
> An inheritance among them which are sanctified (Eph. 1: 11; Col. 1: 12),
> By the faith which is unto Me" (Eph. 1: 15; Phil. 3: 9; Col. 2: 5; 1 Tim. 3: 13; 2 Tim. 3: 15).

This definition of Paul's future ministry is here for the *first time* given with clearness. He did not commence with this ministry, for he had no commission to do so. What he did is explained in verse 20: he witnessed in Damascus, Judaea, Jerusalem, and among the Gentiles "that they should repent and turn to God, and do works meet for repentance", and furthermore, "saying none other things than those which the prophets and Moses did say should come" (verse 22). This is in entire harmony with the Apostle's words in Acts 20 on the eve of his captivity. In verses 17-21 he reminds the Ephesians how he had taught them, "testifying both to the Jews and to the Greeks, repentance toward God, and faith toward our Lord Jesus Christ". But a change was imminent; he would see their face no more. Bonds and imprisonment lay before him; he was about to enter upon the second phase of his ministry; so he continues in verse 24:

> "None of these things move me, neither count I my life dear unto myself, so that I might finish my course with joy (2 Tim. 4: 7), and the ministry which I have received of the Lord Jesus, to testify the gospel of the grace of God" (*i.e.* Acts 26: 18).

Thus we find that the Apostle Paul's second ministry was severed from his first ministry by his Roman imprisonment, the cessation of gifts, the definite leaving of Israel, and turning to the Gentiles apart from Israel. This first ministry, with its miraculous accompaniments, terminated in Acts 28: 24-28. From that point he ceased to be bound for the hope of Israel, and became the prisoner of Jesus Christ for "you Gentiles", and an ambassador in bonds for the Mystery of the gospel.

The claim to the exclusive apostleship of the dispensation of the Mystery is not only made by Paul in Ephesians 3: 1-10, but repeated in Colossians 1: 24-26. Not only does he tell us that his ministry is connected with a purpose from "before the overthrow of the world", but he further says that it is connected with a promise made before the "age-times". In order that the reader may be enabled to see clearly the repeated claim of the Apostle, we will place side by side a translation of two passages where the expression "age-times" occurs:

Titus 1: 1-3

"Paul, a servant of God, but an apostle of Jesus Christ, according to the faith of God's elect, and the knowledge of the truth which is according to godliness, upon hope of eternal life, which God, who cannot lie, promised before *age-times*, but hath manifested in His *own peculiar* seasons His Word by means of the *heralding*, wherewith I am entrusted, according to the commandment of our Saviour God".

2 Timothy 1: 9-11

"Who hath saved us, and called us with an holy calling, not according to our works, but according to His *own peculiar* purpose and grace, which was given to us in Christ Jesus before *age-times*, but hath now been made manifest by the appearing of our Saviour Jesus Christ, who hath abolished death, but hath shed light on immortal life through the gospel whereunto I have been appointed a *herald*, and apostle, and teacher of the Gentiles".

The *promise* is here linked with the *purpose* "made before the age-times", which in turn are both found in Ephesians 1: 3, 4. By comparing the two passages given above, we shall see that Paul's commission "now" is in the "peculiar season", "His own times", and that this present dispensation is linked not with the period covered by the Acts, but with that period designated "before the age-times", and "before the overthrow of the world".

In 1 Timothy 2: 6, 7 the Apostle speaks of his ministry in relation to the present time, "Who gave Himself on behalf of all, to be testified in its *own peculiar seasons*, whereunto I am appointed herald, and Apostle (I speak the truth and lie not), a teacher of the Gentiles in faith and truth". The last words, veiled in the Authorised Version by the rendering "faith and verity", link this passage with Titus 1: 1-3, for there we read of the Apostle's commission as being connected with the *faith* of God's elect, and the knowledge of the *truth*.

The opposition to Paul's three-fold office of herald, apostle, and teacher of the Gentiles led to the denial of the truth of the Mystery, as may be observed in the following passages:

> "All they which are in Asia have *turned away* from me" (2 Tim. 1: 15).
> "Who concerning the truth have *erred*" (2 Tim. 2: 18).
> "They shall *turn away* their ears from the truth" (2 Tim. 4: 4).
> "Some shall *depart* from the faith" (1 Tim. 4: 1).
> "Some have *erred* concerning the faith" (1 Tim. 6: 21).

Repeated warnings are given concerning "profane and vain babblings" (1 Tim. 6: 20, 21; 2 Tim. 2: 16, 23). In 1 Timothy 1: 4 (R.V.) we read, "Neither give heed to fables and genealogies (*cp.* Titus 1: 10-14 *Jewish*, and 1 Tim. 1: 7 *law*), which minister arguings rather than (further) a *dispensation of God* which is in (or by) faith". This dispensation has nothing to do with "Jewish fables and commandments of men"; its great essentials are the faith and the truth. Those who err concerning the truth overturn the faith of some (2 Tim. 2: 18). Those who are ever learning and never able to come to a knowledge of the truth are also disapproved concerning the faith. The special features of Paul's ministry are further emphasized by reading the opening verses of his epistles to Timothy and Titus:

> *1 Timothy 1.*
> "Paul, an apostle of Christ Jesus, by command of God our Saviour, and Christ Jesus our *hope*".
> *2 Timothy 1.*
> "Paul, an apostle of Christ Jesus, through the will of God, according to the *promise of life* in Christ Jesus".
> *Titus 1.*
> "Paul, a servant of God, but an apostle of Jesus Christ, according to the faith of God's elect, and the knowledge of the truth which is according to godliness; upon *hope of eternal life*, which God, who cannot lie, *promised* before age-times".

These passages go to show the peculiarly exclusive character of Paul's commission, and of the present dispensation. Why is it that believers occupy themselves with the political and social "gospels" which are coming into favour everywhere, rather than consider these important passages? Satan will do anything rather than allow the child of God to realize *the* truth, *the* faith, *the* teacher, and *the* dispensation which concern him so vitally.

The ministry of the Apostle Paul, its varied stages, and all things connected with it, are worthy of a volume to itself, but sufficient has been said to enable us to see the difference that there is between the ministry of the twelve, and the ministry of Paul and those associated with him. We have seen two sets of ministry.

The Prophets (Heb. 1:1, 2).	In times past.	To the fathers.
The Son (Heb. 1:1, 2).	In the last of these days.	To the fathers (Rom. 15: 8), confirming the prophets.
The Apostles (Heb. 2:3, 4).	In the "Acts of the Apostles".	To the Jews, Samaritans, and Gentiles, confirming the words of the Son.

The promise of a still further revelation and ministry (John 16: 12-14), is fulfilled in:

Acts 20:22-24. Acts 26:16-18. 1 Tim. 2:7 2 Tim. 1:9, 10. 2 Tim. 4:17. Titus 1:1-3, etc.	The ministry of Paul, after the setting aside of Israel in Acts 28:24-28.

These distinct ministries are related to the two distinct spheres of redemptive purposes — the earth and the heavenlies; and with the two chosen instruments of blessing — Israel and the church, the Body of Christ. Each has its own set of instructions, its own order of ministry, its own gospel, and its own hope. The confusion of those things which differ is largely the cause of failure in Christian teaching; the understanding is darkened, and things appear contradictory. O that we may be enabled to see and receive the truth, for the truth will set us free!

When we step over the boundary line of Acts 28, we find ourselves in a dispensation differing from all that has gone before in many particulars. The first thing we notice is that instead of being connected, as the Abrahamic promises were, with the period known as "since the overthrow of the world", this dispensation is linked to a promise and purpose dating from "before the overthrow of the world" (Eph. 1: 3, 4). Further, the blessings of the Abrahamic covenant were connected with the earth. Abraham looked forward to the *city* which hath the foundations, which was to come down out of heaven; the *land* was to be his inheritance in resurrection.

Should the reader doubt the statement that the earth was the sphere of the Abrahamic blessing, the Bible is before him, let him search and see. He will find nothing in the Old Testament or in the

Scriptures relating to the kingdom and Israel, which teaches about being blessed in the heavenlies. This is the second peculiarity of the present dispensation, its blessings are "*in heavenly places*" in Christ (Eph. 1: 3). The special characteristic, however, to which we desire first to draw particular attention, is that this dispensation and its peculiar favours were never revealed in the Scriptures written before Acts 28; they constituted a secret hidden away by God from all ages and generations, and were not revealed until Israel was rejected, and Satan was thus *apparently*, but only apparently, triumphant.

The evil one had so worked on the hearts of men that the true King had been rejected, and had gone back to heaven; the proper subjects remained unrepentant, and a complete stop had come to the progress of the purpose of God. It was just here that the wonderful wisdom of God was revealed. Out of all this apparent chaos He produced His brightest jewel. Instead of being thwarted, it gave Him the foreknown opportunity of setting in motion the heavenly side of redemptive purposes, so that when the Lord once more takes up the earthly people — Israel — the two sections of the purpose of the ages (the earthly and the heavenly) will then run out their course together. O the depth of the riches, both of the wisdom and knowledge of God!

The epistle to the Ephesians contains a record of more than one secret or mystery, and we must be careful to "prove the things that differ", lest we fall into the snare which so often entraps the unwary. We are safe if we will always believe that God *means* what He *says*. Generalizing, like spiritualizing, is fatal to true interpretation. The word "mystery" (Secret) will be found in Ephesians in the following passages, and the several occurrences will be found exactly to correspond with each other, and emphasize their distinctive meanings:

A 1:9. The mystery of His will. The reconciliation of all things (Col. 1:20)
  B 3:3. The Mystery. Christ and His church
    C 3:4. The mystery of Christ. The Head
    C 3:9. The dispensation of the Mystery. The members
  B 5:32. The great mystery. Christ and His church.
A 6:19. The Mystery of the gospel. The reconciliation.

We will first devote our attention to the references which occur in Ephesians 3. Great harm has been done by many who otherwise have sought rightly to divide the Word, by confounding "the Mystery", with "the mystery of Christ". If we will carefully study the passage we shall see that the Apostle, as is often the case with his writings, inserted a parenthetical passage (indeed the first 13 verses of chapter 3 are entirely parenthetical), as can be seen by comparing 3: 1 with 3: 14 and 4: 1:

"For this cause I Paul, the prisoner of Jesus Christ for you Gentiles".

"For this cause I bow my knees".

"I therefore, the prisoner of the Lord".

This is characteristic of the epistles of Paul. The first nine verses of Ephesians 3 contain a passage complete in itself, having the mystery of Christ and the dispensation of the Mystery distinct, yet connected, as its foci. This will be more clearly seen if we note the structure of the passage, viz.:

A 2. The *dispensation* of the grace of God.
  B 3. The *Mystery* made known *to* Paul
    C a 4. The *mystery* of Christ
      b 5. Apostles the Ministers (plural)
    C a 6. The *Mystery* of this dispensation
      b 7. Paul the minister (singular)
  B 8. The *Mystery* made known *by* Paul
A 9. The *dispensation* of the Mystery (R.V.).

The Revised Version, following the best manuscripts, reads "dispensation" for "fellowship" in verse 9. Notice the two members A and *A*. In the one we have the dispensation of the grace of God given to Paul for the Gentiles, and this is explained in the answering member (verse 9) to be the dispensation of the Mystery. Members B and *B* declare that this Mystery was made known *to* Paul, and *by* Paul exclusively, "that I should enlighten *all*". Members C and *C* deal with the two mysteries and their two respective ministries.

The mystery of Christ, which had been slowly unfolding itself in the pages of Scripture, reaches its zenith in this final revelation of God's purposes. Christ is the centre of all the redemptive purposes of God, whether earthly or heavenly, whether to do with Israel or the church. His glorious exaltation had never been perceived by inspired writers of Scripture "as it is now revealed unto His holy apostles and prophets". In verses 6 and 7 Paul turns from contemplating the mystery of Christ to that which was so intimately connected with the heavenly phase of His glorious exaltation, viz., the present dispensation. That was something peculiarly given to Paul, "whereof I was made a minister", "that I should enlighten *all*".

Paul knew what it was to have enemies watching his words. He realized that to him had been committed the present dispensation. He never flinched from his stewardship, but he sought by every means to vindicate his claim. He commences to tell his readers in chapter 3 of this peculiar honour, but breaks off to refer them back to chapters 1 and 2 as his credentials, asking them to observe the fulness of his knowledge in the mystery of Christ, and saying, practically, If I prove to you that I am ahead of all others in my knowledge of this subject, you may be more ready to believe my claim to have received exclusively the revelation of the Mystery to be justifiable. He then takes up the thread again in verse 6. By using two kinds of type we may follow his argument better:

> "If ye have heard of the dispensation of the grace of God which is given me to you-ward, how that by revelation He made known unto me the *Mystery* (as I wrote before in a few words (viz., in Eph. 1), whereby when ye read ye may understand my knowledge in the *mystery of Christ*, which in other ages was not made known unto the sons of men as it is now revealed unto His holy apostles and prophets by the Spirit), that the Gentiles should be fellow-heirs, and fellow members of the same body, and fellow-partakers of His promise in Christ, by the gospel whereof I was made a minister, according to the gift of the grace of God given unto me by the effectual working of His power. Unto me, the less than the least of all saints, has this grace been given, that I should preach among the Gentiles the untraceable riches of Christ, and to enlighten all as to *what* is the dispensation of the Mystery which has been hidden away from the ages by God, Who did all things create: in order that *now*, unto the principalities and powers in the heavenlies, might be made known the exceeding complex wisdom of God, according to the purpose of the ages which He made in Christ Jesus our Lord" (Eph. 3: 1-11).

It would be difficult to find words that would more strongly express the secret, and unsearchable character of the present dispensation:

Here are riches that are	*unsearchable*	(verse 8).
Here is a dispensation which is	*secret*	(verse 9).
This secret was effectually	*hidden*	(verse 9).
The wisdom there is	*very complex*	(verse 10).
The whole was only discovered by	*revelation*	(verse 5).
And Paul was commissioned to	*enlighten all*	(verse 9).

If these words mean what they say, how foolish, nay, how blindly ignorant is the boast of many that they can find all about the so-called Mystery in the Psalms, Isaiah, Matthew, or Acts. If God hides, who can find? If He desires to keep a secret, who can wrest it from Him? If to Paul was given the exclusive commission of enlightening *all*, how can we expect to know about it if we exclude his writings and ignore his commission? The present dispensation was given to Paul. He claims it in Ephesians 3: 1-11, and *substantiates* his claim by the teaching found *only* in his epistles. The first chapter of Colossians contains an equally definite statement concerning this present dispensation, and its hitherto secret character, " ... for His body's sake, which is the church, of which I became a minister, according to the dispensation of God which is given to me with a view to you, to complete the Word of God, the Mystery, which has been hidden since the ages, and since the generations (*cp.* Genesis and its eleven *generations*), but now is made manifest to His saints" (Col. 1: 24-26).

The reader will observe the same exclusive claims, the same emphasis upon the hidden and secret character of this dispensation, and will also mark the additional clause, that this Mystery "completes the Word of God". The word "complete" is rendered "fulfil" in the Authorised Version, and if we transpose the syllables we shall get nearer to the meaning, "fill-full", or "complete". We pointed out at the end of chapter 4 that the epistles of Paul written since Acts 28 formed a group by themselves, the remainder of the Bible being taken up with the redemptive purposes as pertaining to Israel and the earth. The earthly section, however, is but one side of this mighty subject; the heavenly section needed a revelation too; this was given to Paul, and committed to writing. He could say that the dispensation given to him *completes* the purpose of the Word of God.

A noticeable example, showing how the Lord Jesus rightly divided the Word of truth, is found in Luke 4: 19, 20. The passage in Isaiah, from which He read, makes no apparent allowance for the interval which comes in between "the acceptable year of the Lord", and "the day of vengeance of our God". The Lord, however, "shut the book", and the day of vengeance will not commence until He Himself "opens the book" again, as recorded in Revelation 5. The interval is "filled" by the dispensation of the Mystery. The following passages are given as a sample of the way in which the present interval of over 1,900 years is passed over in the Scriptures written concerning the kingdom:

> Isaiah 9: 6; Isaiah 53 in the middle of verse 10; Isaiah 61: in the middle of verse 2 (*see* above); Daniel 9: 26, 27; Hosea 3: 4, 5; Zephaniah 3: 7, 8; Zechariah 9: 9, 10; Matthew 10: 23; Luke 1: 31, 32; 1 Peter 1: 11.

The long interval between "the sufferings, and the glories", between "the acceptable year of the Lord, and the day of vengeance of our God", is passed over and apparently ignored. Earthly kingdom truth has no recognition of the present dispensation of the Mystery.

We will now consider "the mystery of Christ", mentioned in Ephesians 3. The unfolding of this mystery began with the words of Genesis 3. The Seed of the woman shall bruise the serpent's head. It developed in grandeur and scope as time went on. The Seed of the woman was later revealed as being also Abraham's Seed, in whom all families of the earth should be blessed. Still later we find it revealed that this same blessed One is also to be the Seed of David, and Heir to his throne. Thus each age saw added glory and honour predicted concerning the coming Saviour.

Perhaps Old Testament revelation reaches its zenith in the messianic prophecies of Isaiah. He sees by faith not only the Seed of the woman, the Seed of Abraham, the Seed of David, but *Emmanuel*, which being interpreted is, "God with us"! Yet *Emmanuel* is immediately connected with *Emmanuel's land*. What higher knowledge of the mystery of Christ can be found in the Old Testament than is expressed by the words, "The wonderful Counsellor, the mighty God, the Father of the Ages, the Prince of Peace"? And yet the limitation is at once observed, for such a glorious One as is here described is immediately connected with the throne of *David* (Isa. 9: 6, 7).

Psalm 110, which even sees Christ at the right hand of God as a Priest after the order of Melchisedec, places Him there but temporarily, "until" His enemies are made His footstool, for "out of *Zion*" the rod of His strength is to be sent. Daniel's wonderful vision of the Ancient of Days, and the glory of His throne, and the investiture of Messiah with sovereignty, is entirely connected with the earthly, Abrahamic, and Davidic sphere. He:

> "beheld the Son of man come with the clouds of heaven . . . and there was given unto Him dominion, and glory, and a kingdom, that all peoples, nations, and languages should serve Him . . . And the kingdom, and dominion, and the greatness of the kingdom *under the whole heaven* shall be given to the people of the saints of the Most High" (Dan. 7).

However far-reaching the vision may be, whether it stay at the millennial kingdom, or reach forward to the new creation, one thing is evident, *the heavenly and present glory of Christ*, which is vitally connected with the Mystery of the one Body in heavenly places, was unknown "as it is *now* revealed". If we will but pause to think, the fuller revelation of the glory of Christ becomes a necessity. When Israel rejected their King, and were in turn temporarily rejected by Him, how could the Apostle Paul proclaim the new teaching of the one Body, unless he clearly set forth Christ's present position at the right hand of

God? Closely allied therefore to the revelation of the secret concerning Christ's present heavenly glory is the secret of the one Body, the church of the Mystery (Eph. 3). This Body has no relation to the "things on the earth"; its sphere is "in the heavenlies in Christ". This constitutes one of the many points of difference between the church of the Mystery, and the church connected with the kingdom of the heaven.

In the Sermon on the Mount, *e.g.*, we read, "The meek shall inherit the *earth*" (Matt. 5). Meekness is a grace which is enjoined under the present dispensation also, but it has attached to it other promises and blessings. Meekness is necessary before we can endeavour to keep the unity of the Spirit (Eph. 4); meekness must be found in the servant of the Lord who would teach others the truth of the Mystery. We are no longer directed to the inheritance of the earth, but our hearts and minds are directed to the heavenlies, to His inheritance in the holiest of all (Eph. 1: 18), to the heavenly places.

The five occurrences of the words "heavenly places" in Ephesians are as follows:

A 1:3. Spiritual blessings
 B 1:20. Christ raised far above principalities, and powers
  C 2:6. Christ and His church raised and seated in the heavenlies
 B 3:10. The church a witness to principalities, and powers
A 6:12. Spiritual wickednesses.

(The words of Eph. 6:12, "high places" are the same as those rendered "heavenly places" in the other passages).

In connection with this blessed portion of our study, we may consider the import of another closely related word, the word translated "saints". Fifteen times does the word "*hagios*" occur in Ephesians. Fifteen is 5 × 3, the number of grace and divine perfection, and these occurrences are linked to the five occurrences of the "heavenly places" in the same epistle. There is one form of this word "saint", which we believe conveys a fuller and deeper meaning than is at first sight apparent.

The genitive plural of *hagios* with the article, is *ton hagion*, whether it be masculine, feminine, or neuter, and is translated in the Authorised Version "of the saints". But inasmuch as *hagion* stands for the neuter gender as well as the masculine and feminine, the context must be considered before we decide whether the reference is to holy people (the saints), or to holy places or things. If we turn to Hebrews 9: 23, 24 we may gather sufficient Scriptural evidence to help us. The verses read as follows:

> "It was therefore necessary that the patterns of things in the heavens should be purified with these, but the heavenly things themselves with better sacrifices than these. For Christ is not entered into the holy places made with hands, which are the figures of the true, but into heaven itself, now to appear in the presence of God for us".

What is meant by the *better sacrifices*? We know that under the law many sacrifices were offered, "but Christ, after He had offered *one* sacrifice for sins for ever, sat down on the right hand of God" (Heb. 10: 12). By the figure of speech named *Heterosis*, or as some call this phase of it,"the plural of majesty", the plural is used for the singular to indicate the supreme greatness of the subject. Hence, "better sacrifices" mean "the infinitely better sacrifice", "holy places" mean "the most holy place", "the holy of holies". The typical holiest of all is next said to be the figure of the true or real one, which is defined as "heaven itself".

Coming back to the words *ton hagion* we see that it may mean "of the holiest of all", which is "heaven itself", making a parallel with the term "heavenly places". Reading Ephesians 2: 19 therefore with this in mind, we have, "Now therefore ye are no more strangers and foreigners, but fellow-citizens of the heavenly holiest of all, and of the household of God". This immediately sheds light upon another passage. "Fellow-citizens" is the one word *sumpolitai*, while the word translated "conversation" in Philippians 3: 20 is *politeuma*, and should be rendered "citizenship" (this word is from *polis* = a city, which we retain in our words "metropolis", "politics", etc.). Philippians 3: 20 reads, "Our citizenship is in heaven", the true holiest of all, and is exactly parallel with Ephesians 2: 19.

Another passage which receives deeper meaning is Colossians 1: 12, "Giving thanks unto the Father, who hath made you sufficient to be partakers of the inheritance of the holiest of all in the light". Believers are not going to inherit "saints", but the heavenly holiest of all in the light. This lifts the believer above the things of time and sense. What has he to do with ordinances, types, shadows, ceremonies? All these have passed away with the earthly kingdom and Israel. The inheritance, the blessing, and the sphere of all our spiritual activities are "above, where Christ sitteth on the right hand of God". We are living under an economy of grace that is unparalleled in its riches and its glories. It reaches out beyond the confines of Israel, it mounts up above the earth and its re-generation, it does not recognize distinctions of race or blood, all are viewed as dead in trespasses and sins, and all who believe are equally "quickened, raised, and seated together with Christ".

In Ephesians 3: 6, 7 we have the Mystery defined in the threefold position of believers during this present dispensation. "That the Gentiles should be fellow-heirs, and of the same body, and partakers of His promise in Christ by the gospel, whereof I was made a minister". The full force of these words is lost owing to the difficulty in translating one word by the same English equivalent throughout. Prefixed to the words "heirs", "body", and "partakers" is the little word *sun*, meaning "together", "with", viz.

sugkleronoma........................ heirs together
sussoma................................ a body together
summetocha.......................... partakers together.

If we could but put ourselves back into the period when Gentiles were glad to come and gather the crumbs that fell from the masters' table (the masters being Israel), we should be able to appreciate more fully the grace revealed in the thrice repeated word "together". The middle wall of the partition was not fully broken down until the commencement of the dispensation of the Mystery.

Israel has always had the pre-eminence among the nations. When the millennial kingdom comes the Gentiles will not be "fellow-heirs" with Israel in the sense of equality. Israel shall be "the head and not the tail, and they shall be above only, and they shall not be beneath" (Deut. 28: 13). When the day of Israel's blessing comes, "strangers shall stand and feed their flocks, and the sons of the alien shall be their ploughmen and vinedressers, but Israel shall be named the priests of the Lord, and men shall call them ministers of our God" (Isa. 61: 5, 6). Moreover, "the nation and kingdom which will not serve Israel shall perish". This distinction is seen even in the Acts of the Apostles. When Peter received the command to go to Cornelius, it was with a great deal of fear as to the consequences which might ensue from visiting a Gentile. His trepidation is visible in his opening words to Cornelius, for he prefaced his address by saying, "Ye know how that it is an unlawful thing for a man that is a Jew to keep company or come unto one of another nation, but God hath showed me that I should not call any man common or unclean" (Acts 10: 28).

If the Body began at Pentecost, it seems incredible that Peter, endued with the "power from on high", and used so remarkably as the early chapters of the Acts testify, should be so blindly ignorant of the first principles of the church as revealed through the later epistles of Paul. Could Paul be credited with either faith or reason if the words of Acts 10: 28 were found in his church revelations? Assuredly not, yet Acts 10 supplies us with more than one example of the great difference observable between the messages and ministries of these two equally inspired Apostles. Peter said, "In every nation he that feareth Him (God), and worketh righteousness is accepted with Him", to a man who, though "devout" (Acts 10: 2), and "just" (verse 22), needed to hear words whereby both himself and all his house should be *saved* (Acts 11: 14)! So convinced were they to whom Peter explained his mission to Cornelius, that they were obliged to say, "Then hath God to the Gentiles also granted repentance unto life" (verse 18). Surely these words tell us plainly that neither Peter, the twelve, nor those with them had any conception of the truth as revealed afterwards to the Apostle Paul.

The Gentiles after this were admitted into the number of those saved, but even then a difference was made between Jewish and Gentile believers. This may be seen in Acts 15: 19-21. Circumcision was not demanded of the Gentile believer as a necessity for entrance into the assembly, although circumcision was practised by the Jewish believers (*cp.* Acts 16: 3). The middle wall of partition was still standing. When we come to the epistle to the Ephesians we find no such distinctions; grace, not race; heavenly places in Christ, not inheriting the earth, or being blessed with faithful Abraham. In the dispensation of the Mystery basic and dispensational positions are the same; circumcision, uncircumcision, Jew, Gentile, all distinctions are levelled in the grave of sin (Eph. 2: 1), and buried with Christ. Thus it is that when the Apostle speaks of the Mystery, he declares all distinctions at an end. The Gentile believer equally with the Jewish believer was a fellow-heir. The inheritance before them was not like that before Israel, where the Jew had pre-eminence; all alike were fellow-heirs, all alike were fellow-members of the one Body. The Jewish believer had no priority; he was no nearer to the Lord, than the Gentile fellow-member. Further, they were equal partakers of the promise in Christ Jesus by the gospel of which Paul was made a minister.

It is important to notice that the word "promise" is singular, not plural. To Israel pertained the "promises" (Rom.9), but the promise referred to in Ephesians 3: 6 is entirely distinct from them. It is, however, connected with the gospel of which Paul was the minister, who claimed the exclusive privilege and grace of being the chosen vessel through whom the revelation of the Mystery should be made. The fellow-partaking in this promise must not be confounded with the unequal partaking by the Gentile believers which characterized the promises made unto the fathers. This promise is further emphasized in Titus 1: 1-3. It is the promise made before the age-times, before Abraham, before Adam, before the overthrow of the world. The church of the Mystery, the one Body, is entirely severed from all that pertains to earthly promises and blessings.

We shall further seek to show it has no rites or ceremonies, and that it is as distinct from the Abrahamic and earthly kingdom purpose as the heavens are above the earth. Sufficient has been said in this chapter to give an indication of this difference; we proceed in our next to analyse a passage which is often made a cause of stumbling, viz., Hebrews 6: 1, 2.

Note: To assist our readers to distinguish between the mystery of Christ revealed to the prophets and the Mystery revealed only to Paul i.e. the Church of the One Body, we have used a small 'm' for the former and a capital 'M' for the latter in our exposition.

CHAPTER THIRTEEN

Hebrews 6 and its dispensational position

"Therefore leaving . . . let us go on . . . not laying again" (Heb. 6: 1). Whatever subsequent study may reveal, nothing can alter the fact that the Apostle does not merely say "let us go on", but he also says "leave". There are many who assert that in Hebrews 6: 1 and 2 we have the "fundamentals of our faith". Some push this even further, and assert that "no one can be recognized as a teacher who does not hold to and teach these six things". Such would certainly turn the Apostle Paul away, for he distinctly exhorted the Hebrews to *leave* them.

What were they told to leave? If we are using the Authorised Version we shall read, "Therefore leaving the principles of the doctrine of Christ". It must be evident to all that something is wrong here. This certainly is not at the dictation of the Spirit of truth whose mission was to glorify Christ. However the translators could allow such a perversion, or the Revisers could give such a strange alternative, must be answered by others wiser than the writer. The word translated "doctrine" is the Greek word *logos*. Originally meaning a word, it came to mean a narrative, and is the very word translated "treatise" by the Authorised Version and Revised Version in Acts 1: 1. The word *logos* occurs twelve times in Hebrews, and in several of the passages the term means "account" or "record". It is translated *account* in Hebrews 13: 17, "they must give *account*". It is rendered in Hebrews 4: 13, "with Whom we have *to do*", and should have been rendered "with Whom we have an *account*". It is rendered "account" In Philippians 4: 17.

Again, to translate *arche* by "principles" is a double violation of its meaning. It is in the singular number, whereas the Authorised Version and Revised Version render it by the plural, and moreover in every other occurrence of the word in Hebrews it is rendered either by "first", or "beginning". Literally rendered the words of the verse are, "Wherefore leaving the word of the beginning of the Christ, let us go on toward perfection". If we now read *account* for "word", all is clear and Scriptural. "Leaving the account (narrative or treatise) of the beginning of Christ". If we ask the question as to what is the account or narrative referred to, the answer is supplied by the opening words of the Acts of the Apostles. In fact Green translates the words, "The former *account I composed*, O Theophilus, of all things that Jesus *began* both to do and teach". The former *account* is the Gospel of Luke. Here we arrive at something tangible. The Gospel narratives are a *beginning*, but "perfection" and completeness must be sought elsewhere.

In the case of the earthly kingdom, the perfection or maturity is found in the New Covenant. In the case of the heavenly section, the perfection is found in the epistles of the Mystery. The exhortation of this epistle (Hebrews) goes no further than the superiority of the New Covenant over the old, but sufficient is said concerning the glory of Christ in His present exalted position to enable the believing Jew (if God permitted him) to step out into the perfect grace and blessedness of the one body with its heavenly blessings. The book of Acts is the second volume, of which the first volume is the Gospel by Luke, and it is utterly futile to attempt to understand Vol. 2 until we have mastered in some degree the meaning of Vol. 1. "The record of the beginning of the Christ" is mentioned in Hebrews 2, "How shall we escape if we neglect so great salvation, which at the first *began* to be spoken by the Lord?"

The words translated "perfect" and "perfection" are from the Greek word *telos*, "the end", which is so translated in Hebrews 6: 8. This is in contrast to the "beginning". Not only were the Hebrew believers to *leave* the record of the beginning of Christ, and go on unto perfection, but they were also told not to lay again the foundation of doctrines enumerated in the verses following. These doctrines, six in number, are arranged as follows:

Doctrines	
Repentance. Faith.	Internal and doctrinal
Baptisms. Laying on of hands.	External and elemental.
Resurrection. Judgment everlasting.	Future.

Some reader may be saying, Where is this writer leading us? Are we to leave repentance and faith? Are we to give up the vital doctrine of the resurrection? Is eternal judgment to be abandoned for some universalist teaching? Let us not be hasty in coming to a conclusion: we must "prove all things, and hold fast that which is good". Moreover, we had a "preliminary sketch" in the teaching of the Apostle Paul (2 Tim. 1: 13), so let us reverently, yet faithfully, consider the things which these Hebrew believers were expected not to lay again.

(1) Repentance from dead works

Does this mean that we are to have no sorrow for sin, no departing from iniquity? No! "Repent" is the key-word of the gospel of the kingdom. John Baptist, the Lord Jesus and Peter alike commenced their ministries with this word. Let the reader turn to Ephesians, let him read through the six chapters, and note down every occurrence of the words "repent" and "repentance"; he will not find one occurrence. Let him continue through Philippians and Colossians; the result will be the same. Why is it that this word, so frequent in the Gospels and the Acts, is so rigorously excluded from these epistles which give the foundation teaching of the present dispensation? Is it not that the Lord, by omitting this key-word of the mediatorial kingdom, would lead us to observe that we are in an entirely different dispensation?

We shall find by turning to Hebrews 9: 14 that Paul who told them to leave "repentance from dead works", had a very satisfactory reason, and one which glorified the Lord Jesus Christ. "How much more shall the *blood of Christ* ... purge your conscience from dead works"! Reader, which is better, the oft repeated repentance, or the once completed purgation? Let Hebrews 10: 1-14 answer the question. This is in harmony with Colossians 2: 13, "Having forgiven you *all* trespasses". The Apostle's standard is an infallible test for doctrine so far as we are concerned, and the striking ring "He shall glorify *Me*" is surely heard here.

(2) Faith toward God

If it seemed strange to speak of leaving the doctrine of repentance, it must sound doubly strange to speak of not laying again the foundation of "faith toward God". We may be perfectly sure that the Apostle who so emphasized justification by faith is not advocating its abandonment here. Let us again apply the touchstone. How does Paul speak of faith in the epistles?

"The faith of *Jesus Christ*" (Gal. 2: 16).
"The faith of the *Son of God*" (Gal. 2: 20).
"The faith of *Jesus Christ*" (Gal. 3: 22).
"By faith of *Jesus Christ*" (Gal. 3: 26).
"Your faith in the *Lord Jesus*" (Eph. 1: 15).
"By faith of *Christ*" (Phil. 3: 9).
"Your faith in *Christ*" (Col. 2: 5).
"The faith which is in *Christ Jesus*" (1 Tim. 3: 13).
"Through faith which is in *Christ Jesus*" (2 Tim. 3: 15).

By reading the contexts of the above passages it will be seen that all the blessings of the gospel are not only vitally connected with "faith", but faith which *rests in Christ*! Justification, resurrection life, the sonship and salvation, are all spoken of as resulting from faith which has *Christ* for its object.

By birth, by nationality, by their very laws, customs, and distinctions, the Jews were continually reminded that Jehovah was the *God of the Jews*. Every Jew prided himself upon that fact, so much so, that Paul had to write, "Is He not the God of the Gentiles also"? (Rom. 3: 29). But this national faith toward God, though it ministered to their pride, could not save them. In the parable of the Pharisee and the Publican we have a vivid example of this. The Pharisee had "faith toward God", otherwise he would never have troubled to go to the Temple and say what he did. The Publican*, however, realized that this vague, general recognition of God was not sufficient for his need. Notice the words of his prayer. "God be propitious (mercy upon the ground of sacrifice) to me the sinner". Here was faith not only in God, but in the divine provision for sin. The fact that from earliest childhood these Hebrews had heard of God and read His law was in some measure a stumbling-block to them. They did not realize that they needed a Saviour as much as the Gentiles. The Gentile, on the other hand, had no national faith to rest upon; he cast himself upon the unconditional mercy of God in Christ.

The Lord Jesus when on earth had said, "Ye believe in God, believe *also* in Me" (John 14: 1). To trust in the God of one's fathers is a poor substitute for that faith which owns Him as the "God of *my* salvation". The epistle to the Hebrews emphasizes the necessity of the sacrificial and high priestly work of Christ. All who come unto God for salvation come unto God "by Him" (Heb. 7: 25). The Apostle would lead them away from this crippling pride and national faith to grasp something of the one faith, the unity of the faith of Ephesians 4, which comprised a "full knowledge of the Son of God", and "the mature man". Truly, once again, we see that Paul was leading them on to maturity.

(3) The doctrine of baptisms

The order of the words in the original is "baptisms of doctrine" (or instruction). The word "of" may be the Genitive of relation, and mean that these baptisms were related to instruction and doctrine, for the ordinances of every dispensation have always had a deeper value than the mere ritual observance. The most important word for our

*The Publicans had so far left the religious standing of the Jews as to be classed with the Gentiles. *Cp*. "a heathen man and a publican" (Matt. 18: 17).

consideration is "baptisms". We notice that it is in the plural, contrasting with the one baptism of Ephesians 4. The Apostle here says, "Leave ... not laying again ... the doctrine of baptisms". In Ephesians he says, "Endeavour to keep ... one baptism".

We would first direct attention to the two other passages of Scripture where the word "baptisms" occurs. (1) In Hebrews 9: 10 it is translated "washings":

> "The first tabernacle ... was a figure ... in which were offered both gifts and sacrifices that could not make him that did the service *perfect* as pertaining to the *conscience* (which stood), only in meats and drinks, and *divers baptisms,* and *carnal ordinances* imposed until the time of reformation".

God has used the same word here as in Hebrews 6: 2, and has placed it in such a context that nothing but blindness or wilfulness can bring it into the present dispensation of heavenly and spiritual blessings. It is related to carnal ordinances which touched the flesh, but not the conscience, and is placed in full contrast with that which is perfect. (2) The only other occurrence of this word is in Mark 7: 4 to 8:

> "And when they come from the market, except they baptize they eat not. And many other things there be which they have received to hold, as the *baptisms* of cups, and pots, and brazen vessels, and tables ... Howbeit, in vain do they worship Me, teaching for doctrines (same word as in Heb. 6: 1), the commandments of men. For laying aside (same word as *leaving* in Heb. 6: 1) the commandment of God, ye hold the traditions of men".

It is striking to see that the Apostle in Hebrews takes up the very words of the Lord in the Gospel. The Lord had said that among the doctrines of men which they held was the "doctrine of baptisms", and that they had "left" the commandment of God to "hold the traditions of men". The Apostle says, reverse all this, leave the doctrine of baptisms for the revealed Word of God. What have we found hitherto? The "baptisms" used in Hebrews 9: 10 have one meaning. They formed part of "carnal ordinances" imposed by God, which made none "perfect". Again, the word occurs in Mark 7: 4, and designates the "ceremonial cleansings" imposed by the traditions of the elders. Thus, whether imposed by God or men, these baptisms were carnal ordinances, and had no place in "that which is perfect or mature".

A careful comparison of Hebrews 9: 10 with Hebrews 10: 1-4 will show, by the repetition of such words as "conscience" and "perfect", that these ordinances were contemporary with the Levitical sacrifices, and both passed away together. The epistle to the Hebrews is the first Scripture which reveals that the sacrifices appointed by God were to cease; so also with the ordinances which formed a part of the appointed service.

There is another consideration which demands our attention here. The plural form "baptisms" exactly fits the state of things which obtained during the Pentecostal dispensation, and of no other period but that covered by the Acts of the Apostles can it be predicated that there were baptisms of more kinds than one. The words relating to baptism in the Greek are as follows:

Bapto, to dip (John 13:26; Rev. 19:13).
Baptizo, to render things *bapto.*
Baptismos, the act of dipping or washing (Mark 7:4, 8; Heb. 6: 2; 9: 10 only occurrences).
Baptisma, the result of *baptismos* (occurs 22 times).
Baptistes, the one who baptizes.

In Mark 7: 4 the word *baptizo* is rendered "wash", and in Luke 11: 38, "washed". The reference in each case is to ceremonial cleansing, as the contexts show.

Among the definitions of baptism which we find in the Word is "*John's baptism*" (Matt. 21: 25; Acts 1: 22; 18: 25). What doctrine or instruction was there in "the baptism of John"? Mark 1: 4 supplies an answer in the words, "John did baptize in the wilderness, and preach the baptism of repentance for the remission of sins". This baptism involved (1) a confession that they needed cleansing (Mark 1: 5; Matt. 3: 6), and (2) repentance. This, the key-word of the gospel of the kingdom, was essential for national blessing, and the establishment of the kingdom (Deut. 30: 1-5; 1 Kings 8: 46-49; Mal. 4: 5, 6; Acts 3: 19-26).

Ceremonial cleansing, under the law, was always performed by the person himself (*cp.* Exod. 40: 31; Lev. 11: 40; 2 Kings 5: 14). John's baptism had therefore a somewhat novel feature. John came like Elijah (Matt. 11: 14; Luke 1: 17). The baptism of John was the outward sign of inward repentance. It necessarily implied that those who submitted to his baptism believed that John was "sent from God", and that his baptism was "from heaven". Hence, those who rejected the witness of God concerning the King and kingdom, rejected the counsel of God, being not baptized of John (Luke 7: 30). The next important thing to observe is that John's baptism was ordained to "make manifest" the Messiah to Israel (John 1: 31). The moment John's baptism had accomplished this, he and his baptism passed away. "He must increase, but I must decrease". The work of the fore-runner was done. One further item of importance arising out of John 1: 31 is that it was entirely connected with *Israel.* No Gentiles were sought; he confined his testimony to the people of the kingdom.

The Lord Jesus not only took up the cry of the Baptist, "Repent, for the kingdom of heaven is at hand", but He also baptized with water in a way similar to that of John. In John 3: 22-26 we read, "Jesus came and His disciples into the land of Judaea, and there He tarried with them, and baptized". As John was baptizing at the same time in AEnon, a dispute arose "on the part of John's disciples with the Jews about purifying". The question of the Jews does not prove that baptism was a ceremonial cleansing, but it shows how a contemporary witness viewed the ordinance. In one or two other passages in the Gospels we read of baptism in connection with the ministry of the Lord Jesus and the twelve. One is John 4: 1-3, where we read that Christ avoided the administration of baptism Himself, and another is Matthew 28: 19:

> "Go ye therefore, and teach all nations, baptizing them into the name of the Father, and of the Son, and of the Holy Ghost, teaching them to observe all things whatsoever I have commanded you, and lo, I am with you alway, even unto the consummation of the age".

The command in Matthew 28: 19, 20 is to "make all nations disciples", or "disciple all nations"; it does not contemplate the individual so much as the whole. It is also based upon the ground that "all power is given unto Me in heaven and in earth". When the words of Revelation 5: 12 etc., are fulfilled, and the Lord Jesus takes up His great power, and returns in judgment, then Israel will become the great missionaries to the nations (Isa. 66: 19), and Matthew 28: 19, 20 will then be put into practice. No word is here about the gospel; we have teaching, and observation of commands. Further, the period is referred to as "the end of the age", which Matthew 24 and 25 explain, and which leaps over the interval of the present dispensation altogether. In Mark 16: 15-17 we read:

> "Preach the gospel to every creature. He that believeth, and is baptized shall be saved . . . and these signs shall follow, etc".

Two things press for notice here; belief and baptism are linked together. It does not say, "He that believeth shall be saved", but "He that believeth, *and is baptized* shall be saved". The inference is that they who preach this gospel cannot recognize any as being *saved* who have not been baptized. Further, this gospel and this baptism were to be accompanied with "signs and wonders". A reference to Matthew 10 will show that this is none other than the gospel of the kingdom, and a glance at Acts 2: 38-41 will show that this gospel and this baptism were perpetuated. The preaching of the Baptist had been:

> "I indeed baptize you with water unto repentance, but He that cometh after Me is mightier than I . . . He shall baptize you with holy spirit and fire" (Matt. 3: 11).

During the Gospels we find water baptism, and the promise of baptism in spirit. During the Acts we find water baptism and the baptism in spirit together. During the present period we find *no* water baptism, but the baptism in spirit only. It may be demonstrated thus:

Gospels.	Acts period.	Mystery.
Water baptism.	Water and spirit baptisms.	Spirit baptism.

During the Acts of the Apostles water baptism is of frequent mention. Just as John preached concerning "Him that was to come", so Peter preached concerning One who *had come*, and all who believed the testimony concerning His coming, death, and resurrection were baptized in the name of the Lord Jesus (Act 10: 48; 19: 5). Before Pentecost it was "unto John's baptism"; after Pentecost it was "unto the Name of the Lord Jesus".

This baptism in water was associated with the signs and wonders promised in Mark 16: 17-20 and Acts 10: 45, 46. I quote the following paragraph from an interesting pamphlet entitled: "The One Baptism of the Church Age", by *Amplius*, because it so concisely puts before us the case regarding Paul's connection with water baptism:

> "The relation of the apostle Paul to this baptismal ceremony is of prime importance. It would appear that after his baptism at Damascus (Acts 9: 18), he went on with his gospel preaching for fourteen years without the use of the water ceremony. There is no hint of baptism at Antioch, the new centre; nor at Antioch in Pisidia, or Derbe, or Lystra, in connection with his first missionary journey. It was only after he had been up to Jerusalem and 'received the right hand of fellowship' from the twelve that we have any record of baptism connected with his ministry (compare Galatians 2: 1-10, and Acts 16: 11-33). The nation of the Jews was not yet cast off; the kingdom testimony was still addressed to it; and Paul making himself

'a Jew to the Jews', appealed to the nation as well, simply doing, in fellowship with them, what the twelve had received authority to do, and this went on until the awful sentence on Israel was pronounced by Paul himself at Rome (Acts 28: 23-28), and the judicial blindness fell which has continued until now" (pp. 18 and 19).

The important question touched upon in chapter 11 demands careful consideration. Does the term "the baptism of the Spirit of the Pentecostal dispensation" mean the same thing as the baptism of Ephesians 4? The two baptisms (that of water and of spirit) are found together in the Acts. Note the words of Peter:

"Repent, and be baptized every one of you in the name of Jesus Christ for the remission of sins, and ye shall receive the gift of the Holy Spirit" (Acts 2: 38).

"Then they that gladly received his word were *baptized*, and the same day there were *added* about three thousand souls" (Acts 2: 41).

We sometimes meet Christians who tell us that they have received the baptism of the Holy Ghost, or that they have received the "second blessing". Second blessings are delusions, resulting from undispensational ideas. The charter of the church commences with the fact that God "*hath* blessed us with *all* spiritual blessings". What then is the baptism of the Spirit as spoken of in the Acts? A comparison of Acts 1: 5 with 11: 14—16 will make one thing clear, viz., that it is connected with the baptism of John and his prophecy concerning Christ. Although we have set out these passages in a preceding chapter, we repeat them here for the sake of clearness:

"And began to *speak* with other tongues" (Acts 2: 1-4).
"When Simon *saw* . . . the Holy Spirit was given" (Acts 8: 18).
"They *heard* them speak with tongues" (Acts 10: 44-46).
"They *spake* with tongues and prophesied" (Acts 19: 6).

1 Corinthians 12: 1-27 should be read together with these passages.

Ministering the spirit and working miracles are connected with justifying faith in Galatians 3: 5, 6. Those who contend for the identity of this baptism with that of Ephesians throw over all evidence of their justification, unless they too can work miracles to establish it, *if* the Acts period is present truth. The baptism of 1 Corinthians 12 is essentially connected with miracles and supernatural gifts; it is not so now. When that gospel, which included water baptism, was preached by divine authority, its terms were, "They shall lay hands on the sick, and they *shall* recover". Let those who will have it that there is but one piece of God's good news, but one phase of the baptism of the Spirit, and that water baptism is truth for the time, prove it. It was easy enough in the days of the Apostles: God is not less able now, the world is still as bad as ever, and the witness would be very acceptable. The proposition carries with it its own refutation.

What is the baptism of the Spirit? The Lord defines it for us in Acts 1. "Ye shall be baptized by *pneuma hagion*" (holy spirit = the *gifts*, not the Giver Himself (Acts 1: 5)). "Ye shall receive power, the holy spirit having come upon you" (Acts 1: 8). "Ye shall be endued with power from on high" (Luke 24: 49). The distinction between holy spirit, which is the "power from on high", and the Holy Spirit, Who gives the gift, is seen in the fulfilment of the promise of Acts 1: 5 and 8, in Acts 2: 4:

> "And they were all filled with *pneuma hagion* (holy spirit, the power from on high), and began to speak with other tongues as the Spirit (the Holy Spirit Himself) gave them utterance".

The baptism of the Spirit may be rendered in the terms of Acts 1: 8 as, "power coming from God upon His people". This power may take different forms under different administrations. To-day, the one baptism unites the believer to his glorified Lord. The "power from on high" is none the less real because it does not manifest itself in outward and visible signs. The signs unseen by human eyes may be clearly visible to the "principalities and powers in heavenly places", unto whom the church manifests the manifold wisdom of God (Eph. 3: 10).

This power, which has been exerted on our behalf, is defined as being "according to the working of His mighty power which He wrought in Christ, when He raised Him from the dead, and set Him at His own right hand in the heavenlies". When we believed we were "sealed by that holy Spirit of the promise". This gives the members of the one body such "power from on high" that they can "hold the Head", "keep the unity", "wrestle against principalities and powers". I do not need the gift of "tongues" to overcome the wiles of the devil. While many are spending their strength over these gifts of a past dispensation, the main issues are neglected.

This leads us on to the consideration of the next item of Hebrews 6.

(4) The laying on of hands.

Acts 8: 12-18 makes the connection between water baptism, and the laying on of hands very apparent. "They were baptized", then "they laid hands upon them, and they received *pneuma hagion*" (holy spirit, the *gifts*). "Simon saw that through the laying on of the Apostles' hands, *pneuma hagion* was given". Again, in Acts 19: 6 we read, "When Paul had laid his hands upon them, *pneuma hagion* came upon them, and they spake with tongues and prophesied". In Acts 28: 8, "Paul prayed and laid hands upon him and healed him". These things have ceased and passed away. After Acts 28, although we have the record of several who were sick, we have no record of anyone healing them by the laying on of hands. After Acts 28 we read of believers receiving the seal of the Holy Spirit of the promise, but never, that such was given by the laying on of hands. "Not with hands" might be an appropriate inscription written over the present dispensation. As we have seen, the "gifts" to-day are directly given by the ascended and glorified Lord (Eph. 4: 8-11), without the interposition of man at all.

Paul reminded Timothy of a past act in 1 Timothy 4: 14 and 2 Timothy 1: 6, but when he tells Timothy to "do the work of an evangelist", there is no need or warrant for the "laying on of hands". The instruction, "lay hands suddenly on no man" (1 Tim. 5: 22), has reference to the custom which signified approval (as in Acts 13: 3); no gifts were conferred thereby, and none are specified as necessary in the "qualifications" given in 1 Timothy 3. Thus again we see that even in the setting aside of this ceremony, a ceremony which was once accompanied by such mighty power, a "confirmation" in the true sense of the word (Mark 16: 20 and Heb 2: 3), the believer is led to see the fulness that is his in Christ alone.

(5) The resurrection of the dead

The reader may have experienced several shocks since commencing this chapter, but we can conceive of none greater than to be told that the Apostle here taught the Hebrew believers to "Leave . . . not lay again . . . the resurrection of the dead". Nothing can be more certain than that Paul would never tamper with the "foundation of God" as the "hope" of the believer — resurrection. Yet there must be something hidden beneath the surface to account for so remarkable a statement as that given in Hebrews 6 in the Authorised Version and Revised Version. We make a great mistake when we assume that the resurrection as taught by the Pharisees, that believed by the generality of the Jews and the disciples, and that proclaimed by the Apostles, were all one and the same. We must carefully follow the actual "words which the Holy Ghost teacheth", if we would understand Hebrews 6: 2.

The words translated "the resurrection of the dead" in Hebrews 6: 2 are in the original *anastasis nekron*. Let us trace the use of these words in other passages. We are aware that one of the great differences between the Sadducees and the Pharisees was that the former denied the resurrection, whereas the latter believed it (Matt. 22: 23-31). In Acts 23: 6 we read, "Men and brethren, I am a Pharisee, the son of a Pharisee, of the hope and resurrection *of* the dead (*anastasis nekron*) I am called in question". Again in Acts 24: 21 he says, "touching the resurrection *of* (the) dead (*anastasis nekron*) I am called in question". In reference to this Paul had said "believing all things which are written in the Law and in the Prophets, and have hope toward God, *which they themselves* also allow, that there shall be a resurrection of the dead, both of the just and the unjust". These passages give us the belief of the orthodox Jew, founded upon the Law and the Prophets.

John 11: 24 shows us that the sister of Lazarus entertained the same belief. "Martha said unto Him, I know that he shall rise again in the resurrection *at the last day*". The account of the beginning of Christ gives Christ's own words on this same subject in John 5: 28, 29. "The hour cometh in the which all that are in the graves shall hear His voice, and shall come forth, they that have done good, unto the resurrection of life, and they that have done evil, unto the resurrection of judgment". Hitherto, all the passages quoted are in keeping with Hebrews 6: 2. Turning now to Mark 9: 9, 10 we shall discover something which will throw light upon Hebrews 6:

> "And as they came down from the mountain, He charged them that they should tell no man what things they had seen, till the Son of man were risen *from among* the dead (*ek nekron*); and they kept *that* saying with themselves, questioning one with another what the rising *from* the dead should mean".

If the Pharisees, Martha and the Jews generally believed the resurrection of the dead, we may be certain that these disciples believed it too. What then was their difficulty? Wherein was the need for questioning? "*That* saying" certainly contained a problem for them, and it is found in the little word "from".

They, in common with the majority, believed in a resurrection of the dead *at the last day*, but this statement as to a resurrection "out from among the dead" was something new. In Luke 16: 31 Christ said, "If they hear not Moses and the Prophets, neither will they be persuaded though one rose *out from among the dead*" (*ek nekron*). The sign of the prophet Jonah was the only sign which God would vouchsafe to that sinful generation. After the Lord Jesus had been crucified, buried, and raised from the dead, the words of Christ in Luke 16: 31 proved only too true.

The Apostles, during their ministry in the Acts, ephasized the resurrection of the Lord, but it was rejected. We have such words from

Peter concerning Christ, "Whom God raised up"; "this Jesus hath God raised up". In connection with the healing of the lame man (Acts 3: 13-15) Peter says "God ... hath glorified His Son Jesus ... God hath raised Him *out from* among the dead" (*ek nekron*). The Sadducees were grieved that "they taught the people, and preached through Jesus the resurrection *out from* among the dead" (Acts 4: 1, 2, 10).

We find the expression again in Romans 1: 4, "By the resurrection *out from* among the dead". The epistles of the Mystery reveal, as one of the blessings peculiar to themselves, that the believer in Christ will be raised *out from* the dead, even as was the Lord Himself. Philippians 3 teaches this plainly. Starting at verse 4 Paul summarizes his position as a Pharisee. Then following his wondrous conversion he declares, "What things were gain to me, them I counted loss for Christ". Among the "gains" he enumerates is this one of resurrection. As a Pharisee he held the orthodox belief in a resurrection *of* the dead. The time came, however, when he gave up that belief, not to become a Sadducee, but to be a participator in the "blessed hope" of a resurrection *out from* among the dead.

Right at the end of the Acts of the Apostles, Paul is seen connecting himself with the "hope of Israel" (Acts 28: 20). Immediately after the mighty dispensational change he comes forward as the Apostle of another hope. His words in Philippians 3: 11 literally rendered are, "If by any means I may attain unto the *out-resurrection (exanastasis ton ek nekron)*, that which is *out from* among the dead". Rotherham translates the word *exanastasis*, "the earlier resurrection". This prior or earlier resurrection out from among the dead is connected in Philippians 3: 14 with the "prize of the calling on high", or the "upward calling", and in verse 21 with the changing of "the bodies of our humiliation that they may be fashioned like unto the body of His (Christ's) glory". The "better resurrection" of Hebrews 11: 35 is, of course, the direct alternative to the resurrection of Hebrews 6. The hope of 1 Thessalonians 4 and 1 Corinthians 15 may also be considered as a special resurrection and rapture, but the emphatic words are reserved for the hope of the present dispensation, as shewn above from Philippians 3.

Do we wonder that the Apostle desired the Hebrew believers to leave the idea of a general resurrection for the blessedness of this "better" or "out-resurrection", and all that pertained thereto?

(6) Eternal judgment

The *olam*, *aion*, or age give us the underlying idea in the Hebrew and Greek words translated "eternal" and "for ever". This word formed a conspicuous feature in the literature and teaching of the Rabbis. It is not to our purpose to launch upon "the sea of abstractions" which constituted the traditions which made void the Word of God. The teaching concerning the intermediate state and kindred subjects seemed to fascinate the religious mind of old, even as it has done in modern times.

Some reflection on the hoary traditions of the elders concerning the "gulf fixed", and the "parched tongue" mentioned by Christ in Luke 16 may be seen in Josephus' treatise on Hades, and in many of the Rabbinical writings. The subject of eternal judgment, so conspicuous in many writings, is not emphasized unduly in the epistles of grace. In 2 Thessalonians 1: 9 the Apostle speaks of "everlasting (or eternal) destruction", but destruction is not perpetual existence in agony.

Let the reader go carefully through the epistles of Paul, and make a list of the expressions which he uses regarding the punishment and judgment of the finally impenitent. The very facts collected will be of themselves witnesses to the reason why he urged these Hebrew believers to leave such doctrines. Some very truthfully urge that the Apostle does not say in Hebrews 6 "eternal torture", but "eternal *judgment*". Supposing the passage to be divested of all traditions, what does it mean? The word translated "judgment" is *krima*. In Paul's epistles written after Acts 28 it occurs twice, viz., 1 Timothy 3: 6, and 5: 12. It will be seen that neither of the passages have much to do with "eternal judgment".

Krino, the verb "to judge", occurs three times in these epistles. Colossians 2: 16, and Titus 3: 11 have manifestly no reference whatever to the subject. This leaves the only other occurrence (2 Tim. 4: 1) as being in any way parallel with Hebrews 6: 2. *Krisis*, "judgment", occurs but once in these epistles, viz., 1 Timothy 5: 24. *Krites*, "judge", but once, viz., 2 Timothy 4: 8, the reference being to the Lord as Judge, concerning the awarding of the prize, even as in Colossians 2: 16. Out of over 200 occurrences of the different derivations of *krino*, "to judge" the Apostle Paul uses in the later epistles seven, four of which have no reference to the future judgment upon unbelievers, and further, in the epistles to the Ephesians, Philippians, and Colossians the words are absent, with the exception of the case cited in Colossians 2: 16, which does not apply.

Din olammim, "judgment of the ages", is the eleventh fundamental article of the Jewish creed. It is also interesting to remember that two of the Targums, as a supplement to that speech which they suppose defective, "And Cain said to his brother Abel" (Gen. 4: 8), add a disputation between the brothers about "eternal judgment".

The Apostle speaks of this subject in the same way as he does concerning "baptisms". There were the divine ordinances, and there were the human traditions connected therewith. The first had to be left because the dispensation had changed, the second, because they made void the Word of God. Just in the same way does the Apostle deal with eternal judgment. In the first place, God is the Judge, not man, and in the second place, much has been read into the Word on that dread subject which is untrue. Note the passages in Hebrews where Paul uses the word "eternal", every one of which, except Hebrews 6: 2, having reference to redemption, and not to judgment:

"Eternal salvation" (Heb. 5: 9).
"Eternal judgment" (Heb. 6: 2).
"Eternal redemption" (Heb. 9: 12).
"Eternal Spirit" (Heb. 9: 14).
"Eternal inheritance" (Heb. 9: 15).
"Eternal covenant" (Heb. 13: 20).

The Apostle would urge them to leave their reasonings concerning judgment for the blessed, and to them personal, realities concerning redemption. "Vengeance is Mine, I will repay". The Hebrew believers, like many Christians to-day, were too fond of apportioning out the future judgment upon those who did not believe with them, or belong to their race and creed. This Paul would alter. Leave it with God, see to the "eternal kingdom", the "eternal life", the "eternal glory" which you may be missing by your over-zeal concerning "eternal judgment".

If we accepted the dictum of the majority, then one of the very fundamentals of our faith has been forgotten in the sevenfold unity of the Spirit. Some room ought to have been found for "eternal punishment". The reader must of course choose which he will accept, the sixfold foundation of Hebrews 6, or the sevenfold unity of Ephesians 4. The unity of the Spirit has regard to "that which is perfect" or mature; the sixfold foundation is connected with that which is not perfect, and not fullgrown.

We feel that we ought not to close this chapter without seeking to lay before the reader the Scriptural meaning and usage of the Hebrew and Greek words which are translated "for ever" and "eternal". We can best illustrate the need for a consistent rendering by noting the occurrences of the word *aion* in Ephesians:

"This *world*" (1:21).
"The *course* of this world" (2: 2).
"The *ages* to come" (2: 7).
"From the beginning of the *world*" (3: 9).
"*Eternal* purpose" (3: 11).
"Throughout all *ages world without end*" (3: 21).
"Rulers of the darkness of this *world*" (6: 12).

The words emphasized in the above quotations are in each case the word *aion*. The Authorised Version has rendered *aion* throughout the New Testament by the words "world", "course", "age", "eternal", and in conjunction with the prepositions *apo*, *ek*, *eis* (meaning respectively, "from", "out of", and "into"), it gives "since the world began", "from the beginning of the world", "for ever", "for evermore", "ever", "for ever and ever", "while the world standeth", "world without end".

If we have no theology to uphold, and if furthermore we count the judgment of men as a very small thing, it is possible that we might venture to wonder how it is that one word can be translated "since the world *began*", and also be rendered "world *without* end". Or again, how the word which is rendered "this world" can also mean "for ever", and "eternal". The reader of the original Scriptures would read exactly the same word in Ephesians 1: 21 as he would in Ephesians 3: 9, the only difference being that in the first instance the word is singular, while in the second it is plural.

The English reader has in the Authorised Version the rendering of man's idea, instead of a consistent translation of the word used by God. We cannot spare time to give many examples, but Matthew 24 and 25 supply one instance of faulty rendering. In Matthew 24: 3 we read, "the end of the world". This clearly shows that the word *aion* (translated "world") *may* have an *end*, yet turned into an adjective we find it translated by words intended to express a state that *never* ends, for in Matthew 25: 46 it is rendered with punishment, "everlasting", and with life, "eternal". Further, there are three important passages where the word *aionios* is joined to *chronos*. The passages are Romans 16: 25, 2 Timothy 1: 9, and Titus 1: 2. The Authorised Version translates the words thus, "since the world began", and "before the world began". The Revised Version has rendered the same passages "through times eternal", and "before times eternal", and has gone to the other extreme, for how can one conceive of a period *before* eternity? What are we to do with a word that at one breath can mean a limited period of time, and also eternity?

If the translators had been consistent, we should have read "age-times" instead of "times eternal", "this age" instead of "this world", "unto the ages" instead of "for ever", and "the end of the age" instead of "the end of the world". If we turn to *Dr E. W. Bullinger's* Lexicon and Concordance we read that:

> "*Aion* is from *ao, aemi,* to blow, to breathe, the life that wastes away in the breathing of our breath, life as transitory, then the course of life, an age or generation. *Aion* always includes a reference to life, filling time or a space of time. Accordingly, the unbounded time in which the history or life of the world is accomplished, and hence, the world, or filling the immeasurable contents of immeasurable time".

A reference to *Liddell and Scott's* Lexicon will give ample confirmation of this definition. How comes the word which denotes that which has both beginning and end to mean that which is eternal? For a man to look forward into the future may be futile and vain; he can only see so far as God's revelation allows. Age upon age lies before his view, and seeing no end, and not being able to conceive of one, he calls that space which exceeds his tiny perspective — eternity! whereas to Him Who sitteth in the heavens it is but one short stanza in His dealings with men, angels, and the universe.

We are not, however, to import into the word *aion* the meaning of the pagan Greek, neither have we any need, for in the Septuagint Version we find the word frequently used to translate the Hebrew word *olam*, and to understand this word will help us to understand the other. We are indebted to the studies of another (A. E. Knoch) for the list of passages given hereunder. First we call attention to the translation of the words *me-olam*, "from everlasting".

Used of God	*Used of Man*
Ever of old (Psalm 25:6).	Of old (Gen. 6:4).
From everlasting (Psalm 41:13).	In old time (Josh. 24:2).
Even from everlasting (Psalm 90:2).	Of old (1 Sam. 27:8).
From everlasting (Psalm 93:2).	Of old (Psalm 119:52).
From everlasting (Psalm 103:17).	Long time (Isa. 42:14).
From everlasting (Isa. 63:16).	Since the beginning of the world (Isa. 64:4).

We have not given all the passages, these being enough to help us to see the fitness of the remark, "There is a startling inconsistency here". When applied to God it is always "ever" or "everlasting", but when applied to men it is *never* so rendered. Why? Because in no case will the sense bear it. Man and his history do *not* stretch back to a dateless past eternity. No nation, no prophets have been "from everlasting". If a translator would be guilty of tampering with the Word and prerogatives of God should he render *meolam* "from everlasting" when referring to man in the past, why should he be called a greater heretic for questioning the propriety of using the word *olam* to mean a future eternity when applied to man? The one case is by the nature of things impossible; the future still awaits us, and man has ventured his own opinion, tacked it on to the Word of God, and, usurping the solemn authority of that Holy Word, has swayed the minds, influenced the faith and stifled the consciences of thousands.

We believe that the word *olam* never carries with it the idea of eternity in any passage of Scripture. Any reader who possesses a Hebrew Concordance can turn up many passages (we give just a few by way of illustration). Exodus 21: 5, 6, "If the servant shall plainly say . . . I will not go out free . . . his master shall bore his ear through with an aul; and he shall serve him *for ever*". The context tells us that this has reference to a "Hebrew servant". Now if we read Leviticus 25: 40 concerning the Hebrew servant, we find it written, "He shall serve thee unto the year of Jubilee", when his service ends, and he is not merely free to go out himself, but to take his wife and children with him. In 1 Samuel 1: 22 Hannah, speaking of Samuel, says "I will bring him, that he may appear before the Lord, and there abide *for ever*". Hannah interprets for us these words "*for ever*" in her vow recorded in verse 11, "I will give him unto the Lord all the *days of his life*".

There is no room for the word "until" in our conception of the term "for ever", yet we read in Isaiah 32: 14, 15, "The forts and towers shall be for dens *for ever* . . . *until* the spirit be poured upon us". Scripture never contradicts itself. If our renderings make any appearance of inconsistency, so much the worse for our renderings; let us alter them, but never let us tamper with the Word or the words of truth.

Revelation 21: 22 tells us of a future period when there will be "no temple", yet if we believe the translators of the Authorised Version we shall have a difficulty, for both temple, priesthood, and sacrifices are said to be "*for ever*". We give a reference for each, trusting that the interested reader will search out more for himself (Ezek. 37: 26; Exod. 40: 15; Numb. 18: 8). One more consideration of this Hebrew word, and we leave this section of our study for something less controversial.

The word *olam* is followed in many instances by the words *va ed*. What is the meaning of this added expression *va ed*? The Authorised Version variously renders *ed* by "for", "till", "to", "until", "unto", "yet", *e.g.*:

"Shalt eat bread *till* thou return unto the dust" (Gen. 3: 19)
"Since that time even *until* now" (Ezra. 5: 16).

Va is the Hebrew equivalent for "and". This brings us to the strange expression, "For ever and yet further". That the Hebrew conveys this idea of some period beyond that covered by *olam* is brought out in the Septuagint, which renders the expression, *le olam va ed* by *ton aiona, kai ep aiona, kai eti* (Exod. 15: 18), which translated reads, "the age, and upon the age, and still". *Eti* is translated in the Authorised Version by the word "*yet*" 51 times, besides "further", "still", etc.

There is another consideration to be kept in mind, and that is the fact that *aion* is often rendered in the plural. If the singular can mean "for ever", how can we translate the plural? If we will but render the word *aion* consistently throughout by the word "age", all will be clear. We can have the expression "unto the age", and "unto the ages of the ages" without doing violence to sense, but "eternities of eternities" and "eternity past and eternity future" is simply unintelligible. We may well ask, What is the meaning of the word *olam* that is translated *aion* by the Septuagint?

The root idea of the word *olam* is something secret or hidden (*see* Psalm 90: 8, "secret sins", Eccles. 12: 14, "secret thing"). Because the period is undefined and unknown, man has jumped to the conclusion that it is "for ever", forgetting that he has limited knowledge and that there *may* be ages beyond his ken. Look at Ecclesiastes 3: 11, the Authorised Version says, "He hath set the world in their heart". If we translate the word *olam* with regard to the root sense of something secret, we shall read, "He (God) hath made everything beautiful in its season, (but) He hath even put *obscurity* in the midst of them, that man cannot find out the work that God doeth from the beginning to the end".

We could go further, but will desist; sufficient has been laid before the reader to show that *aion* is the Greek rendering of the Hebrew *olam*, and that *olam* signifies a period of time whose end is undefined, or hidden from man, but which is by no means "everlasting", for instances have been given above of things which *have come to an end*, which were to be "unto the age" (*le olam* is translated in the A. V. "for ever"). Added to this we have the 20 passages wherein we read *le olam va ed* (translated "for ever and ever"), which really means, "unto the age of undefined limits, and yet further".

It will be seen from the usage and meaning of these two words (*olam* and *aion*), that the ages had a beginning, and that they will have an end. There is a purpose or plan in connection with the ages, that purpose being intimately connected with redemption. It includes, as we have seen, "things in heaven, and things in earth". Once, "before the times of ages" sin was unknown; its entry into God's universe led to the development of the purpose of the ages". That purpose, including both Israel and the church, is now in process. The time will come when the last age of the ages will have arrived. Then in that dispensation of the fulness of the seasons Christ will head up all things, Christ will reconcile all things, and the ages will terminate with the accomplishment of redemptive purposes — "God all in all".

In Ephesians 1: 10 we have Christ in relation to the universe as *Head.*

In Philippians 2: 10 we see Him acknowledged in His name of *Saviour.*

In Colossians 1: 20 we see Him as *Reconciler.*

At this conjunction of the purposes of God the heavenly and earthly sections become united, but during the working out of these things, the heavenly and the earthly, the church and the earthly kingdom are kept quite distinct.

Some may imagine that by these observations the eternal security of the believer is attacked. This is by no means the case; this is unquestionably settled by such emphatic words as "incorruptible", "immortal", and by the promise of Christ in John 14: 19. We now turn to the seven passages wherein *aion* occurs in Ephesians.

The moment we leave the words of man for the words of God, the seven occurrences of the word *aion* are found to be in perfect order, and in harmony with the completeness of the testimony of this epistle of the Mystery. Reason and logic cannot argue out the dispensational dealings of God.

> "By *faith* we understand that the ages (if we translate 'worlds', what do we mean? Are the stars 'worlds' — some think so — but does Scripture warrant the thought?) were fitted together by the spoken word or command of God, so that that which is seen should not take its origin from things which appear" (Heb. 11: 3).

It is idle and vain to speculate concerning the termination of the ages; these things belong unto the Lord, that which is revealed is for us. Let us then not darken the revelation by faulty traditions, however respectable and aged they may be.

Aion in Ephesians

A 1:21. Rulers of this and future *ages*. Subject to Christ.
 B 2:2. The *age* of this world. Satanic energy (*energō*).
  C 2:7. In *ages* to come. Display of divine grace (future)
   D 3:9. The Mystery, hid from the *ages* by God
  C 3:11. The purpose of the *ages*. Display of divine wisdom (now)
 B 3:21. The generations of the *age* of the *ages*. Divine energy (*energō*).
A 6:12. Rulers of the darkness of this *age*. Withstood by Christians.

Here we have order, whereas man by his endeavours has produced confusion. The great central figure of the structure, the member that is unique and that stands alone, is D, *The Mystery, hid from the ages by God*. This is the pivot, the hinge of the whole, even as it is the theme of divine revelation during this age.

Space will not allow anything more than a most casual reference to another passage which illuminates Hebrews 6. That passage is 1 Corinthians 2 and 3. Let the reader study the parallelism of these two passages. We give as a guide the following key words:

1 Cor. 2 and 3	*Heb. 5 and 6*	*Eph. 2 and 4*
(1) Babes (3:1).	Babes (5:13).	Babes (4:14).
(2) Milk (3:2).	Milk (5:13).	—
(3) Meat (3:2).	Meat (5:14).	—
(4) Perfect (2:6).	Perfect (5:14; 6:1).	Perfect (4:13).
(5) Foundation (3:11).	Foundation (6:1).	Foundation (2:20).
(6) Fire (3:13).	Fire (6:8)	—
(7) Six things erected (3:12).	Six-fold elements (6:1, 2).	Seven-fold unity (4:3-6).

"The first principles" of Hebrews 6 are likened to "milk", which is not the food for "perfect" or "full grown men". This is the teaching of 1 Corinthians 2 and 3. Paul could not give the Corinthians even a hint of the Mystery, for they were carnal; he could only feed them with milk. Immediately after the revelation of the unity of the Spirit, and the unity of the faith, the Apostle says, "that ye be no longer babes" (Eph. 4: 14).

If the reader still prefers Hebrews 6 to Ephesians 4, we must leave him to his choice. Certain it is he cannot have both. To go on unto perfection he must leave these things behind. The issues that have been raised in this chapter are of supreme importance. None are more conscious than the writer that his exposition is wholly inadequate to fully open out the treasures of the grace of God to the Gentiles. All that he can do is to place these things before the reader, praying that the Lord may give a knowledge of the truth.

We had hoped to have had a chapter devoted to the consideration of the "unity of the Spirit" as set forth in Ephesians 4, and to have contrasted the sixfold foundation of Hebrews 6, with the sevenfold unity of Ephesians 4. Lack of space has compelled us to omit several items, but we give the following extract from the unprinted chapter, so that the reader may be able to consider the two passages together:

God has not left us in ignorance as to what this unity consists of, for verses 4-6 are God's own definition of what the unity of the Spirit really is. The insertion of the words, "there is", both in the Authorised Version and Revised Version of Ephesians 4: 4, tends to prevent the reader from seeing that these verses are explanatory. There are seven items in this unity, and they are arranged as follows:

A One *Body*
  B One *Spirit*
    C One *Hope*
      D One *Lord*
    C One *Faith*
  B One *Baptism*
A One *God* and *Father*.

CHAPTER FOURTEEN

Ordinances, the Lord's Supper, the Lord's Day and the First Day of the Week

In the preceding chapter we compared and contrasted two passages wherein the distinctions between the Judaistic Christianity of the believers who were "zealous for the law", and the seven-fold unity of the Spirit of those who had believed the truth of the Mystery were brought out. There the subject of baptism came before us, and we found that it was vitally connected with the earthly kingdom and the gospel preached by Peter and the twelve.

In 1 Corinthians the Apostle Paul tells us that he baptized several believers of that church, but adds words which go to show that water baptism did *not* form a part of the commission which he had received from the Lord (1 Cor 1: 14-17). The carnal believers were turning a divine ordinance into a party shibboleth, gathering around the names of those who had baptized them as around party leaders. This Paul abominated with his whole soul. There is a statement, however, in verse 17 which demands careful attention. "Christ sent me not to baptize, but to preach the gospel". Not one of the Apostles who received the commission of Christ as recorded in Mark 16: 15-20 could ever say these words. Their commission was to "preach the gospel, *and* baptize". Paul could say, "Christ sent me *not* to baptize, *but* to preach the gospel".

Paul for a time laboured in conjunction with the twelve at Jerusalem, and while he did so he preached the gospel of the kingdom, the hope of Israel, and their baptism which accompanied it. His full apostleship, however, awaited the setting aside of Israel and the kingdom, and it is not until after Acts 28 that we find Paul, the Apostle of the dispensation of the Mystery, proclaiming *one* baptism, and perfect emancipation from all ordinances. The one baptism whereby a believer of the present dispensation is made a member of the one Body is the work of the Holy Spirit, "without hands" and without ordinances uniting the believer, on resurrection ground, to the risen Saviour, burying his "old man" in the burial of Christ, in the baptism wherewith Christ was baptized into death (Matt. 20: 22, 23).

The epistles written to Timothy and Titus contain explicit directions to the leaders in the churches, "that they may know how they ought to behave in the house of God", but we look in vain for any direction, warning, or instruction concerning Baptism or the Lord's Supper. There are one or two facts which we must consider before taking up the subject of the Lord's Supper in detail.

Closely allied to this ordinance of the Lord's Supper in 1 Corinthians 11 is the chapter on spiritual gifts (1 Cor. 12), and the two references to the ministry of women (1 Cor. 11: 2-16 and 14: 34-36). We have already alluded to the difference observable in relation to ministry in chapter 11, so we will not repeat the quotations again here. The contrast observable is decisive and important. At Corinth we are met with spiritual gifts at every turn, possessed by believers who were addressed as being "carnal", and to whom the deeper things of God could not be revealed (1 Cor. 2). In the churches supervised by Timothy and Titus there is not a single *mention* or *expectation* of gifts at all, the only qualifications being those of godliness and morality. 1 Corinthians 12 and 14 are inspired truth, but these chapters would be *utterly useless*, so far as practical advice is concerned, to Timothy and Titus in the regulation of the churches under their care.

We have another important item to consider. While we find some things, such as water baptism, supernatural gifts, and the Lord's Supper omitted from the epistles of the Mystery, we find some things which obtained under the Pentecostal dispensation repeated. This is valuable information. It tells us that where a doctrine or a practice is to be carried over from the past dispensation into the present, then the Apostle Paul was inspired to *say so*.

1 Corinthians 11 and 14	*1 Timothy 2: 8-14*
"Let your women keep silence in the churches, for it is not permitted unto them to speak, but to be under obedience, as also the Law saith" (*cp.* Gen. 3: 16).	"I will therefore that men (Greek = males in contrast to females) pray". "I suffer not a woman to teach, nor to usurp authority over the man, but to be in silence. For Adam was first formed, then Eve, and Adam was not deceived, but the woman, being deceived, was in the transgression" (*cp.* Gen. 3: 13).

Here it will be observed that the primeval conditions which were brought about by the fall are not altered by the introduction of the dispensation of the Mystery. The relation between the man and the woman must still be maintained "because of the angels" (1 Cor. 11:

10), and because of the "principalities and powers in heavenly places" (Eph. 3: 10).

If it be not invidious to compare the importance of one Scripture with another, we now ask, are not the ordinances of Baptism and the Lord's Supper, and the teaching concerning spiritual gifts, as important as the silence or ministry of women in the church? If so, and none will deny it, how is it that the Apostle is inspired to repeat the instruction concerning the ministry of women, and *inspired to omit* any reference to these other equally important subjects? We see only two possible answers. One is that he forgot to mention it, which is a complete denial of the doctrine of inspiration; the other is that he repeated any doctrine or practice which was to be perpetuated, and omitted any reference to those which passed away with the dispensation of the earthly kingdom.

Further, not only does Paul definitely omit any reference to these ordinances, but he most emphatically teaches that all these external observances are done away in Christ. Let us look at Ephesians 2: 13-22, which is arranged as follows:

A1 B He is our peace
  C Who has made the both one (*ta amphotera*)
    D And has broken down the middle wall of the enclosure
      E The enmity abolished in His flesh
    D The law of the commandments in decrees, bringing to naught
  C In order that He might create in Himself the two into one new man (*duo*)
B Making peace
A2 F And that He might fully reconcile
  G The both in one body (*tous amphoterous*)
    H By means of the cross
      I Slaying the enmity
    H And having come, preached peace to those far off, and to those nigh
  G The both through Him (*oi amphoteroi*)
F Have access by one Spirit unto the Father.

We cannot stay to fully consider the teaching of this glorious passage. Let the reader compare the related sections together. The central sections of the structure particularly claim our attention now, viz., D, E, *D*, and H, I, *H*. In both we find reference to enmity abolished, and the first section declares that enmity to have been connected with the middle wall of the enclosure. This middle wall has reference to the *chel*, which separated the court of the Gentiles from the court of Israel in the temple. Upon the wall of this enclosure was a tablet bearing a Greek inscription, which may be translated as follows:

> No one being a foreigner may enter within the enclosure around the holy place. Whoever is apprehended will himself be to blame for his death which will certainly follow.

(A cast of the Greek inscription may be seen in the British Museum).

The charge that Paul had taken Trophimus into the court of Israel was *literally* false, but spiritually was most true, for that is just what his gospel accomplished. The middle wall of enclosure which was in the temple at Jerusalem perpetuated the distinction between Gentile and Jewish believers. All distinctions have now been obliterated; in the heavenly holiest of all there is no middle wall of partition, *both* have access by one Spirit unto the Father.

We have to enquire to what does the middle wall refer? What was there which acted like a barrier between the Jewish and Gentile believers? The answer is found in the corresponding clause *D*, "the law of commandments in decrees". The word *dogma*, which we have translated "decrees", is translated "ordinances" in the Authorised Version. It occurs only five times in the New Testament: Luke 2: 1; Acts 16: 4; Acts 17: 7; Ephesians 2: 15; and Colossians 2: 14. The cognate word *dogmatizomai* occurs but once, viz., Colossians 2: 20, "*subject to ordinances*". The Hebrew equivalent of this word means, "to confine, to restrain, to bind as with cords" (*cp*. Gen. 39: 20; 49: 11), "to bind as by a vow" (Numb. 30: 3). This helps us to understand the nature of the "decrees". They are restraints and bonds imposed either by man or God. Two of the occurrences given above refer to the decrees of Caesar. One is the passage in Ephesians 2: 15 under consideration, with its parallel passage in Colossians 2: 14. This leaves but one other passage, viz., Acts 16: 4.

What were the decrees which were ordained by the apostles and elders at Jerusalem? In Acts 15 we have the record of the decree sent forth by the apostles and elders at Jerusalem in relation to the problems arising in connection with the believers among the Gentiles. James, speaking in reference to this, says:

> "Wherefore, my sentence is, that we trouble not them which from among the Gentiles are turned to God (regarding the law of Moses and circumcision, *cp*. Acts 15: 1-5), but that we write unto them that they abstain from the pollutions of idols, and from fornication, and from that which is strangled, and from blood. For

> *Moses* of old time hath *in every city* them that preach *him*, being read in the synagogues every sabbath day. Then it pleased the apostles and elders, with the whole church, to send chosen men of their own company" (Acts 15: 19-22).

Then follows the letter which was agreed upon.

The words "it pleased", "it seemed good" (verses 22, 25, and 28) are phases of the verb *dokeo* (to think), which gives the word "dogma". A dogma, decree, or ordinance was something which "seemed good", arising out of the thoughts of those possessing it. Some dogmas are good, because framed by God. Some are bad, because framed by man. Some are good for the appointed time, but become "weak and beggarly elements" if misapplied; such were the commands of the law (*cp*. Gal. 4).

These decrees sent from Jerusalem absolved the Gentiles from obedience to the law, and the rite of circumcision, but they only made the difference between the two felt all the more. The Jewish believers were still the "circumcision", and the Gentile believers the "uncircumcision", and this, while it was consistent during the dispensation of the Acts, is utterly hostile to the spiritual and heavenly unity which is now in force. This fleshly distinction was entirely removed when the present dispensation was ushered in. Those who are "called circumcision in the flesh made with hands" have no place in the dispensation of the Mystery. Colossians 2: 8-15 supplies a valuable note here.

> "Beware lest any one lead you off as a spoil, by means of a vain deceitful philosophy, according to the traditions of men, according to the religious elements of the world, and not according to Christ, for in Him dwells all the fulness of the Godhead bodily, and ye are in Him filled full, Who is the Head of all principality and authority, in Whom ye were circumcised with a *circumcision not made by hand*, in stripping off the body of flesh in the circumcision of Christ. Having been buried with Him in the baptism, in Whom also ye have been raised together through faith of the inworking of God, Who raised Him from among the dead. And you, being dead to your offences, and to the uncircumcision of your flesh, He hath quickened together with Him, having forgiven you all trespasses; having blotted out the handwriting of the decrees which was against us, and hath taken away the same from the midst, having nailed it to His cross, having stripped off the principalities and authorities, He made of them a public example, celebrating a triumph over them thereby" (Col. 2: 8-15).

We shall understand this triumph the better if we examine a passage in Ephesians 4. Its relation to the unity of the Spirit may be seen by the following:

A The unity of the Spirit
  B The measure. The gift of Christ
A The unity of the faith
  B The measure. The fulness of Christ.

Ephesians 4: 8, 9 are the opening verses of a new section dealing with "diversity" of gifts. In 1 Corinthians 12 we noticed on pages 154 — 157 that the diversities of gifts were attributed to "the one and self-same Spirit, dividing to every man severally as He will". In Ephesians 4 we find that the gifts come from the one Lord, instead of the one Spirit.

The passage of Scripture here quoted is Psalm 68: 18. Psalm 68 is one of the thirty-one Psalms forming the second book of the Psalms, which answers to the book of Exodus. The theme of this Exodus book of Psalms is "Israel's redemption". This Psalm was handed over for public use in the worship of God, and used at the Feast of the Passover. There is a yet further link with the Exodus in the occurrence in this Psalm of the name *Jah* (verse 4), a name of God closely associating Him with accomplished redemption. It occurs for the first time in Exodus 15: 2, and for the first time in the Psalms in this 68th Psalm.

Exodus 15 records the Song of Moses and the children of Israel, which they sang on the borders of the Red Sea after the overthrow of the hosts of Pharaoh.

> "I will sing unto the Lord, for He hath triumphed gloriously, the horse and his rider hath He thrown into the sea.
>
> The Lord (*Jah*) is my strength and my song, and He is become my salvation.
>
> Pharaoh's chariots and his host hath He cast into the sea.
>
> Who is like unto Thee, O Lord, among the gods?"

Let us notice that the Lord not only "triumphed gloriously" over Pharaoh, but also "among the *gods*": the fallen angels, demons, and spiritual powers ranged under Satan received a premonitory judgment. Exodus 12: 12, "Against all the *gods* of Egypt I will execute judgment". David speaking of the same deliverance and judgment says, "And what one nation in the earth is like Thy people Israel . . . which Thou redeemedst to Thee from Egypt, from the nations and their *gods*?" (2

Sam. 7: 23). In 1 Corinthians 10: 20 we learn that "the things which the Gentiles sacrifice, they sacrifice to demons, and not to God", and it was against these invisible powers that the plagues of Egypt were directed, as much as against their ignorant and deluded devotees. Returning to Psalm 68 we read:

> "The chariots of God are twenty thousand, even thousands of angels, Jehovah among them (hath ascended from) Sinai into the Sanctuary. Thou hast ascended on high, Thou hast led captivity captive, Thou hast received and given gifts among men. Yea, for the rebellious also, that the Lord God might dwell among them. Blessed be the Lord . . . Blessed be God" (Verses 17—19 and 35).

Here we have the voice of praise in connection with the triumphant ascension of the ark of God to its resting place, looking forward to the day when the type shall be fulfilled in reality, when the kingdoms of this world shall have become the kingdoms of the Lord, and of His Christ:

> "Sing unto God ye kingdoms of the earth; oh sing praises unto the Lord. Selah. To Him that rideth upon the heaven of heavens, which were of old" (Psalm 68: 32, 33).

The Apostle Paul had a knowledge of the mystery of Christ which surpassed any revelation given to prophets or apostles before Him (Eph. 3: 4). He could see that just as the overthrow of Pharaoh and his host and of the gods of Egypt was typical of the final overthrow of antichrist, his host, and Satan in relation to the chosen people Israel, so the words of Psalm 68 supplied an analogy regarding the heavenly triumph of Christ, which is connected with the heavenly sphere of redemptive purposes revealed now in the epistles of the Mystery. Psalm 68: 17, 18 appears with fuller meaning to the apostle than David or the prophets of old could discover (*cp.* Eph. 3: 5). Not only does it speak of a triumph over earthly foes, but over heavenly powers also.

With the exception of the one reference in Romans 8: 38, the epistles to the Ephesians and Colossians are the only passages of Scripture which tell us anything about these mighty beings in relation to redemption. While the earthly side of God's purposes was running its course, these heavenly powers are not mentioned except in a casual way, but the moment that we enter the present dispensation of heavenly purposes and heavenly places, we are at once confronted with these spiritual powers, and with Christ's complete triumph over them. The complete subjugation of these evil powers by the cross of Christ is seen in Colossians 2: 10-15 already quoted above:

"And ye are in Him filled full, Who is Head of all principality, and power ... stripping off the principalities, and powers, He made of them an open example, celebrating a triumph over them by it (the cross)".

To the same effect is 1 Peter 3: 22. Speaking of Christ raised from the dead it says, "Who is gone into heaven, and is on the right hand of God, angels and authorities and powers being made subject to Him". Of a truth we can sing unto the Lord, for He hath *triumphed gloriously*.

This is the burden of the words, "He led captivity captive". Victorious generals and kings were wont to display their triumphs by chaining the captives taken to their chariots. The Lord Jesus, having triumphed over the powers of darkness, chained the vanquished host to His glorious chariot, and led them triumphantly through the heights of heaven. Not only did the Lord "ascend up far above all heavens" proclaiming His triumph, but He also "descended into the lower parts of the earth". The ascent was literal: why should we spiritualize the descent?

Peter, who supplies us with the passage already quoted that Christ had ascended, "angels and authorities and powers being subjected unto Him", also tells how, in connection with this same triumph, the Lord, after He was "made alive by the Spirit" (and therefore speaking of His resurrection, and not His humiliation), went even unto the spirits in prison, and made a proclamation. These spirits were disobedient in the days of Noah, and were placed in prison to await their judgment. Of a similar nature to this is the reference in 2 Peter 2: 4 and Jude 6. The angels that sinned were cast down to Tartarus, and delivered into chains of darkness. "The angels that kept not their own *principality* ... He hath reserved unto the judgment of the great day in perpetual chains of darkness".

The triumph of the Lord was complete. Beings in heaven, on earth, and under the earth were compelled to bear witness to the fact that He had "triumphed gloriously", even as they will yet again join in the climax confession that Jesus Christ is *Lord*, in the day that is coming.

The enmity of the law of commandments concerning ordinances or decrees is slain by Christ in the cross (Eph. 2). The handwriting of the decrees, which was against us, Christ has cancelled by nailing it to His cross (Col. 2). As we have seen, this is also related to the heavenly triumphs of the Redeemer, the stripping off of principalities and powers taking place at the same time. We may understand the practical effect which such deep doctrine is to have, by reading Colossians 2: 16-23:

> "Let no one therefore be judging you in eating, or drinking, or in respect of a feast, or new moon, or sabbath, which are a shadow of things about to be (*i.e.*, the millennium), but the body of Christ".

We must pause a moment here. The Authorised Version says, "the body *is* of Christ", supplying the verb to make sense. Does it need it? The passage conveys the true sense by omitting the word "is". We have taken the word "body" as being antithetical to "shadow" (and so of course it is), but it is more. We are not to be concerned about eating and drinking, fasts and feasts, etc., but with the Body of Christ, the spiritual unity, the one Body of Ephesians 4. This is further emphasized if we note how these few verses are arranged, viz.:

A 16, 17 —. Let no man judge you respecting obsolete observances.
  B — 17. Hold to the truth pertaining to the Body of Christ.
A 18. Let no one beguile you of your reward with philosophic deceits.
  B 19. Hold the Head.

The snare will be seen the better if we carefully translate verses 18 and 19, remembering that the word "worshipping" is translated elsewhere "religious" (Acts 26: 5; and James 1: 26, 27):

> "Let no man deprive you of your prize, having pleasure in the religious or ceremonial humility which pertains to angels, taking his stand upon things which he hath seen, vainly puffed up by the mind of his flesh, and not holding the Head, etc".

The trap laid by the evil one is very subtle. He would direct our attention away from Christ to ourselves, and then, seeing our own failures, lead us to seek to help our spiritual life by means of ordinances and observances, and to assume a humility practised by the angels, and relinquish the "boldness of access", and the "unveiled face", which are the glories of our calling. We have no need to stand with veiled face as the angels do. It is a ceremonial humility which is not pleasing to God. We have been raised "far above all principality and power", and are seated with Christ at the right hand of God. If we take our stand upon "things seen", and "things made with hands", we shall inevitably become hereby "religious", and relinquish our high calling. The moment we turn our eyes away from Christ to ourselves, that moment, Peter-like, we begin to sink:

> "Which sort of things has indeed an *appearance* of wisdom (*cp.* verses 8 and 3) in self-devised religious observances, and humiliation (of mind), and discipline (of body), yet are not really of any value to remedy indulgence of the flesh" (Col. 2: 23).

Colossians 3: 1-5 gives the true way to mortify the members on the earth, viz., by setting our mind on things above, and Colossians 2: 20 says:

> "If ye have died together with Christ from the religious elements of the world, why as though alive in the world do ye subject yourselves to decrees or ordinances, (such as) touch not, taste not, handle not, all which things are to perish with the using, according to the commandments (Matt. 15: 9 and Mark 7: 7 are the only other occurrences), and doctrines of men?"

Thus by reading the whole of Colossians 2 we shall find that by our relation to the death of Christ, by grace, we are completely raised above all ordinances, whether human or divine. Ordinances have regard to the flesh, but "we are the circumcision who worship God in spirit, who boast in Christ Jesus, and have *no confidence in the flesh*" (Phil. 3: 3; read also verses 2 and 5).

Colossians 3 takes us one step further in this teaching. Not only have we died with Christ, and been raised with Him (and note the baptism here has just as much to do with us as the circumcision), but we have also been raised together. Hence chapter 3 opens, "If, therefore, ye have been raised together with Christ, seek the things which are above, for ye died, and your life is hid together with Christ by God". Consequently we are not to act "as though living in the world" (Col 2: 20).

Circumcision in the flesh cut off the Israelite from the surrounding nations of the world. Christ, by the cross, was cut off out of the land of the living, cut off from Israel, and from all things pertaining to "this creation". As "Firstborn of all creation", and "Firstborn from the dead", He became Head of a new creation (hence emphasis on "create" in Eph. 2: 15). Believers in him are "cut off" from the flesh, and all things pertaining thereto, by the circumcision of Christ (*i.e.* His death). They are a new creation.

The various rites, ceremonies, ordinances, and observances both of divine and traditional authority made inseparable barriers between the two classes of believers. These have gone, gone completely. No Jewish "*chel*" or "*soreg*" divides the Jewish believer from the Gentile. No tablet threatens the Gentile believer with death if he dare to claim equality with the Jew, for "by one Spirit" they both have "access unto the Father", through Christ. Both, equally, are fellow-heirs, fellow-members of the Body, and fellow-partakers of His promise in Christ by the gospel (Eph. 3: 6).

Thus, if the early church had always kept true to the teaching of the Apostle of the Mystery, we should never have had the perplexities, the schisms, and the tyrannies that have sprung up in the fruitful soil of ordinances. The entire omission of all reference to water baptism, and the Lord's Supper in the epistles of the Mystery, the definite statement in Ephesians 4 as to the *one* baptism, and the weighty words of Colossians 2 and Ephesians 2 against ordinances in connection with the heavenly calling, would have been enough for any mind. As it is, tradition has had such sway, that we fight against our very liberties, we hug to ourselves the fetters of man, as though they were of precious gold, while the "riches of the glory" remain unclaimed and unknown. Consequently we realize that it is not sufficient for us now that the Apostle Paul has *omitted* any reference to the Lord's Supper from the Mystery epistles; it is not enough that he has written Ephesians 2: 15; and Colossians 2 and 3. We must lay the matter before the reader still more emphatically. One would think, by the prominence men give to it, that the Lord's Supper would be referred to on almost every page, or at least in every book of the New Testament. We find it referred to in the Gospels; but by no means certainly, in the Acts, for the term "the breaking of bread" can by no means be made to refer to the Lord's Supper except by merest inference, and finally in the first epistle to the Corinthians.

Our first consideration must be, when and under what circumstances was it instituted? Matthew 26: 26-30 supplies the information:

> "And as they were eating (*i.e.* eating the Passover, *see* verses 17 and 19), Jesus took bread (*i.e.*, a Passover loaf of unleavened bread), and blessed, and brake, and gave to the disciples, and said, Take, eat, this is My body. And He took a cup, and gave thanks, and gave to them, saying, Drink ye all of it, for this is My blood of the new covenant, which is shed for many for the remission of sins. But I say unto you, I will not drink henceforth of the fruit of the vine, until that day when I drink it new with you in My Father's kingdom. And when they had sung an hymn, they went out into the Mount of Olives".

Thus we see that the Lord's Supper is connected with the Jewish Feast of the Passover, and by reading 1 Corinthians 11: 23-26 we see that henceforth this Feast was not merely to recall the deliverance from the bondage of Egypt, but to "shew forth the Lord's death", which in 1 Corinthians 5: 7 is further interpreted by the words, "For even Christ our Passover hath been sacrificed for us". Both Matthew 26 and 1 Corinthians 11 tell us that the wine typified the blood of the *New Covenant*. What is this New Covenant? Is it connected with the

Mystery hidden since the age-times? Is the New Covenant a secret only revealed now, or is it a matter of Old Testament knowledge? Let us turn to Jeremiah 31:

> "At the same time (*i.e.* 'the latter times', 30: 24), saith the Lord, I will be the God of all the families of *Israel*, and they shall be My people . . . again I will build thee, O virgin of *Israel* . . . O Lord save Thy people, the remnant of *Israel*. Behold, I will bring them from the North country, and gather them from the coasts of the earth . . . a great company shall return thither . . . for I am a Father to *Israel* . . . He that scattered *Israel* will gather him, and keep him as a shepherd doth his flock. For the Lord hath redeemed Jacob. Behold, the days come, saith the Lord, that I will sow the house of Israel, and the house of Judah, with the seed of man, and the seed of beast . . . Behold, the days come, saith the Lord, that I will make a *new covenant* with the house of *Israel*, and with the house of *Judah*; not according to the covenant that I made with their fathers in the day that I took them by the hand to bring them *out of the land of Egypt* (hence the connection of the New Covenant with the Passover) . . . But this shall be the covenant that I will make with the house of Israel . . . If those ordinances (sun, moon and stars) depart from before Me, saith the Lord, then the seed of Israel shall cease from *being a nation* before Me for ever. Thus saith the Lord, if heaven above can be measured, and the foundations of the earth searched out beneath, I will also cast off all the seed of Israel for all that they have done, saith the Lord".

These verses are of themselves sufficient to show that the New Covenant is specifically related to the future gathering of Israel back to their land, and that the "church which is His Body" finds no place therein whatsoever. The connection between the Passover and the New Covenant is emphasized both in Matthew 26 and Jeremiah 31. Commentators have pointed out the similarity that there is between the plagues of Egypt, which led up to the Passover, and the redemption of the nation for the first time, as recorded in Exodus, and the plagues which are yet to precede the restoration of Israel, when in a fuller sense "all Israel shall be saved", as recorded in the book of the Revelation.

The opening words of Exodus 20 that introduce the ten commandments repeat the same thing. "I am the Lord thy God, which brought thee out of the land of Egypt, out of the house of bondage". So also Deuteronomy 29: 25, "Then men shall say, Because they have forsaken *the covenant* of the Lord God of their fathers, which He made with them *when He brought them forth out of the land of Egypt*". The first covenant Israel broke, the second (the New Covenant), rests on the work of Christ, and hence His words, "The blood of the New Covenant" (*see also* Jer. 11: 7, 8; Heb. 8; and Isa. 11:

11, 16). We refrain from citing further passages. Those which we have given make it abundantly plain that the New Covenant is linked with the old, which in its turn is connected with the deliverance from Egypt, and both Old and New Covenants are directly connected with the people of Israel, and have nothing in common with the dispensation of the grace of God to the Gentiles, the dispensation of the Mystery. We have not, however, finished with Matthew 26 yet.

The Lord Jesus, in this passage, is seen looking forward to "that day", to "My Father's kingdom". "I appoint unto you a kingdom, as My Father hath appointed unto Me, that ye may eat and drink at My table in My kingdom, and sit on thrones, judging the twelve tribes of Israel" (Luke 22: 29, 30). Where in all this is the remotest hint of the "church of the Mystery"? This kingdom, appointed by the Father, is referred to in Matthew 13: 43, "Then shall the righteous shine forth as the sun in the kingdom of their Father". "Then shall the King say unto them on His right hand, Come, ye blessed of My Father, inherit the kingdom prepared for you from the foundation of the world" (Matt. 25: 34). "Our Father which art in heaven . . . Thy kingdom come" (Matt. 6: 9, 10).

When we pass the "ancient landmark", viz., Acts 28, and read of the kingdom in Ephesians, we do not find "the kingdom of the heavens", or "the kingdom of the Father", but "the kingdom *of Christ* and God" (Eph. 5: 5). In Colossians 1: 13 we read of "the kingdom of the Son of His love". These distinctions are noteworthy, and add their weight to the evidence that goes to show that the kingdom connected with the New Covenant has nothing to do with the present time.

The word *diatheke*, rendered "covenant", "testament" is never used in the New Testament Scriptures apart from Israel. It is absent from the epistles of the Mystery, the *one* occurrence in Ephesians 2: 12 referring to "the time past", when the addressees of "Ephesians" were "aliens from the commonwealth of Israel, and strangers with regard to the covenants of the promise". No covenant is ever mentioned as relating to the "church which is His Body". A promise and a purpose before the age-times there is, but not a covenant either old or new.

In Matthew 26 we read that when the Supper was finished they sang a hymn (which was the set of Psalms known as the *Hallel*), and then went out to the Mount of Olives, the last portion of earth which the Saviour's feet trod before He was received up, and destined to be the first place touched by His feet when He returns to take the kingdom (Acts 1: 12, and Zech. 14: 4). It seems as though everything has been done to link the Lord's Supper with the earthly kingdom, and sever it from the Mystery. If this is the case, can we have any doubt as to who it is that has blinded men's eyes, and made them so zealous for the observance of this ordinance?

Turning to 1 Corinthians 11: 23-26 let us consider the statement, "I have received of the Lord that which also I delivered unto you". If we turn to 1 Corinthians 15: 3 we shall read, "For I delivered unto you first of all that which I also received", or Galatians 1: 11, 12, "For I certify you brethren, that the gospel which was preached of me is not after man. For I neither received it of man, neither was I taught it, but by the revelation of Jesus Christ". Paul continually declares his entire independence of man, both regarding his apostleship and his doctrine. In the church at Corinth there were those who said, "I am of Apollos", and "I am of Cephas", therefore immediately following his words of censure ("I praise you not"), he adds, "For I have received of the Lord", etc.

The greater difficulty, however, is in the words, "Ye do shew the Lord's death till He come". Men say, He has not yet come, therefore we must continue thus to shew forth His death until He does come again. At first sight this is a powerful and logical argument. We have, however, to think for a moment. What was the idea contained in the words "till He come" *when they were written?* The only other epistles then written by Paul were Galatians 1 and 2 Thessalonians. Whether the Corinthians had seen them we cannot say, but we must not read into these earlier epistles the *revelations* given after Acts 28, otherwise they cease to be revelations at all.

Cephas, or Peter, who had some influence at Corinth, gives the second coming of Christ, as it was believed and taught during the Pentecostal times, in Acts 3: 19-21. We have already referred to this passage, so we will not again repeat what we have said, beyond remarking that this coming is connected with the repentance of Israel, the times of refreshing, and the times of restoration of all things which God hath spoken by the mouth of all His holy prophets *since* the age.

Our hope is, on the other hand, connected with a promise given *before* the age-times (*see* Titus 1: 1-3; and 2: 13), which marks it off from the hope of Israel. It was this coming which was the burden of Old Testament prophecy, and connected with the millennial reign of righteousness, and the regeneration of Israel, that was before the Corinthian saints. They had everything in harmony with the kingdom on earth; witness the gifts, the record of which follows immediately upon the passage dealing with the Lord's Supper (1 Cor. 11 and 12). Every one of these Corinthian believers who assembled to partake of the Lord's Supper had some spiritual gift (1 Cor. 14: 26). These gifts and the Lord's Supper were in harmony with the dispensation in which they lived. We have no right to expect the gifts now, for they abruptly ceased at the last chapter of Acts. Why should we pick out *one* item from 1 Corinthians 11 and perpetuate *that*, when we are compelled to confess that the very next verses in 1 Corinthians 12 are written concerning that to which we can lay no claim? When the kingdom on earth became in abeyance, *everything* connected therewith necessarily went with it.*

There is a tradition which is closely allied with the question of the Lord's Supper as it is observed to-day, and it is that the "Lord's day" of Revelation 1: 10, and the "first day of the week" of Acts 20 and 1 Corinthians 16: 2 refer to the day we call *Sunday*. We are told in Revelation 1: 9, 10 that John "came to be in the isle that is called Patmos, because of the Word of God, and the testimony of Jesus (*i.e.* as verse 2 shows, to receive the revelation). "I came to be by (the) Spirit in the Lord's day" (or day of the Lord). This does not mean that John was in a particularly spiritual frame of mind on Sunday, but as in 4: 2; 17: 3 and 21: 10 he was "wrapt (or caught away) by the Spirit" to behold these visions, of which the book of Revelation is a record. Like Ezekiel (Ezek 1: 1), John was carried by the agency of the Spirit into the "day of the Lord". There is absolutely no evidence that "the first day of the week" was ever called "the Lord's day" before the book of the Revelation was written.

Not a few have objected to interpreting the words by "the day of the Lord", because we have the adjective "Lord's" instead of the noun in regimen, "of the Lord". In the first instance, the Hebrew has no such expression as "Lord's"; it must always use "of the Lord". The Greek language, however, like the English, could use either mode of expression, according as the emphasis was required. This liberty has been taken by the Authorised Version in rendering the same Hebrew expression in Haggai 1: 13 by, "the Lord's messenger", and in Malachi 2: 7, "the messenger of the Lord". So also "the Captain of the host of the Lord" (Josh. 5: 14) is the same in Hebrew as "the Captain of the Lord's host" (Josh. 5: 15). The difference between the two modes of expression, "the Lord's day", and "the day of the Lord", is not one of meaning, but of emphasis. Isaiah 2: 12 is the first occurrence of the expression in the Old Testament and supplies the key to the other passages. It is that period of which the book of Revelation is a most marvellous exposition, when "the lofty looks of man shall be humbled, and the haughtiness of men shall be bowed down, and the Lord alone shall be exalted".

---

*The reader should refer back to pages 152-154 for notes on the *parousia*.

The book of the Revelation is the book of the "unveiling". Tradition has robbed the reader of the "key of knowledge", and produced the confusion which has followed (Rev. 22: 18, 19).

Leaving the consideration of the Lord's day, we turn our attention to another expression found in the New Testament and much emphasized by a certain section of Christians, viz., "the first day of the week". The statement and the sentiment of Colossians 2: 16, 17 seem to indicate that a great change has taken place since such a passage as Numbers 15: 32—36 was written:

> "Let no man *therefore* judge (or criticize) you with regard to meat or drink, or in respect of a holy day, or of a new moon, or of the sabbaths, which are a *shadow* of things about to be".

The "therefore" looks back to the previous verses, where the Apostle warns the believer regarding the "rudiments of the world", which stand diametrically opposed to their "completeness in Christ".

Let the believer be taken up with *Him*; let him leave the rites and ceremonies, the ordinances and observances, the traditions and dogmas of men; let him *hold the Head*, and holy days, new moons, sabbaths, fasts, feasts, meats, drinks, and divers baptisms will have no more place with him than a crutch has with an athlete. These days, these feasts, these sabbaths were shadows of a coming age. We have nothing whatever to do with either the past dispensation of shadows, or the future dispensation of their fulfilment; we are connected with a period that intervenes between the breaking off of the dispensational dealings of the Lord with Israel in connection with the earthly kingdom. Our one concern is with those things that are related to Christ *the Head*, and with believers now who are members of *the Body*.

In Romans 14 the Apostle deprecates the censorious and high-handed manner in which some are wont to treat weaker brethren. Whether a man feels *free* to eat "all things", or whether he feels *bound* to abstain from all except "herbs", neither the strong nor the weak is to despise or judge the other, "for God hath received him". He then continues:

> "One man esteemeth every day alike. Let every man be fully persuaded in his own mind. He that regardeth the day, regardeth it unto the Lord, and he that regardeth not the day, to the Lord he doth not regard it".

It will be well if we now consider what days Paul was inspired to authorize. If we search the epistles which particularly concern us, viz., the Prison Epistles, our search will be in vain. We shall find as much instruction concerning the days we are to observe as we found regarding the other elements of a past dispensation. Nowhere throughout the Prison Epistles, the epistles of the Mystery, is there the slightest allusion to any command to observe a day, a season, a feast, or a fast.

Let us seek to understand the expression "the first day of the week". Our first duty will be to place the reader in possession of every occurrence of this expression in the New Testament, viz., Matthew 28: 1; Mark 16: 2, 9; Luke 24: 1; John 20: 1, 19; Acts 20: 7 and 1 Corinthians 16: 2. It will be seen that there are eight occurrences in all, coinciding with the teaching that the first day brings with it resurrection. We must next examine the "*words* which the Holy Ghost teacheth", remembering that omissions and differences of expression are ruled by inspiration of God, that all is of purpose, nothing by chance. In seven of the occurrences the plural form is used, and in one the singular. Mark 16: 9, *prote sabbatou*; Matthew 28: 1, Mark 16: 2, and the rest, *mia sabbaton*. Tregelles reads *mian sabbatou*, singular, in 1 Corinthians 16: 2.

The question which we ask is, What lesson are we to learn from the fact that the Holy Spirit has chosen to use different words in the other references? Man, in his usual perverseness, has fastened upon the *observance of the day*, whereas the Spirit of truth would by His sevenfold use of the other construction direct our hearts to contemplate the *fulfilment of a type*:

> "In the fourteenth day of the first month is the Lord's Passover. And the fifteenth day of the same month is the Feast of Unleavened Bread unto the Lord; seven days ye must eat unleavened bread . . . When ye be come into the land which I give unto you, and shall reap the harvest thereof, then ye shall bring a sheaf of the firstfruits of your harvest unto the priest, and he shall wave the sheaf before the Lord, to be accepted for you; on the *morrow after the sabbath* the priest shall wave it . . . And ye shall count unto you, from the morrow after the sabbath . . . seven sabbaths shall be complete; even unto the morrow after the seventh sabbath shall ye number fifty days, and ye shall offer a new meal offering unto the Lord. Ye shall bring out of your habitations two wave loaves of two tenth deals; they shall be of fine flour, they shall be baken with leaven; they are the firstfruits unto the Lord" (Lev. 23: 5-17).

The contrast between the sheaf of the firstfruits and the wave loaves is well marked. One sheaf, but two loaves. One is pure wheat, the other is "baken with leaven". This important distinction is further emphasized in Leviticus 2: 11-16:

> "As for the oblation of thy firstfruits, ye shall offer *them* unto the Lord, but they shall not be burnt upon the altar for a sweet savour . . . No meal offering shall be made with leaven, for ye shall burn no leaven . . . in any offering of the Lord made by fire . . . And if thou offer a meal offering of thy firstfruits unto the Lord, thou shalt offer . . . green ears of corn dried by the fire, even corns beaten out of full ears. And thou shall put oil upon *it*, and lay frankincense upon *it* . . . *it* is an offering made by fire unto the Lord".

Here again we read of "them" and "it". One is an oblation; the other is a meal offering. One may not be burned; the other must be. The meal offering must not have any leaven, but it has "all the frankincense". We trust that all can clearly see the distinction drawn between the type of Christ, and the type of His people.

"Between the evenings" of that eventful 14th Nisan, Christ our Passover was sacrificed for us, and on the morrow after the Sabbath, while the High Priest went through his empty ritual of waving the sheaf of the firstfruits before the Lord (empty, not only because the type had been fulfilled, but more, because his hands were stained with blood), on that selfsame day the true High Priest with "clean hands and pure heart" had ascended up to His Father, and presented Himself "to be accepted" on behalf of His people. This seems to be implied in the words of Christ in John 20: 17, "Jesus saith unto her, Touch Me not, for I am not yet ascended unto My Father". The same day, but later, He said, "Handle Me" (Luke 24: 13, 33, 36, 39), and eight days after this the Lord bade Thomas, "Reach hither thy finger . . . reach hither thy hand, and thrust it into My side" (John 20: 26, 27).

Fifty days from the day of resurrection brings us to Acts 2. "The day of Pentecost was fully come". Upon this day the second part of the type of Leviticus 2 and 23 began to be fulfilled. The Spirit Who had descended upon Christ like a dove, descended now upon the disciples like fire. He had no leaven; they had. They were not accepted in and of themselves, but only in and through Christ. It will be remembered that the phrase, "the first of the week" (there is no word "day" in the original) occurs but twice outside the Gospels; once in Acts and once in 1 Corinthians 16.

We are all aware that useful as chapter and verse may be, the division of the Scriptures into chapters is at times the occasion of severing that which the Lord has joined together. Therefore before we turn to 1 Corinthians 16, we will read some verses from 1 Corinthians

15, in order to learn the lesson as thoroughly as possible. Chapter 15, as we all know, is almost entirely devoted to the resurrection and its results. Among the many important passages which refer back to type or history are verses 20 and 23:

> "But now hath Christ been raised from among the dead, a *firstfruit* of them who have fallen asleep . . . a *firstfruit* Christ, after that, they who are Christ's at His coming" (*parousia*).

This brings us once again to Leviticus 23. Christ in resurrection, on the first day of the week, fulfilled the type of the *firstfruits* offered at the first of the *weeks*, these weeks numbering seven in all, and ending with Pentecost. If we turn to Deuteronomy 16: 9, 10 we shall find that this period of fifty days ending with Pentecost is called "The Feast of *Weeks*". It was at the commencement of this Feast, day *one* of the weeks that the sheaf of the firstfruits was waved, and Christ the firstfruits was raised from the dead. The emphasis is not so much on the first day of *every* week, but rather on the first day of this *set of* weeks which is singled out from the rest of the year that we have to notice.

Before we go further with the passage in 1 Corinthians 16 we desire to bring forward other important evidence in favour of this interpretation. No reader will require us to prove that the Gospel records of the first day of the week link that day with Pentecost, but what we would point out is this, that *every* instance (whether in the Gospels, Acts, or Epistles) is linked with Pentecost. Proof may be required so far as the passages in the Acts and 1 Corinthians are concerned. Let us turn to Acts 20: 7. "Upon the first of the weeks, when the disciples came together to break bread". We concede for the moment that this may refer to *Sunday*, the so-called "*Lord's day*", any first day of the week throughout the year. A reference to the context will help us to see something further, and something far more important:

> "And we sailed away from Philippi *after the days of unleavened bread*, and came to Troas in five days; where we abode seven days . . . Paul had determined to sail by Ephesus, because he would not spend the time in Asia, for he hasted, if it were possible for him, to be at Jerusalem the day of Pentecost" (Acts 20: 6-16).

If this "first of the weeks" was an ordinary "first day" meeting, why did not Paul meet with the disciples the week previous, seeing that he was in such a hurry to leave them when they were able to meet together? We are aware that many things may have prevented this, but we are also aware that Scripture tells us that Paul was willing to stay a whole week in spite of the fact that he desired, if possible, to be at Jerusalem by Pentecost. Within these few verses we have the three Feasts of the Jews set out in their order:

(1) Unleavened Bread,
(2) First of the Weeks,
(3) Pentecost.

Keeping these thoughts in mind, let us turn again to 1 Corinthians 16. The last verse of the previous chapter is an exhortation based upon the resurrection, and the first verse of chapter 16 is connected therewith. In chapter 5 he refers to Christ as the *Passover*, and draws a lesson from the *Feast of Unleavened Bread*. In chapter 15 he speaks of the *Firstfruits*, and in chapter 16: 8 he says, "But I will tarry at Ephesus until *Pentecost*". Here we have an exact parallel with the order of events as already seen in Acts 20:

(1) Unleavened Bread,
(2) Firstfruits,
(3) Pentecost.

Now let us consider 1 Corinthians 16: 1, 2:

> "Now concerning the collection (not collections) for the saints (*i.e.,* those at Jerusalem, *see* verse 3), as I have given order for the churches of Galatia, even so do ye. *On the first of the weeks* let each one of you put by itself, laying up in whatever degree he may have prospered, that there may be *no collections* when I come".

This last clause shows us that some special offering was intended; not a weekly offering, for the Apostle would not wish that to cease when he came. In 2 Corinthians 9: 1, 2 he says:

> "Concerning the ministry which is for the saints, it is superfluous for me to be writing to you, for I know your forwardness of mind, of which in your behalf I am boasting unto the Macedonians, that Achaia hath been prepared for *a year* past".

Is this referring to weekly offerings? Do not 1 Corinthians 16 and 2 Corinthians 9 refer to the same thing? The Apostle continues with a reference to the harvest, which is quite appropriate to the occasion. "Now he that supplieth seed to the sower, and bread for eating, will supply and multiply your seed for sowing, and cause to grow your fruits of righteousness". Let us turn to Deuteronomy 16: 9-12:

> "Seven weeks shalt thou number unto thee; begin to number the seven weeks from such time as thou beginnest to put the sickle to the corn. And thou shalt keep the *Feast of Weeks* unto the Lord thy God, with the tribute of a free-will offering of thine hand which thou shalt give unto the Lord thy God *according as the Lord thy God hath blessed thee*".

Is not this exactly in harmony with the words of 1 Corinthians 16: 2, "Laying up in whatever degree *he may have prospered*"? How much more valuable does this passage become when we see its relation to Christ the Firstfruits, than if we make it teach something about a "Christian Sabbath". Christ our Passover was connected with the Feast of Unleavened Bread; Christ the Firstfruits was connected with the Feast of Weeks, which, commencing with the unleavened sheaf, concludes with the leavened loaves of Pentecost. There was no need for the church at Corinth to send their "tribute" up to the temple at Jerusalem, but Paul points out another way in which their gratitude may flow out to the poor saints at Jerusalem. If it was the purpose of God that we should observe the first day of the week in the orthodox way, how is it that 1 Corinthians 16: 2 is the only reference to it made by Paul in any of his epistles?

If Paul had been quite silent as to "days" one might have said, at any rate he does not say one way or another. But he is by no means silent. Clearly and solemnly he warns against the observance of days, and adds no qualifying clause whereby we may understand that the first day of the week was to be excepted from his denunciations. If believers in Paul's time really kept the first day of the week instead of the seventh day because of the resurrection, what a splendid opportunity Paul had in Colossians 2 and 3. There he denounces the keeping of Sabbaths as among the "shadows" with which we have nothing to do; he enlarges upon the resurrection of Christ, but says not one word with regard to any day being kept as an alternative to the discarded Sabbath.

In Galatians 4, when the Apostle sought to show the difference between law and grace, what an opportunity he had for pointing out the oft-repeated lesson gathered from the seventh day and the first day; but no, again he denounces the observance of days, and says not a word in their favour. If the observance of the first day of the week is of *divine* appointment, then Romans 14 is inexplicable. It is not a matter of conviction or faith; it is a matter of fact, but that is not the teaching of the fourteenth of Romans. We are convinced that there is neither command nor precedent for the observance of the "Lord's day", or the "first day", as the "Sabbath".

Is it coincidence or inspiration that places every reference to the first of the weeks in between the Feast of Unleavened Bread and Pentecost? Have we *all* we need in Scripture for our instruction, or must we wade through the "Fathers" to find out our church order? But those of our readers who may see with us that there is no such command to observe the first day, must remember the exhortation of Romans 14 not to "despise the one that is weak", and those who still believe that the Lord does command such observing, let them not "judge" those who see the fulness that there is in Christ Jesus.

There may be need for us to say clearly that although we have thus written, and thus believe, yet we do not undervalue the opportunity afforded in the nature of things of meeting with the Lord's people on the first day of the week, and enjoying the fellowship of His saints in worship, prayer, praise, and study. And further, while we consider all days alike unto the Lord, and feel absolutely free to act on the first day as we should on the second, yet we have a responsibility to the weaker consciences of many of our brethren and sisters, and we would carefully guard against any ungracious appearance of bravado.

We believe we have demonstrated that both Acts 20: 7 and 1 Corinthians 16: 2 are capable of a fuller and grander interpretation than the traditional idea can ever lead to. When all this has been weighed in the balances of the sanctuary, let this additional fact be remembered, that every reference to, and every *apparent* authority for, the observance of the day is found in those Scriptures which were written on the other side of the "ancient landmark" of Acts 28. Those who are members of the one Body are warned against the attempts of any one to "spoil them" through the rudiments or elements of the world. "Let no man judge you therefore in meat, or in drink, or in respect of any holy day, or of the new moon, or of the sabbaths". Whatever meaning we may decide the word *sabbaton* to convey in the earlier passages, the Apostle disposes of it in Colossians 2: 16. "Your life is hid with Christ in God". Very well then, "why, as though *living in the world*, are ye subject to ordinances?"

Rotherham, in his translation of Colossians 2: 23, speaks of a "self-devised religious observance". True spirituality is the outcome of unhindered and unfettered enjoyment of the fulness of Christ. Believers of the present dispensation are to be occupied not with the observance of days but with "the day of Christ" (Phil 1: 6), "the day of redemption" (Eph. 4: 30), "that day" (2 Tim. 1: 12, 18 and 4: 8).

There are other "days" that we might have dealt with besides the first day of the week. We suppose that most of our readers are aware of the paganism that clusters round the observance of the 25th

December, and of the undispensational position of those who are called "seventh-day" believers. The observance of "days" is part and parcel of religion: we are not religionists; we believe in a risen, glorified Saviour. *He* constitutes our religion. Let us not spend our time amid the shadows of the past, or the traditions of the present; let us pay no heed to the "self-devised religious observances" of men, but let us set our minds upon things above, where Christ sitteth on the right hand of God. Let it never be said of us, as it was of the Galatians of old, *Ye observe days*.

CHAPTER FIFTEEN

An election within an election

Is membership of the one Body co-extensive with salvation?

We are sure that there is sufficient in the Scriptures to warrant the belief that the reception of the truth of the Mystery is subject to an elective purpose of God, operating within the wider election unto salvation, and we feel that this present volume would be incomplete did we omit this very important phase of dispensational truth. Others before us have had the impression that this is so, but have been hampered by not realizing that the present dispensation did not begin until after Acts 28; consequently they have spoken of an inner election to the "headship" of the one Body. This is the result of including the Body of 1 Corinthians with the Body of Ephesians. We believe that our enquiry will lead us to see that membership of the one Body itself is the object of this elective purpose.

There is another system of teaching which compromises with those who perpetuate undispensational doctrine and observances, believing that we who see the truth of the Mystery should not expose the error of the traditionalists. We might as well extend our charity and encourage the Jew in his legalism. It is not for us to assume the sovereign prerogatives of God. Having seen the truth, we *must* "leave ... and go on to perfection". We have to be concerned with *faithfulness*, even though it should limit the sphere of our so-called *usefulness*.

Some may object at the outset to the idea that the Lord may have chosen some (from among those who are saved) to a peculiarly exalted position. These would doubtless have joined Miriam and Aaron in their resentment against the special call of Moses (Numb. 12: 1-14), but they would have "perished in the gainsaying of Korah" if they had continued in their rebellion against the high calling of Moses and Aaron (Numb. 16: 1-19). Or further, they would have murmured against the exclusive choice of Peter, James, and John to be witnesses of the Transfiguration (Matt. 17), yet their murmurings would not have altered these facts. It must ever be borne in mind, lest we be ensnared with pride, that the elective purposes of God have no room for "good works".

> "When Rebecca had conceived . . . it was said unto her, The elder shall serve the younger". Why?
>
> "For the children being not yet born, neither having done any *good* or *evil*, that the purpose of God according to election might stand, not of works, but of Him that calleth" (Rom. 9: 10-12).

Human responsibility must never be slurred over, but we are convinced that our God is one "Who worketh all things after the counsel of His own will". Human error and satanic guile may be responsible for the eclipse of the truth of the Mystery all down the present age, yet of this we are certain, that none who were predestined by that unalterable counsel of God to "come to a knowledge of the truth" could fail to receive it. Hence we are driven to the conclusion that the time has come when the Lord intends to strip from our eyes the bandages of tradition, and from this time onward to take the graveclothes from many believers who have been marked off to receive the truth so long hidden beneath the rubbish of Christendom's conflicting creeds. The Lord has already given the life-giving command, "Come forth!" and the liberating command , "Loose him, and let him go" (John 11: 43, 44). We believe that "the knowledge of the truth" of the Mystery is only attained by those who are the subjects of this "election within an election". They have received no *revelation*, they possess no new Bible, and they claim no special holiness or learning: the truth lies upon the page of Scripture possessed by all alike, yet apparently seen by few.

Is membership of the one Body co-extensive with salvation? May a man be saved, and yet have never received a knowledge of the truth of the Mystery? These are questions to which we hope to give Scriptural answers as we proceed. In order to manifest more clearly the difference between "faith" (common to all believers), and "knowledge" (possessed by the subjects of this special grace), we venture to lay before the reader the arrangement of the opening verses of the epistle to Titus. It will be seen in the suggested structure (1) that "the faith of God's elect" is described under the member C, d, e, f, and (2) "the knowledge of the truth" under *C, f, e, d*.

It is clear that we are not saved according to our knowledge, yet it is quite certain that none can really believe, hope for, and suffer together with, that which they neither know nor understand. Many have believed with "the faith of God's elect" who have been hopelessly confused concerning the right division of truth. Men like John Calvin, Martin Luther, John Bunyan, or of more recent times, Joseph Irons,

Titus 1:1-4

A a Paul (Name)
  b A servant of God, an apostle of Jesus Christ (Title)
    c According to (1) *faith* (the faith of God's elect); (2) *truth* (the knowledge of the truth)
 B According to godliness
  C d Upon hope of eternal life.
    e Promised by God Who cannot lie.
     f Before age-times
  [*Faith.* — Believed by those who are called "Calvinists".]
  C *f* Manifested in its own seasons
    e His Word by heralding
   d Entrusted to me
  [*Knowledge.* — Denied by most of those so called]
 B According to the commandment of God our Saviour.
A a Titus (Name)
  b Mine own son (Title)
    c According to a common *faith.*

and Charles H. Spurgeon, have been stalwart champions for the faith of God's elect, but if we examine them upon the next item (the knowledge of the truth), they evidence a lack of agreement which leads to confusion. With them kingdom and the church, Israel and the one Body, Abrahamic promises, Zion, and the earth's regeneration are all spiritualized away, yet none of those to whom the knowledge of the truth has been given would think for one instant that they were better than these men of God named above.

The faith of God's elect is explained as comprising three items (*see* structure, member C). It has before it (1) the hope of eternal life, (2) which God, Who cannot lie, promised, (3) before the age-times. These items are enlarged upon in the writings of the great Reformers and Puritans. The knowledge of the truth is explained in a twofold way; (a) it is closely connected with "godliness" (a term which we shall examine shortly), and (b) this truth has (1) a peculiar season for its proclamation, which is now, the present dispensation; (2) it is heralded or proclaimed by the word and words given to (3) the special Apostle of the Mystery — Paul.

Orthodoxy makes no distinction between the proclamation announced in Pentecostal days, or "gospel" times, and the present period; it starts its church at Pentecost, and seeks to rule it by Matthew 18. As to recognizing Paul, the Apostle to the Gentiles, his epistles might as well have never been written, for the place which they are given in its meditation or preaching. If a "text" or a "reading" is wanted, the Gospels, the Acts, the Psalms, etc., are chosen again and again, whereas Ephesians, Philippians, Colossians, Timothy, and Titus are practically a dead letter.

Before passing from this passage we would like to call attention to the word translated "godliness". The word is *eusebeia*, and occurs 15 times in the New Testament. Fifteen is 5 (grace) × 3 (divine perfection). The Pauline epistles contain 10 of these 15 occurrences, still emphasizing 5, the number of grace. The average idea of godliness goes little further than piety, but the word means much more than this conveys to the English reader. It embraces the larger meaning of worship, and may be rendered "the act or state of worshipping well or acceptably". Just as *euaggelion* means *good* message, and *eudokia, good* will, so *eusebia* means *good* worship. Worship to be good must be in harmony with the will of God in reference to the dispensation obtaining for the time. Good worship once demanded the offering of the blood of bulls and goats, but that would not be acceptable now. Good worship once was accepted only at the Temple at Jerusalem, but such is impossible now.

If we read the literature of many of the "bodies" of Christendom, we shall hear many echoes of the Samaritan woman's words (John 4: 20); it is all about where we may or may not worship — the Lord's reply seems to be overlooked. He disposes of both the Samaritan *and* the Jewish centres, and tells us that "God is Spirit, and they who worship* Him *must* worship Him in true spirituality". While so many sorrow over the so-called worship which *must* have its solos, living pictures, politics, ethics, etc., they themselves are often involved in a system of bondage to ceremonies, observances, ordinances, and traditions, perpetuating that which belongs to another dispensation, and failing to offer that worship which is in harmony with the time now present. Those who "resist the truth" are in the context brought into close connection with those who suffer persecution for living in harmony with godliness or proper worship.

This failure to appreciate the spiritual character of the present dispensation is the secret that lies at the root of the bitterness that occurs among those believers who retain any regard for the Word of God. Zealous for God, but not according to the knowledge of the truth, they have instituted a miniature Popery; the "central act of worship" is made an occasion of harshness worthy of a Diotrephes (3 John 9, 10), and the true "place of worship" is unrecognized. Worship to be acceptable must be offered where the great High Priest is. That is entirely independent of place, denomination, or circumstance; many have been received into fellowship *there* who would "defile" some assemblies on earth. "Heaven itself", the true "Holiest of all", is the only place of worship worthy the name. From that assembly none can excommunicate. The binding and loosing of man has no effect there.

---

*This is not the same word as is translated "godliness".

We have often felt, when we have heard of some believers who are called "over-sight" brethren, that the word "over-sight" has more than one meaning, and that while many have been keen over trifles comparable to the tithing of pot-herbs, the weightiest matters concerning the unity of the Spirit, and worship consistent with the dispensation of the Mystery, have been "overlooked".

In 2 Timothy 2 and 3 we read of two classes. One class, to whom the Lord may "peradventure give repentance to the knowledge of the truth", and another, who though "ever learning never come to a knowledge of the truth" ("knowledge" and "acknowledge" in Titus 1: 1; 1 Timothy 4: 3 (verb); 2 Tim. 2: 25 and 3: 7 are the same). The first passage occurs in a setting which is of the utmost importance, especially just now. The arrangement of the passage (2 Tim. 2: 14-26) is as follows:

A 14, 15 a Strive not
 b Study
 c Rightly divide the Word of truth
 B 16. Shun
 C 17, 18. Illustration, "Canker"
 D 19. The sure foundation
 C 20, 21. Illustration, "Vessels"
 B 22, 23. Flee . . . avoid
A 24-26. *a* Not strive
 b Instruct
 c Knowledge of truth, and recovery from snare of the Devil.

It is important that we should realize the purpose of this structural arrangement. It is not merely to excite our curiosity; it is for our instruction. The central member (D) is the important one, and should be studied first. It tells us that in the midst of all the trials and perplexities of this pilgrimage, God's sure foundation standeth. Let those who are troubled remember that and take courage. The door of heaven has not been closed by the shutting of a meeting place; access is still free *there*.

The foundation of God has connected with it (like a seal) the words, "The Lord knoweth them that are His, and let every one that nameth the name of the Lord depart from iniquity". These words are found in a most significant passage in the Old Testament, and supply the key to unlock the whole of the context. The moment we turn to Numbers 16 we shall see that it is directly connected with the "election within an election", and will throw light upon the much-discussed "vessels unto honour and dishonour". Korah and his company rebel against the thought that Moses and Aaron should be favoured with higher privileges than they were, and expressed their feelings by saying:

> "Ye take too much upon you, seeing all the congregation are holy, *every one of them*, and the Lord is among *them*; wherefore then lift ye up yourselves above the congregation of the Lord?"

Moses does not "strive", but falls upon his face. He then speaks to Korah in the words of 2 Timothy 2: 19:

> "Even to-morrow *the Lord will show who are His*" (Numb. 16: 5, *cp.* the Septuagint with 2 Tim. 2: 19 Greek).
>
> "Seemeth it but a small thing with you that the Lord hath separated you (sons of Levi) from the congregation of Israel . . . and seek ye the priesthood also?" (verses 9, 10).

Just before the terrible judgment fell upon Korah and his company, Moses uttered the words which form the second portion of the seal of 2 Timothy 2: 19, "*Depart* I pray you from the tents of these *wicked* men". Surely we can see that the Lord intends us to use this passage in interpreting 2 Timothy 2. The very ones who resented the special choice of Moses and Aaron were themselves specially chosen out of the congregation of Israel. They rebelled against "an election within an election".

On either side of the sure foundation we have the members marked C and *C*, Hymenaeus and Philetus on the one hand, and the great house with its various vessels on the other. We must exercise care here lest we miss the Holy Spirit's meaning. In the first case we have teachers of error, whose word eats like a gangrene. Are the vessels unto dishonour to be reckoned as typifying the same? Much depends upon the force of the little word "but" in verse 20. The injunction had been, "depart from *iniquity*", and lest by over zeal the believer should think that such a title could not possibly mean a fellow saved one, the Apostle reminds him that "in a great house there are *not only* vessels of gold and silver, but also of wood and of earthenware, and some indeed to honour, and some, on the other hand, to dishonour". In other words, he must be prepared to find within the circle of electing grace two classes.

Some will have, by grace, received a knowledge of the truth, while others, though saved, never get beyond the faith of God's elect. All such will "live", but all will not "reign"; some will be "denied" this "honour". It is interesting to note here that Timothy's name is suggestive, as it means "honoured of God"!

Interpreted in the light of Numbers 16 this passage indicates that in the present purposes of God there are some who have been chosen out from the mass of believers; that they have had the eyes of their heart enlightened, that they may *know* what is the hope of His calling, and the truth of the Mystery, while others are left in the traditions of Christendom, saved, yet not so free as they would be did they but "know the truth" (John 8: 32). Orthodoxy has no room in its creed for "one star differing from another star *in glory*", neither has it place for the words "more tolerable" in its conception of future punishment. In order better to illustrate that those under the heading "iniquity" are not the "vessels unto dishonour", we will turn for a moment to 2 Corinthians 6: 14 — 7: 1.

Both 2 Tim. 2 and 2 Corinthians 6 have been mis-used. From both of these passages Christians have drawn arguments about "being separate" from differing Christians, and have not hesitated to use the words "unclean", "defiled", etc., of those who have been accepted by the Lord. Those who have been urged to "come out from among *them*" do not seem to have had enough courage to dare ask to whom the word "them" referred, but have helped on the heart-breaking work of judging one another. The context gives a fearful list as the answer, viz., "unrighteousness", "darkness", "belial", "infidel", "idols" (verses 14-16). Are *these* God's descriptions of His erring children? Such an interpretation is but a murderous, "say now Shibboleth". The true interpretation is lost in this party zeal.

2 Corinthians 6: 17, 18 is not an exhortation to believers, but is a complex quotation from the Old Testament which supplies the exhortation chapter 7: 1, "Having therefore these promises, dearly beloved (!) let us cleanse *ourselves*", etc. It is not so humiliating to be busy cleansing others, and removing the motes from their eyes, but dearly beloved, "let us cleanse *ourselves*". The verb "to cleanse" (2 Cor. 7: 1) and the verb "purge" (2 Tim. 2: 21) are kindred words. So also is the exhortation; he is to purge *himself*.

Two very distinct words are used in 2 Timothy 2. Regarding "iniquity" the believer must "depart" (the word is very emphatic, and is literally "apostatize"), but regarding the vessels unto dishonour, he is to "purge himself". The word "dishonour" needs a little explanation. To the English mind dishonour signifies some positive shame, whereas the word *atimia* means "lack of honour". This can be seen in 1 Corinthians 12: 23, "those members of the body which we think to be *less honourable*" (*atimotera*). The figure of a vessel suggests the theme of our chapter — election. "Hath not the potter power over the clay, *of the same lump*, to make one vessel unto *honour*, and another unto *no honour*?" (Rom. 9: 21). "That the purpose of God according to election might stand" (Rom. 9: 11). The vessels unto "no honour" are those who have never received the "knowledge of the truth", and who are not among those who, like Paul, look forward to the "honour" of "reigning". We will speak more definitely of this later.

The last two verses of 2 Timothy 2 tell us of some who are in the snare of the devil, and that they will "oppose themselves" to those who bear the message of liberty and glory. The servant of the Lord does not strive, he is a vessel of gold or silver, he lets "the potsherds strive with the potsherds of the earth" if they will. He seeks grace to be "gentle toward all, apt in teaching, bearing up under injury and malice (2 Tim. 3: 12), in meekness instructing those who oppose themselves, if God perhaps may sometime *give* them repentance unto a knowledge of the truth, and that being taken alive by Him, they may awake from the snare of the devil unto His (God's) will" (2 Tim. 2: 24-26).

Will the reader refer to the structure of this passage given on page 227; the first and last members will be seen to answer one another. In verses 14 and 15 we find the injunction not to "strive" about words, while in verse 24 we have the commandment not to "strive" with opposers. He who "instructs" (verse 25) has "studied" (verse 15), but the lesson of lessons for us is that "the knowledge of the truth", which delivers from the snare of the devil, and marks one out as a "vessel unto honour", is *the rightly divided Word of truth* (verse 15). Here is the secret of faction and strife. Satan not only opposes the Bible as a whole, but lays a snare for the earnest believer, traps him into undispensational practices, blinds his eyes to the "gospel of the glory of Christ", and the truth of the Mystery, and makes him a tool in his destructive work.

Persecution and religion go hand in hand. Timothy is prepared to receive hard treatment at the hands of those who ought to have received him with open arms. 2 Timothy 3: 12 has been shorn of its true meaning. "All who are willing to live godly in Christ Jesus (or in a manner consistent with the present will of God regarding worship) shall suffer persecution". Some Christians suffer persecution by their endeavour to live in harmony with the "Sermon on the Mount". They read this verse, and find consolation and confirmation, but this is not the meaning of the passage.

In 2 Timothy 3: 10, 11 Paul has made reference to the "persecutions" which he endured, particularly mentioning those which came upon him at Antioch, at Iconium, and Lystra. Why does he specially mention these cities? Why not Jerusalem? The reason is that Antioch, Iconium, and Lystra are associated with a ministry fulfilled in *absolute independence of Jerusalem and the twelve*, and also that the Scripture intimates that it was at Lystra that the Apostle, being stoned to death, was "caught away to paradise" and saw the visions, and heard the words which related to the glory of Christ. Let those who claim consolation from 2 Timothy 3: 12 be consistent. Let them follow Paul in his separate teaching, then they will be entitled to the solace of this passage. The endurance of hardship is repeated several times in relation to the special truth committed to the apostle:

> "Be not thou therefore ashamed of the testimony of our Lord, nor of me His prisoner, but be thou *partaker of the afflictions* of the gospel" (2 Tim. 1: 8).
>
> "The gospel, whereunto I am appointed a herald, and an apostle, and a teacher of the Gentiles. For which cause I also suffer these things" (2 Tim. 1: 11, 12).
>
> "Thou therefore, my son, be strong in the grace that is in Christ Jesus, and the things which thou hast *heard of me* among many witnesses, *the same* entrust thou to faithful men, such as shall be competent to teach others also" (2 Tim. 2: 1, 2).

This true exclusivism disposes of nine-tenths or more of so-called teachers, for they do not even know that Paul had any distinctive message to be passed on.

Paul continues, "Thou therefore endure hardness as a good soldier of Jesus Christ" (verse 3). Then again, after speaking of the gospel which he calls "*My* gospel", the Apostle says, "wherein I suffer hardship, as an evil doer, even unto bonds . . . Therefore I endure all things for the *elects' sakes*, that they may obtain salvation" (verses 9 and 10); yes, but not only salvation, "that they may obtain *the* salvation which is in Christ Jesus *with age-abiding glory*". There is no need for us to begin speculating as to the difference between this salvation and the added glory, for the apostle immediately explains, "if we *died* with Him, we shall also *live* with Him". This is "salvation"; this embraces every believer, whether he has "the knowledge of the truth", or not. "If we *endure* we shall also *reign* with Him". This is the added "glory" and "honour". "Living" is one thing, *reigning* is another. All who reign will live, but not all who live will reign.

The Lord has been pleased to arrange that the present "light affliction, which is but for a moment" (connected in this epistle in a special manner with the teaching committed to Paul), shall "work for us as a far more exceeding age-abiding weight of glory". Some, maybe, will say, this is works, not grace. One thing we know, and that is, it is Scripture, and further, if the Lord had never told us of this high glory we still could not have resisted the truth when He made us see it, but we should have endured affliction sooner than give it up. Shall we say hard things then, if the Lord is pleased to add more of His riches of glory upon those who for a short season are called upon to suffer together with His despised Word?

Believers will either receive the truth and look forward to reigning, or will reject the truth and be denied this honour. "If we deny Him (if we are ashamed of the testimony of our Lord and of Paul His prisoner), He also will deny us". This in no wise touches eternal life, for "if we are faithless, He abideth faithful, for deny Himself He cannot".

We can now proceed a little further. Both Paul and Timothy looked forward to a *crown*, which confessedly symbolizes reigning. The Apostle charges Timothy:

> "Be instant in season, out of season, reprove, rebuke, exhort with all longsuffering (*cp*. 2 Tim. 2: 24-26), and doctrine, for there will come a season when they will not endure sound doctrine, but according to their own desires will, unto themselves, heap up teachers, (because) they have an itching ear, and from the truth they shall turn their ears away, and unto myths will they be turned aside" (2 Tim. 4: 2-4).

Here we have the prophetic picture of our own days. The evil started as recorded in 2 Timothy 1: 15, "All they in Asia "*turned away* from me", and necessarily it ends with the words, "*turn away* from the truth". Does the reader wonder why God has laid upon the hearts of some of His children the burden of this rejected truth, and this rejected Apostle? Apart from the contemplation of these false teachers, Paul addresses Timothy:

> "But thou, be sober in all things, *suffer hardship*, do the work of an evangelist (*cp*. Eph. 4: 11), the ministry that is thine complete" (2 Tim. 4: 5).

The Apostle's approaching death is the reason for this final charge. There is no more Scriptural warrant for "evangelistic succession", than for "apostolic succession", the last word in ministry being 2 Tim. 2: 2, "teachers". Continuing we read:

> "for I am already being poured out as a drink offering, and the season of my release has come,
>
> the noble contest I have contested,
> the race I have finished,
> the faith I have kept,
>
> henceforth there is laid up (same word in Col. 1: 5, 'the hope *laid up* in the heavens') for me the *crown* of righteousness, which the Lord, the righteous Judge, will render unto me in that day, and not to me only, but unto them also that love His *appearing*" (2 Tim. 4: 6-8).

The hope of the Mystery is to be received up in glory. "When Christ, Who is our life, shall *appear*, then shall ye also *appear* with Him in glory". "Looking for that blessed hope and the *appearing* of the glory". Those who look for the *parousia*, or who expect to pass through the tribulation, must not be surprised if they miss this "crown", especially if, by ignoring this special messenger Paul, they are found "denying" (2 Tim. 2: 12), and "ashamed" (2 Tim. 1: 8).

In 2 Timothy 2: 5, 6 there is another reference to a crown "If moreover any man contend even in the games, he is not *crowned* unless he contend according to the rules. The husbandman must labour, before partaking of the fruits". To obtain the "glory" and to "reign" (2 Tim. 2: 10-12), the believer must "keep the rules". The truths of other dispensations will not suffice. We must regulate our worship, our witness, and our warfare according to the teaching of the epistles of the Mystery, or fail. We must:

> "lay aside every weight, and the easily entangling sin, and run with patience the race that *lies before us*, looking off unto Jesus, the Prince-leader and consummator of faith, Who for (*anti*, over against, or corresponding to) the joy that was *lying before Him*, *endured* a cross, despising the shame, and is set down at the right hand of the throne of God" (Heb. 12: 1, 2).

This crown, this race, make us think of the "prize" of Philippians 3. The realization of "an election within an election" will throw great light upon that chapter. Brethren, do you see your calling? If so, "walk worthy" of it. Let the potsherds strive with the potsherds of the earth if they will.

> "Let the peace of God rule in your hearts, to which also ye were called in one body, and be ye thankful" (Col. 3: 15).

CHAPTER SIXTEEN

Summary and conclusion

The reader must feel that all that has gone to make up the present volume is really after all only introductory. We have observed the two distinct lines of redemptive purpose running through the Word of God. We have seen the earthly purpose, dating from the period named "since the overthrow of the world", connected with the covenants and promises made to Abraham, Isaac, Jacob, and David. We have seen how this purpose has reference to a kingdom on earth, and the people of Israel.

The purpose pertaining to the heavens is linked with a period named "before the overthrow of the world", and "before age-times". This purpose was never divulged or made the subject of divine revelation until the time came when Israel and the earthly kingdom purpose were put into abeyance for the time being, as recorded in Acts 28. Then the Apostle Paul entered upon his commission, the dispensation of the Mystery being peculiarly his. He was the instrument through whom the Lord gave us all that we know concerning the Body of Christ, and the hidden purpose relating to the heavens.

What is now required is (a) an examination of those Scriptures which describe that period when God will once again put into operation His purpose regarding the land, the kingdom related to it, and Israel. This would involve an exposition of parts of Isaiah, Jeremiah, Ezekiel, Daniel, the Minor Prophets, and the book of the Revelation; and (b) regarding the heavenly section, a translation and careful study of the epistles of the Mystery, viz., Ephesians, Philippians, Colossians, 1 and 2 Timothy and Titus.

It is evident to all that such a vast field would occupy a volume to itself. Already we have exceeded the space which we originally purposed to occupy, being obliged, as mentioned before, to omit dealing with the "unity of the Spirit", and it would do more harm than good to attempt to condense the most important part of the subject before us into a final chapter. The reader has before him a clue which, if followed, will lead him safely through the paths of divine revelation to the end. A knowledge of the two-fold purpose, and the need for "rightly dividing the Word of truth", will act in the same way as the skein of thread does to a traveller in the catacombs or labyrinths; but just as it would mean disaster and perhaps death to lose the thread which stretches back along the whole of the winding course of the catacombs, so it must mean spiritual loss, shame, and denial if we relinquish our hold upon the thread of safety provided for us in 2 Timothy 2: 15.

We will set out before the eye the double line of purpose noted in the preceding pages, trusting that it may be of use to the reader in gathering up the thoughts that have occupied our attention in this volume.

The redemptive purposes. Their two-fold division.

(1) Two time periods.

Since the overthrow of the world (Matt. 13: 34, 35; 25: 34, etc.).	Before the overthrow of the world (Eph. 1: 3, 4; Titus 1: 1-3; 2 Tim. 1:9).

(2) Two spheres of operation

The Earth (Gen. 12: 1-7; 2 Sam. 7: 11-16; Luke 1:32, 33).	The Heavens (Job 15: 15; Gen. 1:8; Eph. 2: 6; 6: 12; Heb. 9: 23, 24; Col. 1:20).

(3) Two ministries

The Prophets; the Son; the Twelve (Heb. 1: 1, 2; Rom. 15: 8; Heb. 2: 1-4; 1 Cor. 1: 5-7; John 16: 12-14).	Paul, afer Acts 28. (Acts 26: 16-18; 2 Tim. 1: 9-11; 2 Tim. 4: 17; Eph. 3: 1.10).

(4) Two agencies

The kingdom vested in Israel (from Genesis to Acts 28; Daniel and Revelation).	The church of the Mystery (Ephesians, Philippians, Colossians, Timothy, Titus).

(5) Two gospels

The gospel of the kingdom (Matt. 3: 2; 4: 17; 10: 1-10; Mark 16: 15-20; Acts 10).	The gospel of the grace and glory of God (Acts 20: 24; 1 Tim. 1: 11; Rom. 16: 25).

(6) Two hopes

The *parousia* (1 Thess. 4: 16, 17). Rapture or resurrection (1 Cor. 15: 51-58). The millennium (Rev. 20).	"The one hope" (Eph. 1: 18; 4: 4). "Glory", and the *epiphania* (Col. 3: 4; Titus 2:13).

(7) The ultimate

Reconciliation of things on earth, and things in heaven. New heavens and new earth (Eph. 1: 10; Col. 1: 20; 2 Peter 3: 13; Isa. 66: 22; Rev. 21: 1-27).

Pursuing this subject further we should find that the heavenly section is itself subdivided, those heavenly places "far above all" belonging to the Mystery. The ministry of Paul is divided into two, one before and one during his imprisonment. For the present purpose, however, the main outline given will suffice. The fuller subdivision is indicated in the companion volume, *The Apostle of the Reconciliation.*

It will be observed that these two lines of purpose do not interlink until the new creation is reached. We have been too apt to take it for granted that the millennial kingdom is the goal before God and His people. This is not so, however. The millennium is Israel's opportunity, but it is not the final kingdom which will be the culmination of redemptive purposes.

It is the earth with Jerusalem as the centre that is the locality of the millennial kingdom (Isa. 40: 10-11; Rev. 5: 9, 10; Isa. 52: 1, 2, 7-10, and Zech. 14: 16-21). The people of Israel shall "all be righteous", and "offer themselves willingly" (Isa. 60: 21, and Psalm 110: 3 R.V.), but the nations render "feigned obedience" (Psalm 18: 44; 66: 3 margin; Isa. 60: 12, and Zech 14: 18, 19). The Lord Jesus "rules with a rod of iron" (Psalm 2: 9, and Rev. 12: 5), and with "power" (Psalm 66: 7) "in the midst of enemies" (Psalm 110: 2, 5, 6); with "judgment" (Psalms 149: 1-9, and 101: 8); Satan is *bound* (Rev. 20: 2), and sin *restrained.*

In spite of the fact that the Lord and His people reign and rule for a thousand years, the end of that kingdom is well-nigh universal *rebellion* and *destruction* (Rev. 20: 7-10). The millennial kingdom is the period of Israel's exaltation and blessing. While darkness shall cover the earth, and gross darkness the people at first, Israel shall shine in the glory of the Lord (Isa. 60: 1-3). The curse resting upon the whole earth will be removed first of all from the "holy mountain" of Israel (Isa. 65: 25; 25: 6-9), and then extend over the earth.

No dispensation since the world began will have had so many advantages, yet none will so manifest the lesson of the ages, the inability of the creature to stand apart from God. During the millennium there will be on the earth a perfect monarchy, perfect law, perfect administration, and the absence of external temptation. No longer will the "god of this age" rule the religious world; no longer shall the "prince of the authority of the air" control the "course of this age", or energize the children of unbelief; all will come under the mighty sway of the Prince of Peace. Yet that which is begotten of the flesh remains flesh. Only those who are subjects of the new creation, "who are kept by the power of God, through faith unto salvation", will endure.

Satan will find many ready to rise in rebellion at the end of the thousand years. Can *this* be the kingdom for which the disciples were taught to pray, "Thy will be done on earth *as* it is in heaven?" The millennium is the winding-up of the day of man, and the introduction of the day of God. Christ is to rule finally over a kingdom which transcends the millennium as heaven does the earth. It will not end in rebellion, like the millennium; perfection is its purpose and character. Its embrace will not merely reach to the "ends of the earth", but to "things in heaven and things on earth" (Phil. 2: 10; 1 Cor. 15: 24-28). The Apostle Paul gives a three-fold statement relative to this glorious period:

	Reference	*Commences with*	*And finishes with*
(1)	Eph. 1:17-23	Christ. — Resurrection.	The fulness.
(2)	Phil. 2:6-11.	Christ. — Equality with God.	His universal Lordship.
(3)	Col. 1:16-20.	Christ. — Creator.	The rconciliation of all things.

Here a glorious prospect opens out. No imperfection sullies its progress at the close. It starts with resurrection, and marches triumphantly onward to the universal Lordship of the Son of God, and the reconciliation of all things. Almighty power, all-conquering grace, all sufficiency, and all fulness are its dominant notes. This is a kingdom worthy of "the Son of His love".

Ephesians 1 gives us universal *sway*, Philippians 2 universal *recognition*, and Colossians 1 universal *reconciliation*. This kingdom is to be handed over to the Father, and this introduces the eternal state in order that God may be all in all. This redemption will be perfect. Starting in Genesis 1: 1 we see the great God as Creator of heaven and earth, and arriving at the close of divine revelation we see not only God as Creator, but God and creation standing perfect, not in the strength of creaturehood, but in the indefectible stability of redemption. Beyond this we know nothing. What lies before the redeemed after this is known to God only. Of one thing we may be sure: it will be worth all the pain, all the endurance, all the years, all the trouble: we leave it with Him, and rest in Him. Death, and he who hath the power of death, the grave, and all things that offend will have gone. Once again a clean universe will be presented to God, the work of the Son. All tears will be wiped away; no more sorrow, no more sighing, no more pain; these will have passed for ever away with sin which caused them.

This is "The ultimate", the seventh heading of the diagram given in this chapter. Surely, dear reader, your heart goes out to such a God, to such a Saviour? Seeing these things, you will not mind what men think or say. You will begin to forget what is behind for the bright things before, you will seek grace to "know Him", and to realize more than ever before the "calling wherewith you have been called".

Thus we must take leave of one another for the time being. Think not upon the "earthen vessel"; dwell much upon the "treasure" of the Word. If it should be the Lord's will, we may renew our acquaintance in a future volume dealing with these precious things so peculiarly ours;* but if not, let us seek grace to "press toward the mark", "rightly divide the Word of truth", and "live . . . looking for that blessed hope".

---

*See *The Testimony of the Lord's Prisoner* and *In Heavenly Places* by the same author and published by *The Berean Publishing Trust*.

The Purpose of the Ages.

"In the beginning, God —" (Gen. 1:1)

A The beginning. Before age-times.	a *Christ* The firstborn of all creation. The form of God. The image of the invisible God (Col. 1:15; Phil. 2:6). b *Satan* The cherub of the anointing. Priestly and kingly functions (Ezek. 28:12-19). c The overthrow of the world — *kosmos* (Gen. 1:2).
B The ages begin. Paradise lost.	*Earth* d Re-made and blessed (Gen. 1:2-:4). e Subjected to curse. Thorns and thistles (Gen. 3). *Man* f For a little (while) lower than the angels (Psalm 8). g The first Adam a living soul. The image of God (Gen. 1:26; 2:7). h Dominion over the earth (Gen. 1:26). *Usurper* i The Nachash. The shining one (Gen. 3:1). j Ye shall not surely die (Gen. 3:4). k Ye shall be as God (Gen. 3:5). *Hope* l The Seed of the woman (Gen. 3:15).
C The days of Noah. The nations just before the call of Abraham.	m The irruption of the sons of God. The *Nephilim* (Gen. 6). n Preservation in the ark. Noah uncontaminated (Gen. 6:9-8). o Punishment by flood for children of the wicked (Gen. 7, 8). p Spirits in prison (1 Peter 3:19-22; Jude 6).
D Abraham.	q Heir of the world (Christ the Seed) (Gen. 12; Rom. 4:13). r Righteousness by faith (Gen. 15:6).
E Moses.	s First covenant (given after Passover) broken (Jer. 31:32). t Curse pronounced on law-breaker (Deut. 27:26).
F David.	u The kingdom (Christ the Seed) (2 Sam. 7).
G Christ as King of the Jews, born, rejected, and crucified (Matthew).	
H *The Mystery hidden since the ages.*	The church of the Mystery. The present dispensation. Its hopes and blessings spiritual, and in the heavenlies. Inaugurated and completed in "its own season" (Titus 1:1-3), during the period of Israel's rejection (the later Pauline epistles).

C As it was in the days of Noah. The nations just before Israel are saved and blessed.

- *m* Rise of antichrist, the son of perdition (2 Thess. 2; Rev. 13).
- *n* Preservation for those in the Lamb's book of life. Uncontaminated (Rev. 13:8).
- *o* Punishment by fire for worshippers of antichrist (Rev. 14:9, 10).
- *p* The spirits in prison liberated for a season (Rev. 9:14).

D Abrahamic blessings.

- *q* The inheritance entered (Psalm 37; Isa. 60, 61).
- *r* The people all righteous (Isa. 60:21).

E Moses superseded.

- *s* The new covenant based upon the blood of Christ, the true Passover. Never to be broken (Matt 26:28; Jer. 31:31-40).
- *t* The curse removed by the death of Christ (Gal. 3:13).

F Davidic kingdom *u* The millennial reign (Rev. 20).

G Christ comes the second time as King, in power and great glory (Revelation).

B The consummation of the ages. Paradise restored

- *Earth* *d* Restored and blessed (Hosea 2:18-23).
- *e* The curse removed. Instead of the thorn, the fir tree (Isa. 55:13).
- *Man* *f* The man Christ Jesus far above all (Eph. 1).
- *g* The last Adam a life-giving Spirit. The express image of God (Heb. 1; 1 Cor. 15).
- *h* Dominion over heaven and earth (Matt. 28).
- *True Heir* *i* The Lamb is the light of the city, and He is the brightness of the Father's glory (Rev. 21:23).
- *j* Immortality conferred on believers (1 Cor. 15).
- *k* Christ has pre-eminence (Col. 1).
- *Hope* *l* Creation's groan hushed. The Seed of the woman, of Abraham, and of David has come (Revelation).

A The end (1 Cor. 15:24). The purpose of the ages finished.

- *a* *Christ* The Head of all things. Acknowledged as Lord. Firstborn of all creation.
- *b* *The Church* In the heavenly holiest of all. Satan, death and hades destroyed (Rev. 20:10, 14; Heb. 2:14).
- *c* The reconciliation of all things. "As it was in the beginning" (Col. 1:20).

"God all in all" (1 Cor. 15:28).

Index to Subjects

Index to Scripture References

Index to Scripture References — *continued*

Index to Hebrew Words Used

Index to Greek Words Used

Index to Structures Used

THE UNFOLDING PURPOSE OF GOD

by Stuart Allen

"The burden of this book is that Christ's first coming was to Israel as King Priest, to redeem them from their sins and make them agents for worldwide blessing. After the book of Acts, the Jew was put aside temporarily and this age is predominantly a Gentile one. The author maintains that Acts 28 is a dispensational boundary and that the Prison Epistles are the Divine message for the present age. There is much that is good in this book . . .".

The Prophetic Witness

"The greater part of the book consists of an exposition of Paul's captivity epistles, the implication being that God's unfolding purpose is revealed most fully in them . . . readers will find much helpful exposition in its pages".

F.F. Bruce in *The Life of Faith*

"The 260 pages of this volume are filled with devotional teaching and in some cases the writer presents less prominent Bible facts in terms which are both instructive and challenging".

Chas. Presho in *The British Weekly*

"We congratulate the publishers of this book at a price which in these days of high costs combines both quality and quantity . . . Here is a book packed with solid meat for the student of Scripture, well supported by quotations and references from the Word of God".

The Evangelical Preacher

Order from
THE BEREAN PUBLISHING TRUST